Farm Journal's
Best-Ever
COOKIES

Farm Journal's
Best-Ever
COOKIES

By Patricia A. Ward

Book Design by Michael P. Durning

Illustrations by Merry Cassino

Farm Journal, Inc.
Philadelphia, Pennsylvania

Distributed to the trade by
Doubleday & Company, Inc.
Garden City, New York

Other Farm Journal Cookbooks

Farm Journal's Country Cookbook
Farm Journal's Complete Pie Cookbook
Homemade Bread
America's Best Vegetable Recipes
Homemade Candy
Homemade Ice Cream and Cake
Country Fair Cookbook
Great Home Cooking in America
Farm Journal's Homemade Snacks
Farm Journal's Best-Ever Recipes
Farm Journal's Great Dishes from the Oven
Farm Journal's Freezing and Canning Cookbook
Farm Journal's Friendly Food Gifts from your Kitchen
Farm Journal's Choice Chocolate Recipes
Farm Journal's Cook It Your Way
Farm Journal's Complete Home Baking Book
Farm Journal's Meal & Menu Planner Cookbook

Library of Congress Cataloging in Publication Data
Main entry under title:
Farm journal's best-ever cookies.
Includes index.
1. Cookies. I. Ward, Patricia A.
II. Farm journal (Philadelphia, 1956-)
TX772.F37   641.8'654   80-15364
ISBN 0-385-17146-3

Contents

Introduction

Few people I know can resist the brown sugary goodness of a chocolate chip cookie filled with chopped walnuts or a soft, cake-like oatmeal cookie spiced with cinnamon and studded with plump raisins. Farm and ranch women have always known the merits of the homemade cookie—and most country kitchens still have cookie jars filled with the family's favorites.

Nearly every recipe in this collection has proven its worth time and again in farm kitchens across the country, and the others have been especially created for this book in our Farm Journal Test Kitchens. Each recipe has been professionally tested by our home economists, and each cookie sampled by cookie lovers.

In the chapters that follow you'll find recipes for old-fashioned specialties that have been favorites for generations as well as extra-speedy cookies that can be micro-waved in a few minutes or need no baking at all. There are simple recipes for cookies that children will enjoy making almost as much as eating; super-nutritious cookies that taste great and are good for you, too; and cookies especially well suited to lunch boxes, bake sales and long trips through the mail. We've also included dozens of recipes developed with an eye toward thrift, and an abundance of cookies that are simply extravagant, including a glorious assortment of Christmas cookies.

Don't wait for a holiday or a special occasion—create your own by baking a batch of homemade cookies. They're a welcome treat any day of the year.

—Patricia A. Ward

1 | All About Cookies

Almost everyone loves cookies—they're fun to eat and fun to make. Even if you've never baked before, the basic mixing techniques are a snap to learn, and this chapter contains baking tips that will help you turn out a successful batch of cookies every time.

We begin by describing the six basic types of cookies—bar, drop, molded, pressed, refrigerator and rolled. For each one, we include baking tips and a test for doneness. And for ease in recipe selection, each cookie is coded with a symbol indicating which kind of cookie it is (see Six Types of Cookies).

We also describe all the basic utensils needed and explain how to measure the ingredients and mix the dough; you'll find this information useful if you're a novice baker or if you're introducing someone else to cookie baking.

General reminders are included here, too, under Ten Tips for Baking Beautiful Cookies, and the chapter closes with suggestions for storing and mailing cookies.

☐ Six Types of Cookies

Cookie dough can be formed in six ways—all of them easy to learn and requiring no prior baking experience.

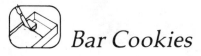 *Bar Cookies*

A bar cookie is a cross between a cookie and a cake. It's the easiest cookie of all to make because no shaping is required—the dough is usually spread or pressed into the baking pan. After baking, the cookies are cooled in the pan and cut into bars, squares, rectangles or diamonds. Best of all, the cookies can be covered and stored right in the pan.

Baking Tips: Don't overmix the dough; mix just until the dry ingredients are absorbed or the cookies will develop hard, crusty tops and a tough texture. Be sure to spread the dough evenly in the pan so that it will bake evenly.

Test for Doneness: Cake-like bars should be baked until the top springs back when touched lightly with a finger, or until a toothpick comes out clean when inserted in the center. Fudge-like bars should be baked until the top is dull, not shiny, and a slight imprint remains when touched lightly with your finger. (There are some exceptions, so check each recipe for its doneness test.)

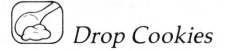 *Drop Cookies*

The soft dough for drop cookies is usually dropped by teaspoonfuls onto a baking sheet. Be sure to allow space between mounds of cookie dough as directed, because the dough spreads as it bakes. After baking, the cookies should be immediately removed from the baking sheet to prevent further baking. (There are some exceptions; see individual recipes.)

Baking Tips: Use an ordinary teaspoon rather than a measuring teaspoon for dropping the cookie dough. Use slightly rounded teaspoonfuls unless the recipe states otherwise, and push the dough from the spoon with another spoon. For even baking, make the drops the same size.

Test for Doneness: Bake until the cookies are delicately browned and a slight imprint remains when touched lightly with finger.

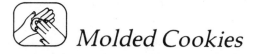 *Molded Cookies*

These cookies are made by using your hands to form rather stiff dough into shapes such as balls or ropes. The balls of dough are either baked as is or flattened with an ordinary drinking glass, the tines of a fork or with your fingers.

Baking Tips: For consistency, use a spoon to measure out small amounts of dough before shaping, or use a ruler to measure the shaped cookie. Dusting your hands with a little flour will help to keep the dough from sticking, although some molded cookies can be shaped with unfloured hands.

Test for Doneness: Bake until the cookies are delicately browned and a slight imprint remains when touched lightly with finger.

Pressed Cookies

These cookies are shaped by forcing the dough through a cookie press into desired shapes. The dough is usually rich in butter or margarine, and will be rather stiff.

Baking Tips: For best results, it's important to keep the dough pliable. If it begins to get too soft, return it to the refrigerator for a short time. (If the dough gets too cold, it will become crumbly.) Follow the manufacturer's directions for your cookie press. Hold the press so that it rests on baking sheet and force the dough out onto the sheet.

Test for Doneness: Bake until cookies are set and delicately browned around the edges. (Some are done as soon as they are set, but not browned; see individual recipes.)

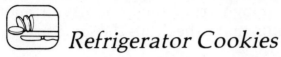 *Refrigerator Cookies*

The stiff dough for these cookies is shaped into rolls, wrapped in waxed paper or aluminum foil, and then thoroughly chilled. Before baking, the rolls are cut into thin slices. Unbaked dough can be stored for one week in refrigerator and up to six months in the freezer.

Baking Tips: Be sure dough is thoroughly chilled, and slice with a thin, sharp knife. Be sure to slice rolls evenly so that the cookies will bake evenly.

Test for Doneness: Bake until the cookies are delicately browned.

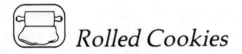 *Rolled Cookies*

These are similar to refrigerator cookies; the dough is usually stiff and chilled in the refrigerator. The chilled dough is rolled out on a floured surface and cut into desired shapes with cookie cutters.

Baking Tips: Roll out only a small amount of dough at one time, keeping the rest in the refrigerator. Roll the dough from the center to the edges, as you would pie crust. Thin dough makes crisper cookies, thicker dough makes softer cookies—and too much rerolling of dough makes tough cookies!

Test for Doneness: Bake until the cookies are delicately browned.

☐ Basic Cookie-Baking Utensils

Just a few basic utensils are needed to turn out perfect cookies every time. You won't need all the utensils described here to make every recipe; some, such as the cookie press, will be used only in certain recipes. Others, such as the pastry blender and pastry cloth, are nice to have, but you can do without them—and we'll explain how.

Assorted Cookie Cutters: These are used for rolled cookies; they should be sharp, with no rough edges. It's best to dip the cutter into flour each time before using.

Baking Pans or Dishes: Standard-sized baking pans and dishes are used in all our recipes. They include:
>   *Metal:* 15½x10½x1"; 13x9x2"; 9" square; 8" square.
>   *Glass:* 13x9x2" (3-qt.); 12x8x2" (2-qt.); 8" square; 9" pie plate.

Baking Sheets: You'll need at least two. Shiny metal baking sheets are best because they reflect oven heat away from the cookies and produce more even browning. Sheets should be flat, with one or two raised sides for easier handling. For delicate, even browning of cookies, baking sheets should be four inches shorter and four inches narrower than the inside of your oven.

Cookie Press: This is a metal tube-shaped utensil with several attachments for making cookies of various shapes. The cookie dough is forced out the opening of the tube onto a baking sheet.

Cooling Racks: You'll need at least two good-sized wire racks. All cookies should be cooled on racks so that air can circulate around the cookies as they cool.

Electric Mixer: Although many of the recipes in this book can be mixed by hand, an electric mixer is recommended for all recipes requiring thorough beating, especially those using the creaming method. (In our Farm Journal Test Kitchens, we use electric mixers mounted on stands, but a portable electric mixer works just as well.)

Flour Sifter or Sieve: A sifter is needed to sift some ingredients before measuring and to help mix dry ingredients together. A large sieve will do.

Knife: A sharp kitchen knife is needed to slice refrigerator cookies and to cut bar cookies; it also can be used to level off dry ingredients when measuring.

Measuring Cups: Two types of measuring cups are needed for accurate measurement. For measuring dry ingredients, nested-type metal or plastic cups are used. They're available in sets of four: ¼ cup, ⅓ cup, ½ cup and 1 cup. For measuring liquids, use glass or plastic measuring cups with ounce measurements marked on the sides. Liquid measuring cups are available in 1-cup, 1-pint and 1-quart sizes. To be accurate, never substitute one type of measuring cup for the other.

Measuring Spoons: You'll need a set of four in these sizes: ¼ teaspoon, ½ teaspoon, 1 teaspoon and 1 tablespoon.

Metal Spatulas: Both a small and a large flat metal spatula are handy for cookie baking. Use them to level off dry ingredients in measuring cups, to spread cookie dough in a baking pan and to remove cookies from baking sheets. A pancake turner also works well to remove cookies from baking sheets.

Mixing Bowls: You'll need several sizes—ranging from 1-qt. to 3-qt.— and they can be of crockery, glass or metal.

Oven Thermometer: It's best to check the temperature of your oven each time you use it. Place the thermometer in the oven and preheat according to manufacturer's directions. Before putting cookies in oven, double-check temperature and adjust as needed.

Pastry Blender: A wire utensil used for cutting a solid fat, such as shortening, margarine or butter, into dry ingredients. If you don't have one, you can improvise by using two table knives.

Pastry Cloth: A pastry cloth makes quick work of rolled cookies; after some flour is rubbed into the cloth, there's little chance that dough will stick as it's rolled out. The cloth should be kept clean, and it should be laundered after every two or three uses. If you don't have a pastry cloth, lightly dust your countertop or board with flour before rolling out the dough.

Pastry Tube: Also called a decorating tube. It consists of an assortment of metal tips designed to make different shaped icing decorations including flowers, leaves and borders. The tip of your choice is placed inside the plastic or paper bag, and the frosting is then spooned into the bag. The frosting is forced out through an opening in the metal tip. Larger tips are used to make meringue cookies or shells.

Rolling Pin: A heavy rolling pin makes it easier to roll out the dough evenly for rolled cookies, but choose one that fits comfortably in your hands. A stockinet cover for the rolling pin will make the process even easier.

Rubber Spatulas: Rubber or plastic spatulas are shaped like a flat paddle and are flexible. They're especially useful for scraping the cookie dough down the sides of the bowl when beating with an electric mixer, for folding ingredients into beaten egg whites or heavy cream and for turning dough out of the bowl.

Ruler: If you want truly professional-looking cookies, a ruler is essential. Use it to measure the thickness of rolled dough or refrigerator cookie slices, to cut bar cookies, and to measure cookie cutters and baking pans.

Timer: A timer is helpful for cookie baking because most cookies are baked for short lengths of time.

Wooden Spoon: Use for general mixing of cookie dough and for stirring dry ingredients into creamed mixture.

☐ How to Measure Ingredients

Dry Ingredients

Baking powder, baking soda, salt: Scoop directly into container with measuring spoon and level off top with edge of metal spatula or knife.

Flour (all-purpose and cake): Sift flour first even if package describes flour as presifted. Carefully spoon flour into nested-type measuring cup; do not shake or pack down. Level off top with edge of metal spatula or knife.

Flour (whole-grain): Don't sift; just stir. Carefully spoon flour into nested-type measuring cup without shaking or packing down. Level off top with edge of metal spatula or knife.

Sugar (brown): Spoon into nested-type measuring cup, pack firmly and level off top with edge of metal spatula or knife.

Sugar (confectioners'): Sift confectioners' sugar, then spoon lightly into nested-type measuring cup. Level off top with edge of metal spatula or knife.

Sugar (white): Spoon into nested-type measuring cup and level off top with edge of metal spatula or knife.

Liquids

Honey, juices, milk, oil, syrups and water: Place liquid measuring cup on level surface, fill to desired mark, and check at eye level, keeping cup on level surface.

Vanilla and other extracts: Pour into measuring spoon.

Eggs: All our recipes are tested with large eggs.

Shortenings

Butter, margarine, shortening and lard: Spoon into nested-type measuring cups and press firmly into cup. Level off top with edge of metal spatula or knife. Butter and margarine packaged in ¼-pound units usually have tablespoon measurements marked on the package; simply cut off the amount needed for recipe. (One-quarter pound equals ½ cup.)

☐ How to Mix Cookie Dough

Every recipe in this cookbook gives precise directions for mixing the dough. Most recipes for cookies are made by the creaming method, so named because the sugar is thoroughly beaten or creamed into the shortening before the rest of the ingredients are added. Here are some general directions for the creaming method of mixing:

•For ease in mixing, be sure to bring shortening, such as butter and margarine, to room temperature before mixing.

•To cream together shortening and sugar, first place the shortening in the mixing bowl. Gradually add the sugar to the shortening, beating constantly with an electric mixer at medium speed. Continue beating until mixture is light and fluffy. (We recommend using an electric mixer for cookie recipes that use the creaming method, but you can mix dough with a spoon if you wish.)

•Next add the eggs and flavoring, beating well with an electric mixer at medium speed.

•Gradually add the dry ingredients. In some recipes, these are added while beating with the electric mixer at low speed. In others, the dry ingredients are stirred in by hand.

☐ Ten Tips for Baking Beautiful Cookies

1. Preheat your oven according to manufacturer's directions, allowing 10 to 15 minutes. Be sure the oven temperature is correct before putting in the cookies.

2. For best results, use the correct size baking pan or baking sheets.

3. Grease baking sheets and pans with shortening or margarine. (Some rich cookies don't require greased baking sheets or pans; see individual recipes.)

4. When placing cookies on baking sheets, leave enough space to allow them to spread. (Each of our recipes tells exactly how much space to allow.)

5. When baking, always place cookies on cool baking sheets so that they don't begin to spread immediately and become misshapen.

6. For more even baking, bake just one sheet of cookies at a time. Place the baking sheet on a rack in the center of the oven. If you prefer to bake two sheets at a time, space the

racks so that the oven is divided into thirds and place one baking sheet on each rack.

7. Bake cookies just until done; don't overbake. Follow the test for doneness in each recipe.

8. Remove cookies immediately from baking sheets to prevent further baking, unless recipe directs otherwise. Use a metal spatula or pancake turner to remove cookies from baking sheets.

9. For even cooling, always cool individual cookies in a single layer on wire cooling racks. Bar cookies should be cooled in their pans on racks. Cooling racks allow air to circulate around the cookies to prevent sogginess.

10. Never stack cookies until thoroughly cooled or they will become misshapen.

☐ How to Store Cookies

For short-time storage: Store crisp cookies in a container with a loose-fitting cover. Soft cookies should be stored in a container with a tight-fitting cover. If cookies tend to dry out, a piece of fresh bread or a wedge of apple in the container will keep them soft.

For longer storage: Use your freezer. Bake cookies as usual and cool thoroughly. Cookies can be frozen in plastic bags, cardboard boxes, baking pans or coffee cans, or simply wrapped in aluminum foil or plastic wrap. Cookies can be frozen up to 12 months with no loss of flavor. To serve, unwrap and thaw 15 minutes at room temperature.

☐ How to Pack Cookies for Mailing

Sending a package of homemade cookies to a special person is one of the nicest personal gifts you can give. To be sure your cookies arrive in best condition—not crumbs—plan their journey carefully.

1. Choose soft, moist cookies. Bars, brownies and drop cookies are best able to withstand a few rough jolts without crumbling.

2. Use a sturdy cardboard packing box. Metal or wooden containers are best for overseas mailing. Line with waxed

paper, aluminum foil or plastic wrap, then crumple pieces of the same material in the bottom of the box to create a cushion. (We don't recommend using popcorn or cereal as packing material because it may attract insects.)

3. Wrap flat cookies in pairs back-to-back in plastic or aluminum foil, with waxed paper in between. Wrap bar cookies individually.

4. Place cookies snugly in box. Between layers of cookies, place a cushion of crumpled waxed paper, foil or plastic wrap. Pack tightly so that cookies can't jiggle around in the box, and top with another cushion of crumpled paper.

5. Tape box securely shut with brown-paper tape if available. Wrap in heavy brown paper and tape with brown-paper tape. Clearly label with address of both receiver and sender. Write "Fragile, Handle with Care" on both sides of the box.

6. For overseas mailing, use air parcel post.

2 | From Grandmother's Kitchen

Remember those special days when the aroma of homemade cookies greeted you at the door when you came home from school? You probably had a favorite cookie that you liked to eat warm from the oven with a tall glass of cold milk— maybe it was a soft applesauce raisin, an extra-crunchy brown sugar refrigerator cookie or a big chocolate chip cookie.

All 45 recipes in this chapter are as good as the cookies you remember from your childhood, because each recipe has been farm-family tested. Like treasured heirlooms, these recipes have been lovingly passed from one generation to the next, many having been in the same family for more than 75 years.

Each recipe in this chapter is an old-fashioned favorite.

We've included 10 different spice cookies, each one a winner, from the extra-spicy Grandmother's Ginger Cookies iced with a light vanilla frosting to the flavorful New England Hermits made in convenient bar form.

For chocolate fans, we've included eight of the best, such as Chewy Fudge Brownies, a basic brownie studded with pecans, and Chocolate Marbled Brownies, made by swirling a cream cheese filling throughout a chocolaty batter. To make them utterly irresistible, the moist bars are frosted with a creamy chocolate icing. If you prefer a chocolate-studded cookie, try Grandmother's Chocolate Chippers; an Illinois woman fondly remembers her grandmother serving them with mugs of hot cocoa.

There are fruit-filled cookies, too: Old-Fashioned Date-Filled Cookies made with a sweet date filling, and Old-Fashioned Filled Cookies, butter cookies with a choice of apricot, prune or fig filling.

No heirloom recipe collection would be complete without the classic sugar cookie and there are seven in this chapter, each one a little bit different. If you prefer a crispy sugar cookie, try Grandmother's Sugar Cookies, Old-Fashioned Rolled Sugar Cookies, or crunchy Butter Crispies, a recipe rediscovered by an Iowa woman in an old Norwegian cookbook. If you're in a hurry, make No-Roll Sugar Cookies, with their crinkled tops glistening with sugar crystals.

As you might expect, many of these are big-batch recipes—some of them yield as many as nine dozen cookies. Examples of these family-style treats are Granny's Best Oatmeal Cookies, large rounds laced with lots of raisins and chopped walnuts; cake-like Buttermilk Chocolate Chip Cookies, an interesting variation of the standard chocolate chip; and Spicy Walnut-Almond Cookies, a recipe originally brought to this country at the turn of the century by a Dutch baker.

No matter which recipe you start with, your own kitchen soon will be filled with the enticing aroma of freshly baked cookies—just as good as you remember.

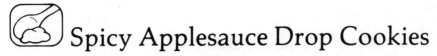 Spicy Applesauce Drop Cookies

This is a favorite recipe of an Oregon farm woman who keeps these cookies on hand for her five grandchildren.

2 c. sifted flour	1 c. sugar
1 tsp. baking soda	1 egg
½ tsp. baking powder	1 c. applesauce
¼ tsp. salt	1 tsp. vanilla
1 tsp. ground cinnamon	½ c. raisins
1 tsp. ground nutmeg	½ c. chopped walnuts
½ c. butter or regular margarine	Confectioners' sugar

Sift together flour, baking soda, baking powder, salt, cinnamon and nutmeg; set aside.

Cream together butter and sugar in bowl until light and fluffy, using electric mixer at medium speed. Add egg, applesauce and vanilla, beating well.

Gradually stir dry ingredients into creamed mixture, blending well. Stir in raisins and walnuts. Drop mixture by teaspoonfuls, about 3" apart, on greased baking sheets.

Bake in 350° oven 12 minutes, or until golden brown. Remove from baking sheets; cool on racks. Sprinkle cookies with confectioners' sugar. Makes 4 dozen.

 Applesauce Fudgies

The addition of applesauce to this chocolate brownie makes it extra-moist and chewy. Keep on hand for unexpected guests.

½ c. butter or regular margarine	¼ tsp. salt
2 (1-oz.) squares unsweetened chocolate	2 eggs
	1 c. brown sugar, packed
1 c. sifted flour	1 tsp. vanilla
½ tsp. baking powder	½ c. applesauce
¼ tsp. baking soda	½ c. chopped walnuts

Combine butter and chocolate in saucepan. Place over low heat, stirring constantly, until melted. Remove from heat; cool slightly.

Sift together flour, baking powder, baking soda and salt; set aside.

Combine eggs, brown sugar and vanilla in bowl. Beat until well blended, using electric mixer at medium speed. Blend in chocolate mixture and applesauce.

Gradually stir dry ingredients into chocolate mixture, mixing well. Stir in walnuts. Pour mixture into greased 13x9x2" baking pan.

Bake in 350° oven 25 minutes, or until top springs back when touched lightly with finger. Cool in pan on rack. Cut into 2¼" squares. Makes 24.

Spicy Apple Squares

Oatmeal, diced apple and walnuts are combined in this old-fashioned spice cookie. These bar cookies are a snap to prepare, too.

1 c. sifted flour	1 c. sugar
1 tsp. baking powder	2 eggs
1 tsp. ground cinnamon	1 c. diced, pared apples
½ tsp. baking soda	¾ c. rolled oats
½ tsp. ground nutmeg	½ c. chopped walnuts
¼ tsp. ground cloves	Confectioners' sugar
⅔ c. butter or regular margarine	

Sift together flour, baking powder, cinnamon, baking soda, nutmeg and cloves; set aside.

Cream together butter and sugar in bowl until light and fluffy, using electric mixer at medium speed. Add eggs, one at a time, beating well after each addition.

Gradually add dry ingredients to creamed mixture, beating well after each addition, using electric mixer at low speed.

Stir in apples, rolled oats and walnuts. Spread batter in greased 13x9x2" baking pan.

Bake in 350° oven 25 to 30 minutes, or until top springs back when touched lightly with finger. Cool in pan on rack. Sprinkle with confectioners' sugar. Cut into 2¼" squares. Makes 24.

Raisin Cookies

Here's a good basic raisin cookie flavored with a dash of nutmeg. You'll find it easy to prepare at the last minute for a dessert.

3 c. sifted flour	3 eggs
1 tsp. baking soda	1 tsp. vanilla
¼ tsp. salt	½ c. hot water
¼ tsp. ground nutmeg	1 c. raisins
1 c. shortening	1 tblsp. flour
1½ c. sugar	

Sift together 3 c. flour, baking soda, salt and nutmeg; set aside.

Cream together shortening and sugar in bowl until light and fluffy, using electric mixer at medium speed. Add eggs, one at a time, beating well after each addition. Beat in vanilla.

Add dry ingredients alternately with hot water to creamed mixture, beating well after each addition, using electric mixer at low speed.

Combine raisins and 1 tblsp. flour. Stir into dough. Drop mixture by teaspoonfuls, about 2" apart, on greased baking sheets.

Bake in 400° oven 10 minutes, or until golden brown. Remove from baking sheets; cool on racks. Makes about 5 dozen.

Applesauce-Raisin Cookies

These soft cookies are lightly spiced with cinnamon and cloves. They're rolled in confectioners' sugar before serving.

2½ c. sifted flour	1 c. sugar
1 tsp. baking powder	1 egg
½ tsp. baking soda	1 c. applesauce
½ tsp. salt	½ c. raisins
½ tsp. ground cinnamon	½ c. chopped walnuts
¼ tsp. ground cloves	1 tblsp. flour
½ c. shortening	Confectioners' sugar

Sift together 2½ c. flour, baking powder, baking soda, salt, cinnamon and cloves; set aside.

Cream together shortening and sugar in bowl until light and fluffy, using electric mixer at medium speed. Add egg and applesauce; blend well.

Gradually add dry ingredients to creamed mixture, beating well after each addition, using electric mixer at low speed.

Combine raisins, walnuts and 1 tblsp. flour. Stir raisin mixture into dough. Drop mixture by teaspoonfuls, about 2" apart, on greased baking sheets.

Bake in 375° oven 12 minutes, or until golden. Remove from baking sheets; cool on racks. Roll in confectioners' sugar. Makes 4 dozen.

Peanut-Raisin Cookies

Ground raisins and peanuts make this cookie unusual. A farm woman rediscovered the recipe in a turn-of-the-century church cookbook.

1½ c. Spanish peanuts	½ c. butter or regular
1½ c. raisins	margarine
1 tsp. cooking oil	½ c. shortening
1½ c. sifted flour	1 c. brown sugar, packed
1½ tsp. baking powder	1 c. sugar
1½ tsp. baking soda	2 eggs

Combine peanuts and raisins. Pour cooking oil into food grinder to ease grinding. Grind peanuts and raisins, using fine blade; set aside.

Sift together flour, baking powder and baking soda; set aside.

Cream together butter, shortening, brown sugar and sugar in bowl until light and fluffy, using electric mixer at medium speed. Add eggs, one at a time, beating well after each addition.

Gradually stir dry ingredients into creamed mixture, blending well. Stir in ground peanut-raisin mixture. Shape dough into 1¼" balls. Place balls, about 3" apart, on greased baking sheets.

Bake in 375° oven 8 minutes, or until golden brown. Cool on baking sheets 2 minutes. Remove from baking sheets; cool completely on racks. Makes 6 dozen.

Spicy Nut and Fruit Squares

Cinnamon, nutmeg and cloves add a pleasant spiciness to these candied fruit and nut bars. A perfect choice for holiday baking.

1¾ c. sifted flour
¼ tsp. baking soda
¼ tsp. salt
½ c. butter or regular
  margarine
1 c. brown sugar, packed
1 egg, separated

1 tsp. vanilla
3 tblsp. sugar
1 tsp. ground cinnamon
1 tsp. ground nutmeg
¼ tsp. ground cloves
1 c. mixed candied fruit
1 c. chopped walnuts

Sift together flour, baking soda and salt; set aside.

Cream together butter and brown sugar in bowl until light and fluffy, using electric mixer at medium speed. Add egg yolk and vanilla; blend well.

Gradually stir dry ingredients into creamed mixture, mixing well. (Dough will be very crumbly.) Press dough into ungreased 13x9x2" baking pan.

Slightly beat egg white in a bowl with a fork. Add sugar, cinnamon, nutmeg, cloves, candied fruit and walnuts; mix well. Spread fruit mixture evenly over dough.

Bake in 350° oven 20 to 25 minutes, or until golden brown. Cool in pan on rack. Cut into 2¼" squares. Makes 24.

Spicy Raisin Bars

A tangy orange glaze highlights these triple-spiced raisin bars. These bars are shaped by spreading the dough on baking sheets.

2 c. raisins
1 c. water
4 c. sifted flour
1 tsp. baking powder
1 tsp. baking soda
½ tsp. salt
1½ tsp. ground cinnamon
1½ tsp. ground allspice

½ tsp. ground nutmeg
1 c. shortening
2 c. brown sugar, packed
3 eggs
1 tsp. vanilla
Orange Glaze (recipe
  follows)

Place raisins and water in 2-qt. saucepan. Cook over medium heat until it comes to a boil. Reduce heat and simmer, covered, 5 minutes. Remove from heat; cool completely.

Sift together flour, baking powder, baking soda, salt, cinnamon, allspice and nutmeg; set aside.

Cream together shortening and brown sugar in bowl until light and fluffy, using electric mixer at medium speed. Add eggs, one at a time, beating well after each addition. Blend in vanilla and cooled raisin mixture.

Gradually stir dry ingredients into creamed mixture, blending well. Divide dough in fourths. Spread each fourth on greased baking sheet, forming a 12x3" rectangle.

Bake in 350° oven 18 to 20 minutes, or until golden brown. Cool on baking sheets on racks. Prepare Orange Glaze. Frost rectangles with Orange Glaze. Cut each rectangle into 12 bars, 1" wide. Makes 48.

Orange Glaze: Combine 4 c. sifted confectioners' sugar, 2 tblsp. melted butter or regular margarine and 4 tblsp. orange juice in bowl. Stir until smooth. Add 1 more tblsp. orange juice, if necessary, to make frosting of spreading consistency.

New England Hermits

This extra-spicy molasses bar cookie with citron, raisins, currants and nuts has changed little since colonial days.

2 c. sifted flour	½ c. sugar
1 tsp. ground cinnamon	2 eggs
¾ tsp. baking soda	½ c. molasses
¾ tsp. cream of tartar	3 tblsp. chopped citron
½ tsp. salt	½ c. chopped raisins
½ tsp. ground cloves	½ c. currants
¼ tsp. ground nutmeg	¼ c. chopped walnuts
⅛ tsp. ground allspice	
½ c. butter or regular margarine	

Sift together flour, cinnamon, baking soda, cream of tartar, salt, cloves, nutmeg and allspice; set aside.

Cream together butter and sugar in bowl until light and fluffy, using electric mixer at medium speed. Add eggs, one at a time, beating well after each addition. Blend in molasses.

Gradually stir dry ingredients into creamed mixture, mixing well. Stir in citron, raisins, currants and walnuts.

Spread mixture evenly in greased 13x9x2" baking pan.

Bake in 350° oven 20 minutes, or until no imprint remains when touched lightly with finger. Cool slightly in pan on rack. While still warm, cut into 3x1" bars. Cool completely. Makes 39.

Date-Oatmeal Sandwich Cookies

Two country favorites combined in one—oatmeal cookies sand-wiched around a sweet date filling. A good old-fashioned treat.

2 c. sifted flour	½ c. milk
1 tsp. baking soda	2 c. quick-cooking oats
½ tsp. salt	Date Filling (recipe follows)
1 c. shortening	Confectioners' sugar
1 c. brown sugar, packed	

Sift together flour, baking soda and salt; set aside.

Cream together shortening and brown sugar in bowl until light and fluffy, using electric mixer at medium speed. Add milk; blend well.

Gradually stir dry ingredients into creamed mixture, mixing well. Stir in oats. (Dough is soft.)

Divide dough in half. Roll out one half of dough on floured surface to ¼" thickness. Cut into 34 rounds, using floured 2½" round cookie cutter. Place rounds, about 2" apart, on greased baking sheets.

Roll out remaining dough. Cut into 34 rounds. Cut out center of each, using 1" cookie cutter or doughnut hole cutter. Place rounds, about 2" apart, on greased baking sheets.

Bake in 350° oven 10 minutes, or until lightly browned. Remove from baking sheets; cool on racks.

To make sandwich cookies: Prepare Date Filling. Spread Date Filling on whole rounds. Sprinkle confectioners' sugar on top of cutout rounds and place on top of other cookies, making sandwich cookies. Makes 34 sandwich cookies.

Date Filling: Combine 1 (8-oz.) pkg. pitted dates (chopped), ¾ c. sugar and ½ c. water in saucepan. Cook over medium heat, stirring constantly, until mixture comes to a boil and starts to thicken. Remove from heat. Mash dates with vegetable masher until smooth. Cool completely.

Old-Fashioned Date-Filled Cookies

A Washington farm wife has fond childhood memories of her mother baking these favorites in the family's wood stove.

2½ c. sifted flour	1 egg
3 tsp. baking powder	1 tsp. vanilla
¼ tsp. salt	½ c. milk
½ c. butter or regular margarine	Date Filling (recipe follows)
1 c. sugar	Sugar

Sift together flour, baking powder and salt; set aside.

Cream together butter and 1 c. sugar in bowl until light and fluffy, using electric mixer at medium speed. Add egg and vanilla; beat well.

Add dry ingredients alternately with milk to creamed mixture, beating well after each addition, using electric mixer at low speed. Cover and chill dough in refrigerator at least 3 hours.

Meanwhile, prepare Date Filling.

Divide dough into fourths. Use one fourth of the dough at a time, keeping remaining dough in refrigerator. Roll out each fourth of the dough on floured surface to 1/8" thickness. With floured 2½" round cookie cutter, cut 18 rounds from each fourth of dough. Place 36 rounds, about 2" apart, on greased baking sheets. Place about 1 tsp. Date Filling in center of each round. Spread filling with back of spoon to flatten. Top each with another round. No need to seal edges because dough is soft and seals during baking. Sprinkle tops of each cookie with sugar.

Bake in 375° oven 10 to 12 minutes, or until golden brown. Remove from baking sheets; cool on racks. Makes 3 dozen.

Date Filling: Combine ½ c. sugar and 2 tblsp. flour in saucepan; mix well. Add 1 c. chopped, pitted dates and 1 c. boiling water; mix well. Cook over medium heat, stirring constantly, until it comes to a boil. Simmer 2 minutes. Remove from heat and cool completely.

Uncle Jim's Oatmeal Cookies

No cookie file would be complete without a good basic oatmeal recipe. This one makes a nutritious snack with a tall glass of milk.

1½ c. sifted flour	1 c. sugar
1 tsp. ground cinnamon	2 eggs
¾ tsp. baking soda	2 tblsp. molasses
½ tsp. baking powder	3 tblsp. sour milk
½ tsp. salt	3 c. rolled oats
¾ c. butter or regular	½ c. raisins
margarine	

Sift together flour, cinnamon, baking soda, baking powder and salt; set aside.

Cream together butter and sugar in bowl until light and fluffy, using electric mixer at medium speed. Add eggs, one at a time, beating well after each addition. Beat in molasses.

Add dry ingredients alternately with sour milk to creamed mixture, mixing well after each addition, using electric mixer at low speed. Stir in oats and raisins. Drop mixture by teaspoonfuls, about 2" apart, on greased baking sheets.

Bake in 350° oven 10 to 12 minutes, or until golden brown. Remove from baking sheets; cool on racks. Makes 6 dozen.

Granny's Best Oatmeal Cookies

Here's the recipe to choose when you need lots of home-style raisin-studded oatmeal cookies. It yields nine dozen.

4¼ c. sifted flour	4 eggs
1 tsp. ground cinnamon	2 tsp. baking soda
1 tsp. ground cloves	1 c. milk
½ tsp. salt	4 c. quick-cooking oats
1½ c. butter or regular margarine	2 c. raisins
3 c. brown sugar, packed	1½ c. chopped walnuts

Sift together flour, cinnamon, cloves and salt; set aside.

Cream together butter and brown sugar in bowl until light and fluffy, using electric mixer at medium speed. Add eggs, one at a time, beating well after each addition.

Stir baking soda into milk. Add dry ingredients alternately with milk mixture to creamed mixture, beating well after each addition, using electric mixer at low speed. Stir in oats, raisins and walnuts. Drop mixture by tablespoonfuls, about 2" apart, on greased baking sheets.

Bake in 350° oven 15 minutes, or until golden brown. Remove from baking sheets; cool on racks. Makes about 9 dozen.

Pineapple Oatmeal Bars

These rich bars with an oatmeal and brown sugar crumb crust, are topped with a luscious layer of pineapple. Delightfully good!

½ c. brown sugar, packed	1 (20-oz.) can crushed pine-
1¼ c. quick-cooking oats	apple in juice, drained
½ c. sifted flour	1 tblsp. cornstarch
¼ tsp. baking soda	½ c. sugar
¼ tsp. salt	½ c. light cream
½ c. butter or regular	1 egg yolk
margarine	

Combine brown sugar, oats, flour, baking soda and salt in bowl. Cut in butter until mixture is crumbly, using a pastry blender. Press mixture into greased 12x8x2" (2-qt.) glass baking dish.

Combine pineapple, cornstarch, sugar, light cream and egg yolk in saucepan. Cook over medium heat, stirring constantly, until mixture is thick. Remove from heat. Pour over crust.

Bake in 375° oven 30 minutes, or until topping is set. Cool in pan on rack. Cut into 3x1" bars. Makes 32.

Coconut Oatmeal Cookies

Flaked coconut is stirred into this oatmeal dough to make the cookies extra-chewy and to give them a nutlike flavor.

1 c. sifted flour	1 c. sugar
1 tsp. baking soda	2 eggs
¼ tsp. salt	1 tsp. vanilla
1 c. melted shortening	1 c. flaked coconut
1 c. brown sugar, packed	2 c. quick-cooking oats

Sift together flour, baking soda and salt; set aside.

Beat together shortening, brown sugar and sugar in bowl until well blended, using electric mixer at medium speed. Add eggs, one at a time, beating well after each addition. Blend in vanilla.

Gradually stir dry ingredients into sugar mixture; mix well. Stir in coconut and oats. Shape dough into 1" balls. Place balls, about 2" apart, on greased baking sheets.

Bake in 325° oven 12 minutes, or until golden brown. Remove from baking sheets; cool on racks. Makes 6 dozen.

Heirloom Brown Sugar Cookies

These crisp, golden brown rounds resemble peanut butter cookies because they're flattened with a fork before baking.

4¼ c. sifted flour	1 c. brown sugar, packed
2 tsp. baking soda	1 c. sugar
2 tsp. cream of tartar	3 eggs
½ tsp. salt	
1 c. butter or regular margarine	

Sift together flour, baking soda, cream of tartar and salt; set aside.

Cream together butter, brown sugar and sugar in bowl until light and fluffy, using electric mixer at medium speed. Add eggs, one at a time, beating well after each addition.

Gradually stir dry ingredients into creamed mixture, blending well. Shape mixture into 1¼" balls. Place balls, about 3" apart, on greased baking sheets. Flatten each with floured tines of fork in one direction.

Bake in 375° oven 10 minutes, or until golden brown. Remove from baking sheets; cool on racks. Makes 6 dozen.

Brown Sugar Refrigerator Cookies

Christmas wouldn't be the same in one Wisconsin family without these crispy cookies—they've been enjoyed for 80 years.

3½ c. sifted flour	2 eggs
1 tsp. baking soda	1 tsp. vanilla
2 c. brown sugar, packed	1 c. chopped pecans
1 c. melted butter or regular margarine	

Sift together flour and baking soda; set aside.

Beat together brown sugar and butter in bowl until well blended, using electric mixer at medium speed. Add eggs, one at a time, beating well after each addition. Beat in vanilla.

Gradually stir dry ingredients into creamed mixture, mixing well. Then stir in pecans. Cover bowl with aluminum foil and refrigerate 1 hour.

Shape dough into 2 (12") rolls, about 1½" in diameter. Wrap each roll in plastic wrap. Chill in refrigerator overnight.

Cut rolls into ¼" thick slices. Place slices, about 2" apart, on greased baking sheets.

Bake in 375° oven 10 to 12 minutes, or until golden brown. Remove from baking sheets; cool on racks. Makes about 8 dozen.

 Old-Fashioned Ice Box Cookies

If you keep a couple of rolls of these pecan cookies in your freezer, you'll be able to bake cookies anytime.

1¾ c. sifted flour	⅔ c. sugar
¼ tsp. salt	1 egg
¾ c. butter or regular margarine	1 tsp. vanilla
	¾ c. finely chopped pecans

Sift together flour and salt; set aside.

Cream together butter and sugar in bowl until light and fluffy, using electric mixer at medium speed. Add egg and vanilla, beating well.

Gradually stir dry ingredients into creamed mixture, blending well. Stir in ¼ c. of the pecans. Divide dough in half. Shape each half into a 6" roll. Roll each in remaining ½ c. pecans. Wrap each roll in waxed paper. Chill in refrigerator overnight.

Cut each roll into 18 slices, about ⅓" thick. Place slices, about 2" apart, on greased baking sheets.

Bake in 350° oven 12 minutes, or until golden brown. Remove from baking sheets; cool on racks. Makes 3 dozen.

Cottage Cheese-Chocolate Cookies

These cottage cheese-flecked chocolate cookies are soft and cake-like. They make perfect dunkers for coffee or tea.

2¾ c. sifted flour	1¾ c. sugar
½ c. baking cocoa	1 c. small-curd creamed cottage cheese
1 tsp. baking soda	
1 tsp. baking powder	2 eggs
½ tsp. salt	1 tsp. vanilla
1 c. butter or regular margarine	

Sift together flour, cocoa, baking soda, baking powder and salt; set aside.

Cream together butter and sugar in bowl until light and fluffy, using electric mixer at medium speed. Add cottage cheese, eggs and vanilla; blend well.

Gradually add dry ingredients to creamed mixture, beating well after each addition, using electric mixer at low speed. Drop mixture by teaspoonfuls, about 2" apart, on ungreased baking sheets.

Bake in 350° oven 10 minutes, or until no imprint remains when touched lightly with finger. Remove from baking sheets; cool on racks. Makes 5 dozen.

Grandmother's Chocolate Chippers

"On cold wintry days my Grandmom welcomed us with these chewy cookies and hot chocolate," an Illinois woman wrote to us.

2½ c. sifted flour	½ c. sugar
1 tsp. baking soda	2 eggs
1 tsp. salt	1 tsp. vanilla
1 c. butter or regular	1 (6-oz.) pkg. semisweet
margarine	chocolate pieces
1 c. brown sugar, packed	

Sift together flour, baking soda and salt; set aside.

Cream together butter, brown sugar and sugar in bowl until light and fluffy, using electric mixer at medium speed. Add eggs, one at a time, beating well after each addition. Blend in vanilla.

Gradually stir dry ingredients into creamed mixture; blend well. Stir in chocolate pieces. Drop mixture by teaspoonfuls, about 2" apart, on greased baking sheets.

Bake in 375° oven 8 to 10 minutes, or until golden brown. Remove from baking sheets; cool on racks. Makes 4½ dozen.

Buttermilk Chocolate Chip Cookies

Buttermilk is used in this variation of a basic chocolate chip cookie. These cake-like cookies keep well.

3 c. sifted flour	1½ tsp. vanilla
1 tsp. baking soda	½ c. buttermilk
1 c. shortening	1 (12-oz.) pkg. semisweet
1 c. sugar	chocolate pieces
1 c. brown sugar, packed	1½ c. chopped walnuts
2 eggs	

Sift together flour and baking soda; set aside.

Cream together shortening, sugar and brown sugar in bowl until light and fluffy, using electric mixer at medium speed. Add eggs, one at a time, beating well after each addition. Blend in vanilla.

Add dry ingredients alternately with buttermilk to creamed mixture, beating well after each addition, using electric mixer at low speed. Stir in chocolate pieces and walnuts. Drop mixture by teaspoonfuls, about 2" apart, on greased baking sheets.

Bake in 350° oven 12 to 15 minutes, or until golden brown. Remove from baking sheets; cool on racks. Makes 9 dozen.

 # Chocolate Marbled Brownies

"This is one of my husband's favorites. He asks me to make these two-toned brownies often," a New York homemaker told us.

1⅓ c. sifted flour	2 (3-oz.) pkg. cream cheese,
1 tsp. baking powder	softened
½ tsp. salt	⅓ c. butter or regular
⅔ c. butter or regular	margarine
margarine	⅓ c. sugar
2 c. sugar	2 tblsp. flour
4 eggs	2 eggs
4 (1-oz.) env. unsweetened	¾ tsp. vanilla
liquid chocolate	Easy Chocolate Frosting
2 tsp. vanilla	(recipe follows)
1 c. chopped walnuts	

Sift together 1⅓ c. flour, baking powder and salt; set aside.

Cream together ⅔ c. butter and 2 c. sugar in bowl until light and fluffy, using electric mixer at medium speed. Add 4 eggs, one at a time, beating well after each addition. Blend in liquid chocolate and 2 tsp. vanilla. Stir in dry ingredients and walnuts. Set aside.

Beat together cream cheese and ⅓ c. butter in small bowl until smooth, using electric mixer at medium speed. Add ⅓ c. sugar, 2 tblsp. flour, 2 eggs and ¾ tsp. vanilla. Beat until smooth.

Spread one half of chocolate batter in greased 13x9x2" baking pan. Spread cream cheese mixture evenly over all. Spoon remaining chocolate batter over cream cheese layer. Use a metal spatula to swirl layers to give marbled effect.

Bake in 350° oven 40 minutes, or until top springs back when touched lightly with finger. Cool in pan on rack.

Prepare Easy Chocolate Frosting. Frost brownies with Easy Chocolate Frosting. Cut into 3x1" bars. Makes 39.

Easy Chocolate Frosting: Combine 2 c. sifted confectioners' sugar, 2 (1-oz.) env. unsweetened liquid chocolate, ¼ c. melted butter or regular margarine, 3 tblsp. milk and 1 tsp. vanilla in bowl. Beat until smooth and creamy, using electric mixer at medium speed.

Chewy Fudge Brownies

"I've been making this easy dessert for over 40 years," wrote an Alabama woman. "It's a hand-me-down recipe from my mother."

¼ c. butter or regular margarine	2 eggs
3 (1-oz.) squares unsweetened chocolate	½ c. unsifted self-rising flour
1⅓ c. sugar	1 tsp. vanilla
	⅔ c. chopped pecans

Combine butter and chocolate in small saucepan. Cook over low heat until melted. Remove from heat. Pour mixture into bowl. Add sugar and eggs. Beat until well blended, using electric mixer at medium speed. Stir in flour and vanilla. Stir in pecans. Spread mixture in greased 9" square baking pan.

Bake in 325° oven 30 minutes, or until a slight imprint remains when touched lightly with finger. Cool slightly in pan on rack. While still warm, cut into 2¼" squares. Cool completely. Makes 16.

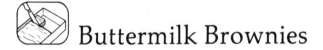

Buttermilk Brownies

Cinnamon-flavored brownies swirled with a creamy milk chocolate frosting. These cocoa-based bars are moist, too.

2 c. sifted flour	1 c. water
2 c. sugar	3 tblsp. baking cocoa
1 tsp. baking soda	½ c. buttermilk
½ tsp. salt	2 eggs
½ tsp. ground cinnamon	1 tsp. vanilla
1 c. butter or regular margarine	Milk Chocolate Frosting (recipe follows)

Sift together flour, sugar, baking soda, salt and cinnamon into bowl; set aside.

Combine butter, water and cocoa in saucepan. Cook over medium heat until butter melts. Remove from heat.

Add cocoa mixture to dry ingredients. Beat 1 minute, using electric mixer at medium speed. Add buttermilk, eggs and vanilla. Beat 1 more minute. (Batter will be thin.) Pour into greased 15½x10½x1" jelly roll pan.

Bake in 350° oven 25 minutes, or until top springs back when touched lightly with finger. Cool slightly in pan on rack.

Meanwhile, prepare Milk Chocolate Frosting. While brownies are still warm, frost with Milk Chocolate Frosting. Cool completely. Cut into 2½x1½" bars. Makes 48.

Milk Chocolate Frosting: Sift 1 (1-lb.) box confectioners' sugar into bowl; set aside. Combine ½ c. butter or regular margarine, 6 tblsp. milk and 3 tblsp. baking cocoa in saucepan. Cook over medium heat until butter melts. Remove from heat. Add to confectioners' sugar with 1 tsp. vanilla. Beat until smooth, using electric mixer at medium speed. Stir in ½ c. chopped walnuts.

 # Deluxe Brownie Fingers

Here's another good brownie recipe for all the chocolate fans in your family. It makes a big batch of 40 good-sized bars.

¼ c. baking cocoa	1 tsp. baking soda
1 c. butter or regular	2 eggs
margarine	1 tsp. vanilla
1 c. water	½ c. buttermilk
2 c. sifted flour	Fudge Frosting (recipe
2 c. sugar	follows)

Combine cocoa, butter and water in 3-qt. saucepan. Cook over medium heat, stirring constantly, until butter is melted. Remove from heat; cool slightly.

Sift together flour, sugar and baking soda. Gradually stir dry ingredients into chocolate mixture, mixing well with spoon. Blend in eggs, vanilla and buttermilk, mixing well. Pour into greased 15½x10½x1" jelly roll pan.

Bake in 375° oven 20 minutes, or until no imprint remains when touched lightly with finger. Cool in pan on rack. Prepare Fudge Frosting. Frost brownies with Fudge Frosting. Cut into 4x1" bars. Makes 40.

Fudge Frosting: Combine 1½ c. sugar, 6 tblsp. butter or regular margarine, 6 tblsp. milk and ½ c. semisweet chocolate pieces in 2-qt. saucepan. Cook over medium heat, stirring constantly, until mixture comes to a boil. Add 20 miniature marshmallows. Boil 1 minute, stirring constantly. Remove from heat. Cool to lukewarm (120°). Beat, until frosting is of spreading consistency, using electric mixer at medium speed.

Butterscotch Brownies

Rich butterscotch bar cookies, swirled with a brown butter frosting and topped with an extra-thin semisweet chocolate glaze.

1 c. sifted flour	½ c. chopped walnuts
1 tsp. baking powder	2 (1-oz.) squares semisweet
½ tsp. salt	chocolate
¼ c. melted butter or regular	2 tblsp. butter or regular
margarine	margarine
1 c. brown sugar, packed	Brown Butter Frosting
1 egg	(recipe follows)
½ tsp. vanilla	

Sift together flour, baking powder and salt; set aside.

Combine ¼ c. butter and brown sugar in bowl. Stir until thoroughly blended. Add egg and vanilla; mix well.

Gradually stir dry ingredients into brown sugar mixture. Add walnuts; mix well. Spread mixture in greased 8″ square baking pan.

Bake in 350° oven 30 minutes, or until top springs back when touched lightly with finger. Cool in pan on rack.

Melt chocolate with 2 tblsp. butter in small saucepan over low heat, stirring constantly. Remove from heat and cool slightly.

Meanwhile, prepare Brown Butter Frosting. Spread Brown Butter Frosting over brownies. Then pour chocolate mixture over the top, slightly tilting pan back and forth to distribute chocolate evenly over surface. When toppings are set, cut into 2″ squares. Makes 16.

Brown Butter Frosting: Melt ¼ c. butter or regular margarine in small saucepan over low heat. Heat butter until it turns a light golden brown. Remove from heat. Stir in 2 c. sifted confectioners' sugar. Then stir in 2 tblsp. light cream and 1 tsp. vanilla. Stir until smooth and of spreading consistency.

Lemon-Coconut Squares

There are many versions of this tangy two-layer bar cookie. The Farm Journal food staff feels this is one of the best ever tasted.

¼ c. butter or regular	1 tsp. vanilla
margarine	¾ c. flaked coconut
1 c. sifted flour	½ c. chopped pecans
2 eggs	⅛ tsp. baking powder
1 c. brown sugar, packed	Lemon Icing (recipe follows)

Cut butter into flour in bowl until mixture is crumbly, using a pastry blender. Press crumb mixture into an ungreased 12x8x2" (2-qt.) glass baking dish.

Bake in 350° oven 12 to 15 minutes, or until lightly browned.

Meanwhile, beat eggs in bowl until light and lemon-colored, using electric mixer at high speed. Gradually beat in brown sugar and vanilla. Stir in coconut, pecans and baking powder. Spread mixture over baked crust.

Bake in 350° oven 20 minutes, or until top is lightly browned. Cool slightly in dish on rack. Prepare Lemon Icing. While still warm, spread with Lemon Icing. Cool completely. Cut into 2" squares. Makes 24.

Lemon Icing: Combine 1 c. sifted confectioners' sugar, 2 tblsp. lemon juice and 1 tsp. grated lemon rind in bowl. Stir until smooth.

Frosted Coconut-Orange Cookies

These chewy coconut cookies are frosted with a creamy orange frosting. They're superb served with a pitcher of icy lemonade.

1¾ c. sifted flour	½ tsp. grated orange rind
¼ tsp. baking soda	½ tsp. grated lemon rind
¼ tsp. salt	3 tblsp. orange juice
½ c. butter or regular margarine	1 tblsp. lemon juice
	1 c. flaked coconut
⅔ c. sugar	Orange Frosting (recipe
1 egg	follows)

Sift together flour, baking soda and salt; set aside.

Cream together butter and sugar in bowl until light and fluffy, using electric mixer at medium speed. Add egg; beat well. Beat in orange rind and lemon rind.

Add dry ingredients alternately with orange juice and lemon juice to creamed mixture, beating well after each addition, using electric mixer at low speed. Stir in coconut. Drop mixture by rounded teaspoonfuls, about 3" apart, on greased baking sheets.

Bake in 350° oven 12 minutes, or until edges are browned. Remove from baking sheets; cool on racks.

Prepare Orange Frosting. Frost cookies with Orange Frosting. Makes 3 dozen.

Orange Frosting: Combine 1⅓ c. sifted confectioners' sugar, ½ tsp. grated orange rind, 1 drop yellow food coloring, ½ tsp. lemon juice and 1 tblsp. orange juice in bowl. Beat until smooth, using a spoon.

Crunchy Peanut Butter Cookies

Most children prefer simple cookies like these peanut butter rounds. Chunky peanut butter adds extra peanut flavor.

3 c. sifted flour	1 c. brown sugar, packed
1½ tsp. baking soda	2 eggs
½ tsp. salt	1 c. chunky peanut butter
1 c. shortening	1 tsp. vanilla
1 c. sugar	

Sift together flour, baking soda and salt; set aside.

Cream together shortening, sugar and brown sugar in bowl until light and fluffy, using electric mixer at medium speed. Add eggs, one at a time, beating well after each addition.

Add peanut butter and vanilla; beat until smooth.

Gradually stir dry ingredients into creamed mixture, mixing well. Shape dough into 1" balls. Place balls, about 2" apart, on greased baking sheets. Flatten each with floured tines of a fork in a crisscross pattern.

Bake in 400° oven 12 minutes, or until golden brown. Remove from baking sheets; cool on racks. Makes about 5½ dozen.

Date Meringue Bars

During baking these interesting bars separate into a chewy date layer on the bottom with a tender meringue-like crust.

¾ c. sifted flour	1 tsp. vanilla
1 tsp. baking powder	2 c. chopped, pitted dates
½ tsp. salt	1 c. chopped walnuts
3 eggs	Confectioners' sugar
1 c. sugar	

Sift together flour, baking powder and salt; set aside.

Beat eggs in bowl until thick and lemon-colored, using electric mixer at high speed. Gradually add sugar, beating well. Blend in vanilla.

Gradually stir dry ingredients into egg mixture, mixing well. Stir in dates and walnuts. Pour mixture into greased 13x9x2" baking pan.

Bake in 350° oven 25 minutes, or until golden brown. Cool in pan on rack. Sprinkle with confectioners' sugar. Cut into 3x1" bars. Makes 39.

 Grandmom's Apricot Squares

No electric mixer needed for this heirloom bar cookie. Just cut butter into dry ingredients, press into pan and spread with jam.

1½ c. sifted flour
1½ c. quick-cooking oats
1 c. brown sugar, packed
¾ c. soft butter or regular
   margarine

1 (10-oz.) jar apricot
   preserves (1 c.)

Combine flour, oats and brown sugar in bowl. Cut in butter until mixture is crumbly, using pastry blender. Press two thirds of crumb mixture into greased 8″ square baking pan, building up sides to make ½″ rim.

Spread apricot preserves over crumb layer. Sprinkle remaining crumbs on top; pat down gently.

Bake in 350° oven 35 minutes, or until golden brown. Cool in pan on rack. Cut into 2″ squares. Makes 16.

Spicy Ginger Cookies

Molasses adds flavor and iron to these old-fashioned spice cookies. The balls of dough are rolled in sugar before baking.

4 c. sifted flour	1 c. shortening
2 tsp. baking soda	1 c. sugar
½ tsp. salt	1 egg
2 tsp. ground ginger	1 c. molasses
½ tsp. ground cinnamon	Sugar
½ tsp. ground cloves	

Sift together flour, baking soda, salt, ginger, cinnamon and cloves; set aside.

Cream together shortening and 1 c. sugar in bowl until light and fluffy, using electric mixer at medium speed. Add egg and molasses, beating well.

Gradually stir dry ingredients into creamed mixture, blending well. Cover and chill in refrigerator 2 hours.

Shape dough into 1" balls. Roll in sugar. Place balls, about 2" apart, on greased baking sheets.

Bake in 350° oven 12 minutes, or until no imprint remains when cookies are lightly touched with finger. Remove from baking sheets; cool on racks. Makes 7½ dozen.

Grandmother's Ginger Cookies

These extra-spicy molasses cookies are flavored with ginger, cinnamon and nutmeg. A vanilla frosting makes them even more appealing.

4 c. sifted flour	1 egg
2 tsp. ground ginger	1 c. molasses
1 tsp. ground cinnamon	2 tsp. baking soda
1 tsp. ground nutmeg	1 c. very hot water
½ tsp. salt	Vanilla Frosting (recipe
½ c. shortening	follows)
1 c. sugar	

Sift together flour, ginger, cinnamon, nutmeg and salt; set aside.

Cream together shortening and sugar in bowl until light and fluffy, using electric mixer at medium speed. Add egg and molasses; beat until smooth.

Dissolve baking soda in very hot water in small bowl; mix well.

Add dry ingredients alternately with baking soda mixture to creamed mixture, beating well after each addition, using electric mixer at low speed. Cover and chill in refrigerator 1 hour.

Drop mixture by teaspoonfuls, about 3" apart, on greased baking sheets.

Bake in 375° oven 8 minutes, or until no imprint remains when cookies are lightly touched with finger. Remove from baking sheets; cool on racks. Prepare Vanilla Frosting. Frost cookies with Vanilla Frosting. Makes 5½ dozen.

Vanilla Frosting: Combine 2 c. sifted confectioners' sugar, 1 tsp. melted butter or regular margarine, 1 tsp. vanilla and 2 tblsp. milk in bowl. Beat until smooth, using a spoon.

Molasses Crinkles

These crunchy molasses cookies have crinkled sugary tops. A real treat when served as an afternoon break.

2¼ c. sifted flour	½ c. butter or regular
2 tsp. baking soda	margarine
1 tsp. ground ginger	1 c. brown sugar, packed
½ tsp. ground cloves	1 egg
¼ tsp. salt	¼ c. molasses
¼ c. shortening	Sugar

Sift together flour, baking soda, ginger, cloves and salt; set aside.

Cream together shortening, butter and brown sugar in bowl until light and fluffy, using electric mixer at medium speed. Add egg and molasses; blend well.

Gradually add dry ingredients to creamed mixture; mix well. Cover and chill in refrigerator 1 hour.

Shape dough into 1" balls. Dip tops in sugar. Place balls sugared side up, about 3" apart, on greased baking sheets.

Bake in 375° oven 10 to 12 minutes, or until no imprint remains when cookies are lightly touched with finger. Remove from baking sheets; cool on racks. Makes about 4 dozen.

Butter Crispies

"The recipe for these crunchy butter cookies was taken from my grandmother's Norwegian cookbook," wrote an Iowa farm woman.

2 c. sifted flour	½ c. shortening
½ tsp. baking soda	1 c. sugar
½ tsp. cream of tartar	1 egg, slightly beaten
½ c. butter or regular	1 tsp. vanilla
margarine	Flaked coconut or sugar

Sift together flour, baking soda and cream of tartar into mixing bowl. Cut in butter and shortening until mixture is crumbly, using a pastry blender. Add sugar, egg and vanilla. Mix well.

Shape dough into 1" balls. Roll in coconut or sugar. Place balls, about 2" apart, on greased baking sheets. Flatten each with drinking glass dipped in sugar.

Bake in 350° oven 15 minutes, or until lightly browned. Remove from baking sheets; cool on racks. Makes 3 dozen.

Old-Fashioned Filled Cookies

You have a choice of fillings when you make these: prune, fig or apricot. Why not try a different one each time you make them?

2½ c. sifted flour	2 eggs
1 tsp. salt	1 tsp. vanilla
1 c. butter or regular margarine	Prune, Fig or Apricot Filling (recipes follow)
1 c. sugar	

Sift together flour and salt; set aside.

Cream together butter and sugar in bowl until light and fluffy, using electric mixer at medium speed. Add eggs, one at a time, beating well after each addition. Beat in vanilla.

Gradually stir dry ingredients into creamed mixture, mixing well. Cover and chill dough in refrigerator overnight, or until firm enough to roll out. Prepare Prune, Fig or Apricot Filling.

Divide dough in half. Use one half of the dough, keeping remaining dough in refrigerator. Roll out first half of dough on floured surface to ⅛" thickness. Cut 30 rounds, using floured 2" cookie cutter. Place rounds, about 2" apart, on ungreased baking sheets. Place 1 tsp. Prune Filling, Fig Filling or Apricot Filling in center of each round.

Roll out remaining dough. Cut 30 (2") rounds. Cut out center of each, using ¾" cookie cutter. Place over filled rounds. Press edges of each cookie with floured tines of a fork.

Bake in 400° oven 8 minutes, or until golden brown. Remove from baking sheets; cool on racks. Flavor of cookies improves if stored overnight in tightly covered container. Makes 2½ dozen.

Prune Filling: Combine 6 oz. pitted prunes (1 c.) and ¾ c. water in small saucepan. Bring to boil over medium heat. Simmer 2 minutes. Cover and let stand until completely cooled. Drain off liquid. Purée prunes in blender until smooth. Combine prunes, ¼ c. sugar, 2 tsp. grated orange rind, ¼ tsp. salt, ¼ tsp. vanilla and ½ c. chopped walnuts; mix well. Makes enough filling for 2½ dozen cookies.

Fig Filling: Grind 12 oz. dried figs (2 c.) in food grinder, using medium blade. (Makes 1 c. ground figs.) Combine ground figs, ⅓ c. orange juice, 2 tsp. grated orange rind, ¼ c. water, ⅛ tsp. salt and ¼ c. sugar in saucepan. Cook over medium heat, stirring constantly, 2 minutes or until thickened. Cool well. Stir in ¼ c. chopped walnuts. Makes enough filling for 2½ dozen cookies.

Apricot Filling: Combine 1 (6-oz.) pkg. dried apricots (1 c.) and 1 c. water in saucepan. Bring to a boil over medium heat. Simmer 5 minutes. Remove from heat. Purée apricots with cooking liquid in blender until smooth. Stir in ½ c. sugar and 2 tblsp. butter or regular margarine; cool completely. Makes enough filling for 2½ dozen cookies.

Amish Sugar Cookies

This big-batch recipe makes seven dozen farmhouse-size sugar cookies. It's a favorite in a Kansas farm family.

4½ c. sifted flour
1 tsp. baking soda
1 tsp. cream of tartar
1 c. butter or regular
   margarine
1 c. cooking oil
1 c. sugar

1 c. sifted confectioners'
   sugar
2 eggs
1 tsp. vanilla
1 c. chopped walnuts
Sugar

Sift together flour, baking soda and cream of tartar; set aside.

Cream together butter, oil, 1 c. sugar and confectioners' sugar in mixing bowl until light and fluffy, using electric mixer at medium speed. Add eggs, one at a time, beating well after each addition. Blend in vanilla.

Gradually stir dry ingredients into creamed mixture, mixing well. Add walnuts. Drop mixture by rounded teaspoonfuls, about 3" apart, on greased baking sheets. Flatten each with greased bottom of drinking glass dipped in sugar.

Bake in 375° oven 10 minutes, or until lightly browned around the edges. Remove from baking sheets; cool on racks. Makes 7 dozen.

Grandmother's Sugar Cookies

For an old-fashioned look, cut rolled dough with a round, scallop-edged cookie cutter. This recipe makes six dozen cookies.

4 c. sifted flour
3 tsp. baking powder
1 tsp. baking soda
½ tsp. salt
¼ tsp. ground nutmeg
1 c. butter or regular
   margarine

2 c. sugar
3 eggs
1 c. dairy sour cream
Sugar

Sift together flour, baking powder, baking soda, salt and nutmeg; set aside.

Cream together butter and 2 c. sugar in bowl until light and fluffy, using electric mixer at medium speed. Add eggs, one at a time, beating well after each addition.

Add dry ingredients alternately with sour cream to creamed mixture, beating well after each addition, using electric mixer at low speed. Cover and chill dough in refrigerator overnight.

Divide dough into fourths. Use one fourth of the dough at a time, keeping remaining dough in refrigerator. Roll out each fourth of dough on floured surface to ¼" thickness. Cut with floured 2½" round cookie cutter. Place rounds, about 2" apart, on greased baking sheets. Sprinkle each with sugar.

Bake in 400° oven 6 to 8 minutes, or until lightly browned. Remove from baking sheets; cool on racks. Makes 6 dozen.

Old-Fashioned Rolled Sugar Cookies

This sugar cookie variation features three eggs and a whole cup of light cream to make the dough double-rich.

6 c. sifted flour	2 c. sugar
4 tsp. baking powder	3 eggs
1 tsp. baking soda	2 tsp. vanilla
1 tsp. salt	1 c. light cream
1 tsp. ground nutmeg	Sugar
1 c. shortening	

Sift together flour, baking powder, baking soda, salt and nutmeg; set aside.

Cream together shortening and 2 c. sugar in bowl until light and fluffy, using electric mixer at medium speed. Add eggs, one at a time, beating well after each addition. Beat in vanilla.

Add dry ingredients alternately with light cream to creamed mixture, beating well after each addition, using electric mixer at low speed.

Divide dough into fourths. Roll out each fourth of dough on floured surface to ¼" thickness. Cut into desired shapes, using floured 2" cookie cutters. Place cookies, about 2" apart, on greased baking sheets. Sprinkle each with sugar.

Bake in 400° oven 10 minutes, or until golden brown. Remove from baking sheets; cool on racks. Makes 7 dozen.

No-Roll Sugar Cookies

To give the cookies a crackled top, a few drops of water are placed on top of each sugar-coated ball before baking.

3 c. sifted flour
1 tsp. cream of tartar
1 tsp. baking soda
1 tsp. salt
1 c. butter or regular
  margarine

2 c. sugar
2 eggs
1 tsp. vanilla
Sugar
Water

Sift together flour, cream of tartar, baking soda and salt; set aside.

Cream together butter and 2 c. sugar in bowl until light and fluffy, using electric mixer at medium speed. Add eggs, one at a time, beating well after each addition. Blend in vanilla.

Gradually stir dry ingredients into creamed mixture; mix well. Cover and chill dough in refrigerator 1 hour.

Shape dough into 1" balls; dip in sugar. Place balls, about 2" apart, on greased baking sheets. Make a slight indentation in each cookie; place 2 to 3 drops water in each.

Bake in 350° oven 20 minutes, or until golden brown. Remove from baking sheets; cool on racks. Makes 4 dozen.

Sour Cream Drop Cookies

A buttery cookie flavored with nutmeg and lemon extract. Sour cream helps keep these heirloom cookies soft and cake-like.

2¾ c. sifted flour	1½ c. sugar
1½ tsp. baking powder	2 eggs
½ tsp. baking soda	½ c. dairy sour cream
½ tsp. salt	½ tsp. lemon extract
¼ tsp. ground nutmeg	Sugar
1 c. butter or regular margarine	

Sift together flour, baking powder, baking soda, salt and nutmeg; set aside.

Cream together butter and 1½ c. sugar in bowl until light and fluffy, using electric mixer at medium speed. Add eggs, one at a time, beating well after each addition. Add sour cream and lemon extract.

Gradually stir dry ingredients into creamed mixture, blending well. Drop mixture by rounded teaspoonfuls, about 3" apart, on greased baking sheets. Sprinkle each with sugar.

Bake in 375° oven 8 minutes, or until golden brown around the edges. Remove from baking sheets; cool on racks. Makes 5½ dozen.

Toffee Pecan Bars

These rich, brown sugar-flavored bars taste just as wonderful when chopped walnuts are substituted for pecans.

1½ c. sifted flour	1½ tsp. vanilla
¾ c. brown sugar, packed	3 tblsp. flour
¾ c. butter or regular margarine	1½ tsp. baking powder
2 eggs	¾ tsp. salt
1½ c. brown sugar, packed	1⅓ c. flaked coconut
	1½ c. chopped pecans

Combine 1½ c. flour and ¾ c. brown sugar in bowl. Cut in butter until mixture is crumbly, using a pastry blender. Press crumb mixture into greased 13x9x2" baking pan.

Bake in 350° oven 15 minutes.

Beat eggs in bowl until lemon-colored, using electric mixer at high speed. Add 1½ c. brown sugar and vanilla; blend well. Combine 3 tblsp. flour, baking powder and salt. Stir dry ingredients into egg mixture; mix well. Stir in coconut and pecans. Spread topping over baked layer.

Bake in 350° oven 30 minutes, or until topping is brown. Cool slightly in pan on rack. While still warm, cut into 3x1" bars. Cool completely. Makes 39.

Rolled Butter Cookies

*Here's a good basic cookie that everyone likes to find in the cookie jar.
Even prettier topped with a pecan half.*

3 c. sifted flour	2 c. sugar
1 tsp. baking soda	2 eggs
¼ tsp. salt	1 tsp. vanilla
1 c. butter or regular margarine	Colored decorating sugar

Sift together flour, baking soda and salt; set aside.

Cream together butter and sugar in bowl until light and fluffy, using electric mixer at medium speed. Add eggs, one at a time, beating well after each addition. Blend in vanilla.

Gradually stir dry ingredients into creamed mixture, mixing well. Divide dough into fourths. Roll out each fourth of dough on floured surface to ⅛" thickness. Cut with floured 2½" round cookie cutter. Place rounds, about 2" apart, on greased baking sheets. Sprinkle each with colored decorating sugar.

Bake in 350° oven 10 minutes, or until lightly browned. Remove from baking sheets; cool on racks. Makes 5 dozen.

Maple Walnut Squares

If you like rich, brown sugary cookies, you'll like these candy-like bars. They taste like a buttery brittle sprinkled with walnuts.

1½ c. sifted flour	2 eggs
¼ c. brown sugar, packed	½ tsp. vanilla
½ c. butter or regular margarine	2 tblsp. flour
⅔ c. brown sugar, packed	¼ tsp. salt
1 c. maple-blended syrup	1 c. chopped walnuts

Combine 1½ c. flour and ¼ c. brown sugar in bowl. Cut in butter until mixture is crumbly, using a pastry blender. Press crumb mixture into greased 13x9x2" baking pan.

Bake in 350° oven 15 minutes.

Meanwhile, combine ⅔ c. brown sugar and maple-blended syrup in small saucepan. Cook over medium heat 5 minutes. Remove from heat. Slightly beat eggs in bowl. Slowly pour hot syrup into beaten eggs, stirring constantly. Then stir in vanilla, 2 tblsp. flour and salt. Mix thoroughly. Pour over baked crust. Sprinkle with walnuts.

Bake in 350° oven 20 minutes, or until lightly browned. Cool in pan on rack. Cut into 2¼" squares. Makes 24.

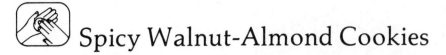 Spicy Walnut-Almond Cookies

Finely ground almonds and walnuts as well as cinnamon, cloves and nutmeg make these thin, rich cookies extra-delicious.

1 c. walnut pieces	½ tsp. ground nutmeg
1 c. blanched almonds	2 c. butter or regular
4½ c. sifted flour	margarine
3 tsp. ground cinnamon	1 c. sugar
¾ tsp. baking soda	1 c. brown sugar, packed
½ tsp. salt	⅔ c. dairy sour cream
½ tsp. ground cloves	Sugar

Grind walnut pieces and almonds in food grinder, using fine blade. Set aside.

Sift together flour, cinnamon, baking soda, salt, cloves and nutmeg; set aside.

Cream together butter, 1 c. sugar and brown sugar in bowl until light and fluffy, using electric mixer at medium speed.

Add dry ingredients alternately with sour cream to creamed mixture, beating well after each addition, using electric mixer at low speed. Stir in ground nuts. Cover and chill dough in refrigerator until firm enough to shape, about 2 hours.

Shape dough into 1¼" balls. Place balls, about 3" apart, on greased baking sheets. Flatten each with greased bottom of drinking glass dipped in sugar.

Bake in 375° oven 8 to 10 minutes, or until golden brown. Remove from baking sheets; cool on racks. Makes 9 dozen.

3 | Cookies in a Hurry

You needn't skimp on flavor or appearance when you want to bake a batch of cookies in a hurry. Farm women know what it is to be busy, and no country-style cookbook would be complete without a collection of timesaving treats to lighten the load of a hectic schedule.

All the cookies in this chapter can be prepared almost as quickly as they'll be eaten: the first 13 recipes need no baking, and the rest require just a few minutes in a microwave oven. Turn to these recipes when there's no time to bake cookies the conventional way or when it's just too hot to turn on your oven.

Some of the no-bake cookies in this chapter need no cooking at all. Peanut-Cocoa Cereal Bars, for example, are made with just five ingredients that are quickly tossed together, chilled and cut into squares. Our version of the traditional Rum Balls is made with crushed vanilla wafers and laced with white rum and orange juice.

Other no-bakes require heating a few ingredients on the range top before mixing together. Chocolate-covered Peanut Logs combine peanut butter-flavored chips, graham cracker crumbs and chopped peanuts. After being shaped into fingers, they're covered with a coating of melted semisweet chocolate—an elegant addition to any dessert plate.

If you've never tried microwaving cookies, start with Microwaved Brownies or Hurry-Up Brownies; you're sure to be delighted with the results. You'll like the convenience of melting chocolate in your microwave oven, too, because there's no need to watch it closely; set the timer as indicated in the recipe and the microwave will do the job without danger of burning.

The home economists in our test kitchens have adapted several traditionally baked cookies to the microwave oven, too, including buttery Thumbprint Cookies, coated with finely chopped walnuts and filled with bright red currant jelly, and the Eight-Minute Lemon Squares with their tangy lemon filling and extra-rich crust dusted with confectioners' sugar. Other favorites are Chocolate Chip Bars, Speedy Peanut Butter Cookies, Microwaved Snickerdoodles and Swedish Tea Cakes. Each of these microwaved cookies resembles its baked counterpart, but often the whole batch of cookies can be microwaved in the time it takes to bake just one sheet of cookies in a conventional oven.

Be sure to watch cookies closely as they microwave because they can overcook in as little as 10 seconds and become hard and dry. Check each recipe, set the timer as indicated and if they're not done—check every 10 seconds.

Whatever the occasion, you'll find each of these super-speedy cookies a marvelous addition to your cookie jar or dessert plate.

Coconut-Date Mounds

These golden cornflake treats are quickly cooked in a skillet—a perfect choice for days when it's too hot to use the oven.

3½ c. cornflakes
1 c. chopped, pitted dates
¾ c. sugar
2 eggs, beaten
1 c. chopped walnuts

1 tsp. vanilla
1⅓ c. flaked coconut
12 red or green candied
   cherries, cut into halves

Crush cornflakes slightly with hands; set aside.

Combine dates, sugar and eggs in 10″ skillet. Cook over medium heat, stirring constantly, until mixture pulls away from the sides of the pan, about 5 minutes. Remove from heat.

Stir walnuts and vanilla into date mixture. Gently stir in cornflakes. Cool slightly, about 5 minutes.

Shape mixture into 1½″ balls. Roll each in flaked coconut. Place on waxed paper-lined baking sheets. Press a candied cherry half in each ball, flattening slightly. Makes 2 dozen.

Peanut Cereal Bar Cookies

When there's no time to bake, these extra-easy peanut butter-flavored bars can be ready in minutes.

1 c. sugar	1 c. peanut butter
1 c. light corn syrup	6 c. high-protein cereal flakes

Combine sugar and corn syrup in saucepan. Cook over medium heat, stirring constantly, until mixture comes to a boil. Boil 1 minute. Remove from heat. Add peanut butter, stirring until well blended. Pour over cereal in bowl. Toss to coat cereal evenly. Spread mixture in buttered 13x9x2" baking pan. Cool completely. Cut into 3¼x1⅛" bars. Makes 32.

Fruited Bran Cookies

These quick, nourishing cookies need no cooking; just mix and refrigerate until time to serve.

2½ c. whole bran cereal	1½ tsp. grated lemon rind
1 (8-oz.) pkg. chopped, pitted dates	1 (14-oz.) can sweetened condensed milk (not
¾ c. golden raisins	evaporated)
¾ c. flaked coconut	2 tblsp. lemon juice
¾ c. chopped, toasted almonds	

Combine cereal, dates, raisins, coconut, almonds and lemon rind in bowl.

Stir together sweetened condensed milk and lemon juice. Combine with bran mixture; mix well.

Divide into fourths. Shape each fourth into a roll, 1½" in diameter. Wrap tightly in waxed paper or plastic wrap. Chill in refrigerator at least 1 hour.

To serve, just cut into ½" slices. Makes about 6 dozen.

Range-Top Cookies

Three favorite cookie ingredients—cocoa, oatmeal and peanut butter—are brought together in this confection-type cookie.

2 c. sugar	2½ c. quick-cooking oats
⅓ c. baking cocoa	½ c. peanut butter
½ c. milk	2 tsp. vanilla
¼ c. butter or regular margarine	

Combine sugar, cocoa, milk and butter in 3-qt. saucepan. Cook over medium heat, stirring occasionally, until mixture comes to a boil, about 10 minutes. Cook 2 more minutes. Remove from heat.

Stir in oats, peanut butter and vanilla. Stir just until blended. Drop mixture by teaspoonfuls on waxed paper-lined baking sheets. Makes 3 dozen.

Chocolate-Peanut Drops

If you have a microwave oven, you can melt the chocolate with the corn syrup in a glass cup in 1½ minutes at the medium setting.

1 (6-oz.) pkg. semisweet chocolate pieces	2 tblsp. confectioners' sugar
¼ c. light corn syrup	⅛ tsp. salt
2 tsp. vanilla	1½ c. dry roasted peanuts

Combine chocolate pieces and corn syrup in small saucepan. Place over low heat and stir until melted. Remove from heat.

Add vanilla, confectioners' sugar, salt and peanuts; mix well. Drop mixture by teaspoonfuls on waxed paper-lined baking sheets. Let stand at room temperature 2 to 3 hours, or until set. Makes 2½ dozen.

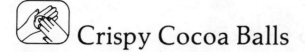

Crispy Cocoa Balls

Rich peppermint-flavored, chocolate butter cream is rolled in crisp cereal for a delightfully different confection.

1 c. butter or regular margarine	⅓ c. baking cocoa
2 c. sifted confectioners' sugar	¼ tsp. peppermint extract
	3 c. toasted rice cereal
	Toasted rice cereal

Cream together butter, confectioners' sugar and cocoa in bowl until light and fluffy, using electric mixer at medium speed. Blend in peppermint extract.

Stir in 3 c. toasted rice cereal. Cover and chill in refrigerator until stiff enough to shape. Shape mixture into 1" balls. Roll each in additional toasted rice cereal. Place on waxed paper-lined baking sheets. Store in refrigerator. Makes 3½ dozen.

Rum Balls

Hide these for a week in a tightly covered container, and the flavor will be even richer when you're ready to serve them.

¾ lb. walnuts	¼ c. orange juice
1 (12-oz.) pkg. vanilla wafers, crushed (about 3¾ c.)	¼ c. white rum
	½ tsp. grated orange rind
⅓ c. honey	Sugar

Grind walnuts in food grinder, using medium blade.

Combine ground walnuts, vanilla wafer crumbs, honey, orange juice, rum and orange rind in bowl. Mix well. Shape into ¾" balls. Roll each in sugar. Place on waxed paper-lined baking sheets. Store in tightly covered container. Makes 5 dozen.

 Mocha Nut Balls

These creamy confection-type morsels can be topped with either pecan halves or halves of candied cherries.

1 (6-oz.) pkg. semisweet chocolate pieces	1¾ c. vanilla wafer crumbs (about 3 dozen wafers)
3 tblsp. light corn syrup	3 c. sifted confectioners' sugar
2 tsp. instant coffee	48 pecan halves
⅓ c. boiling water	

Melt chocolate pieces in top of double boiler over hot water. Remove from heat. Stir in corn syrup. Dissolve instant coffee in boiling water. Stir coffee mixture into chocolate mixture.

Add vanilla wafer crumbs and confectioners' sugar, mixing well. Shape mixture into 1" balls. Place on waxed paper-lined baking sheets. Press a pecan half in the center of each ball, flattening slightly. Makes 4 dozen.

Chocolate-Coconut Balls

An easy, no-mess way to crush vanilla wafers into fine, even crumbs is to put them through a food mill or whirl them in a blender.

2½ c. vanilla wafer crumbs (about 5 dozen wafers)	1 c. flaked coconut
1 c. sifted confectioners' sugar	⅓ c. evaporated milk
2 tblsp. baking cocoa	¼ c. dark corn syrup
1 c. finely chopped walnuts	½ tsp. vanilla
	Sugar

Combine vanilla wafer crumbs, confectioners' sugar, cocoa, walnuts and coconut in bowl. Stir in evaporated milk, corn syrup and vanilla; mix well. Shape mixture into 1" balls. Roll each in sugar. Makes 3 dozen.

 Chocolate-Marshmallow Balls

For a special treat that needs no baking, try these rich marshmallow-filled chocolate balls coated with flaked coconut.

1 (6-oz.) pkg. semisweet
    chocolate pieces
2 c. graham cracker crumbs
1 c. sifted confectioners'
    sugar
2 c. miniature marshmallows

1 c. chopped walnuts
½ c. chopped red candied
    cherries
½ c. milk
1⅓ c. flaked coconut

Melt chocolate pieces in top of double boiler over hot water.

Combine graham cracker crumbs, confectioners' sugar, marshmallows, walnuts and candied cherries in bowl.

Pour melted chocolate and milk over crumb mixture; mix well. Shape mixture into 1″ balls. Roll each in coconut. Place on waxed paper-lined baking sheets. Cover and chill in refrigerator 1 hour, or until set. Makes 3½ dozen.

 Peanut Logs

Chocolate and peanut butter—always a favorite combination. Surprise a peanut butter lover with these chocolate-covered logs.

1 (12-oz.) pkg. peanut
    butter-flavored pieces
½ c. peanut butter
¼ c. butter or regular
    margarine
½ c. milk

2 c. graham cracker crumbs
1 c. chopped peanuts
6 (1-oz.) squares semisweet
    chocolate
3 tblsp. shortening

Combine peanut butter-flavored pieces, peanut butter, butter and milk in top of double boiler. Heat over hot water, stirring occasionally, until peanut butter pieces melt and mixture is smooth.

Combine graham cracker crumbs and peanuts in bowl. Pour melted peanut butter mixture over crumb mixture; mix well. Shape mixture into 2½″ logs, using 1 tblsp. mixture at a time. Place on waxed paper-lined baking sheets. Cover and chill logs in refrigerator 1 hour.

Combine chocolate and shortening in top of double boiler. Heat over hot water, stirring occasionally, until chocolate melts. Spoon chocolate over logs, completely covering tops and sides. Store in refrigerator. Makes 3 dozen.

 Peanut-Cocoa Cereal Bars

Chocolate corn cereal mildly flavors this double-peanut confection, which features chunky peanut butter and coarsely chopped peanuts.

1 c. chunky peanut butter
2 tblsp. butter or regular
   margarine, softened
1¼ c. sifted confectioners'
   sugar

3 c. chocolate-flavored corn
   puffs
1 c. coarsely chopped
   peanuts

Line 8" square baking pan with aluminum foil, bringing foil up over pan edges.

Blend together peanut butter, butter and confectioners' sugar in bowl. Mix in cereal, crushing it slightly, using hands. Press mixture into foil-lined pan. Sprinkle with peanuts and press in peanuts firmly. Cover and chill in refrigerator several hours.

To serve, pull up foil to remove confection from pan. Cut into 2x1" bars. Makes 32.

Graham Cracker Bars

An unusual no-bake confection made by sandwiching a brown sugar mixture between whole graham crackers. It's topped with an icing.

30 graham crackers
1 c. brown sugar, packed
½ c. butter or regular
   margarine
½ c. milk
1 c. flaked coconut
1 c. graham cracker crumbs

2 c. sifted confectioners'
   sugar
5 tblsp. melted butter or
   regular margarine
3 tblsp. dairy half-and-half
½ tsp. vanilla

Line bottom of greased 13x9x2" baking pan with 15 of the graham crackers.

Combine brown sugar, ½ c. butter, milk, coconut and graham cracker crumbs in saucepan. Cook over medium heat, stirring constantly, until mixture comes to a boil. Cook 10 minutes more, or until thickened. (Mixture burns easily.) Remove from heat.

Spread hot mixture evenly over graham crackers in pan. Top with remaining 15 graham crackers.

Beat together confectioners' sugar, 5 tblsp. melted butter, dairy half-and-half and vanilla in bowl until smooth, using electric mixer at medium speed. Spread mixture over graham crackers in pan. Cover with waxed paper. Chill in refrigerator overnight. Cut into 3x1" bars. Makes 39.

Chocolate-Nut Bars

Graham cracker crumbs, chocolate and pecans are combined with sweetened condensed milk to give extra richness.

1½ c. graham cracker
  crumbs
1 (14-oz.) can sweetened
  condensed milk (not
  evaporated)

1 (6-oz.) pkg. semisweet
  chocolate pieces
¾ c. chopped pecans
½ tsp. vanilla

Combine graham cracker crumbs, sweetened condensed milk, chocolate pieces, pecans and vanilla in bowl; mix well. Spread mixture in greased 8″ square glass baking dish.

Microwave (high setting) 8 minutes, or until top of mixture is dry, giving dish one-quarter turn three times. Cool in dish on wooden board or heat-proof counter. Cut into 2x1″ bars. Makes 32.

Frosted Molasses Squares

Molasses colors these spicy microwaved cookies a golden ginger so that the lack of browning isn't noticed.

1½ c. sifted flour
1½ tsp. baking powder
1 tsp. ground cinnamon
½ tsp. salt
¼ tsp. baking soda
¼ tsp. ground cloves
½ c. shortening

½ c. sugar
1 egg
½ c. light molasses
½ c. water
Confectioners' Sugar Icing
  (recipe follows)

Sift together flour, baking powder, cinnamon, salt, baking soda and cloves; set aside.

Cream together shortening and sugar in bowl until light and fluffy, using electric mixer at medium speed. Add egg, beating well. Blend in molasses and water.

Gradually stir dry ingredients into creamed mixture, blending well. Spread in greased 12x8x2″ (2-qt.) glass baking dish.

Microwave (high setting) 7 minutes, or until a wooden pick inserted in center comes out clean, giving dish one-quarter turn three times. Cool in dish on wooden board or heat-proof counter. Prepare Confectioners' Sugar Icing. Frost bars with Confectioners' Sugar Icing. Cut into 2″ squares. Makes 24.

Confectioners' Sugar Icing: Combine 1½ c. sifted confectioners' sugar, 5 tsp. milk and ½ tsp. vanilla in bowl. Beat until smooth, using a spoon.

Apricot-Coconut Bars

Bright bits of apricot fleck these golden oat bars—a snap to prepare and microwave in just four minutes.

½ c. butter or regular margarine	¼ c. light corn syrup
1½ c. quick-cooking oats	½ c. chopped dried apricots
½ c. brown sugar, packed	½ c. flaked coconut
	½ c. chopped pecans

Place butter in 8" square glass baking dish. Microwave (high setting) 2 minutes, or until melted. Stir in oats, brown sugar, corn syrup, apricots, coconut and pecans. Press mixture firmly into same dish.

Microwave (high setting) 4 minutes, or until lightly browned, giving dish one-quarter turn three times. Cool in dish on wooden board or heat-proof counter. Cut into 2x1" bars. Makes 32.

Orange-Frosted Coconut Bars

To sliver orange rind, peel a thin layer of skin from orange, using a vegetable peeler. Slice into thin strips.

1 c. sifted flour	½ tsp. baking powder
¼ c. brown sugar, packed	¼ tsp. salt
⅓ c. butter or regular margarine	1 tsp. vanilla
2 eggs	1 c. chopped walnuts
1 c. brown sugar, packed	½ c. flaked coconut
2 tblsp. flour	Orange Icing (recipe follows)
	Slivered orange rind

Combine 1 c. flour and ¼ c. brown sugar in bowl. Cut in butter until mixture is crumbly, using pastry blender. Press into bottom of 12x8x2" (2-qt.) glass baking dish.

Microwave (high setting) 4 minutes, giving dish one-quarter turn once. Cool in dish on wooden board or heat-proof counter 5 minutes.

Meanwhile, beat eggs slightly in another bowl, using electric mixer at medium speed. Add 1 c. brown sugar, 2 tblsp. flour, baking powder, salt and vanilla; beat until blended. Stir in walnuts and coconut. Pour over baked layer.

Microwave (high setting) 4½ minutes, or until set, giving dish one-quarter turn twice. Cool in dish on wooden board or heat-proof counter. Prepare Orange Icing. Frost bars with Orange Icing. Sprinkle with slivered orange rind. Cut into 3x1" bars. Makes 32.

Orange Icing: Combine 1 c. sifted confectioners' sugar, 3½ tsp. orange juice and 1 tsp. lemon juice in bowl. Beat until smooth, using a spoon.

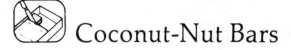 Coconut-Nut Bars

These will continue to cook as they cool, so remove them from the microwave while the topping is still moist.

¾ c. sifted flour	2 eggs
½ tsp. baking soda	¾ c. brown sugar, packed
½ tsp. salt	1 tblsp. flour
⅓ c. butter or regular margarine	1 tblsp. lemon juice
	¾ c. flaked coconut
⅓ c. brown sugar, packed	½ c. chopped walnuts
¾ c. quick-cooking oats	

Sift together ¾ c. flour, baking soda and salt; set aside.

Cream together butter and ⅓ c. brown sugar in bowl until light and fluffy, using electric mixer at medium speed. Gradually stir dry ingredients and oats into creamed mixture, blending well. Press into bottom of waxed paper-lined 8" square glass baking dish.

Beat eggs in another bowl, using electric mixer at high speed. Stir in ¾ c. brown sugar, 1 tblsp. flour, lemon juice, coconut and walnuts. Spread over oat mixture.

Microwave (high setting) 5 to 7 minutes, or until set, giving dish one-quarter turn twice. Cool in dish on wooden board or heat-proof counter. Cut into 2x1" bars. Makes 32.

Eight-Minute Lemon Squares

This version of a favorite two-layer bar features a rich buttery crust and a tangy lemon filling topped with confectioners' sugar.

1 c. sifted flour	1 c. sugar
¼ c. sifted confectioners' sugar	3 tblsp. lemon juice
	1 tsp. grated lemon rind
⅓ c. butter or regular margarine	1 tblsp. flour
	½ tsp. baking powder
2 eggs	Confectioners' sugar

Combine 1 c. flour and ¼ c. confectioners' sugar in bowl. Cut in butter until mixture is crumbly, using pastry blender. Press mixture into bottom and ½" up sides of 8" square glass baking dish.

Microwave (high setting) 4 minutes, or until set, giving dish one-quarter turn once.

Combine eggs, sugar, lemon juice, lemon rind, 1 tblsp. flour and baking powder in bowl. Beat until blended, using electric mixer at medium speed. Pour over crust.

Microwave (high setting) 3½ minutes, or until top is bubbly, giving dish one-quarter turn twice. Cool in dish on wooden board or heat-proof counter. When cool, sprinkle with confectioners' sugar. Cut into 2" squares. Makes 16.

Peanut-Oatmeal Bars

If you want a crisp cookie, serve these bars as soon as they cool. For a softer cookie, cover with foil and serve the next day.

½ c. sifted flour
½ c. quick-cooking oats
¼ tsp. baking soda
¼ tsp. salt
3 tblsp. butter or regular
   margarine
¼ c. peanut butter

½ c. brown sugar, packed
1 egg
½ tsp. vanilla
⅓ c. semisweet chocolate
   pieces
2 tsp. peanut butter
3 tblsp. chopped peanuts

Stir together flour, oats, baking soda and salt; set aside.

Cream together butter, ¼ c. peanut butter and brown sugar in bowl until light and fluffy, using electric mixer at medium speed. Add egg and vanilla, beating well.

Gradually add dry ingredients to creamed mixture, beating well after each addition, using electric mixer at low speed. Spread mixture in 8" square glass baking dish.

Microwave (high setting) 3 minutes, or until top is no longer wet, giving dish one-quarter turn twice. Cool in dish on wooden board or heat-proof counter.

Combine chocolate pieces and 2 tsp. peanut butter in 1-c. glass measuring cup. Microwave (medium setting) 2 minutes, or until chocolate melts. Spread over bars. Sprinkle with chopped peanuts. Cut into 2x1" bars. Makes 32.

Seven-Layer Bars

There's no mixing with these bars; just layer the ingredients into the baking dish and they're ready to microwave.

½ c. butter or regular
   margarine
1½ c. graham cracker
   crumbs
1 c. chopped walnuts
1 (6-oz.) pkg. semisweet
   chocolate pieces

1 c. peanut butter-flavored
   pieces
1⅓ c. flaked coconut
1 (14-oz.) can sweetened
   condensed milk (not
   evaporated)

Place butter in 12x8x2" (2-qt.) glass baking dish.

Microwave (high setting) 1 minute, or until melted. Layer ingredients in this order: graham cracker crumbs, walnuts, chocolate pieces, peanut butter-flavored pieces and coconut. Pour sweetened condensed milk over all. Do not stir.

Microwave (high setting) 8 minutes, or until lightly browned, giving dish one-quarter turn twice. Cool in dish on wooden board or heat-proof counter. Cut into 3x1" bars. Makes 32.

Chocolate Chip Bars

Chocolate chip cookies, in convenient bar form, take only four minutes to cook in the microwave oven.

1¼ c. sifted flour	⅓ c. brown sugar, packed
½ tsp. baking powder	1 egg
½ tsp. salt	1 tsp. vanilla
½ c. butter or regular	1 (6-oz.) pkg. semisweet
margarine	chocolate pieces
⅓ c. sugar	

Sift together flour, baking powder and salt; set aside.

Cream together butter, sugar and brown sugar in bowl until light and fluffy, using electric mixer at medium speed. Add egg and vanilla, beating well.

Gradually stir dry ingredients into creamed mixture, blending well. Stir in ⅔ c. of the chocolate pieces. Spread mixture in 8" square glass baking dish.

Microwave (high setting) 4 minutes, or until a wooden pick inserted in center comes out clean, giving dish one-quarter turn twice. Cool in dish on wooden board or heat-proof counter.

Place remaining chocolate pieces in 1-c. glass measuring cup. Microwave (medium setting) 2 minutes, or until melted, stirring once. Spread over bars. Cool completely. Cut into 2x1" bars. Makes 32.

Swedish Tea Cakes

You can microwave three dozen of these cookies in a fraction of the time you'd need to bake them in a conventional oven.

2¼ c. sifted flour	⅓ c. sugar
¼ tsp. salt	1 tsp. vanilla
1 c. butter or regular	¾ c. chopped walnuts
margarine	Confectioners' sugar

Sift together flour and salt; set aside.

Cream together butter and sugar in bowl until light and fluffy, using electric mixer at medium speed. Blend in vanilla.

Gradually stir dry ingredients into creamed mixture, blending well. Stir in walnuts. Shape mixture into 1¼" balls. Arrange 9 balls in ring, equally spaced, on 10" round of cardboard covered with waxed paper. Place cardboard in microwave oven on inverted saucer.

Microwave (high setting) 2 minutes, or until set, giving cardboard one-quarter turn once. Let stand 2 minutes on cardboard. Slide waxed paper from cardboard to wooden board or heat-proof counter. When cool, roll in confectioners' sugar. Makes 3 dozen.

 Microwaved Snickerdoodles

Traditional sugar cookies, mildly flavored with cinnamon, are tender and crisp when microwaved.

1¾ c. sifted flour	¾ c. sugar
1 tsp. cream of tartar	1 egg
½ tsp. baking soda	½ tsp. vanilla
⅛ tsp. salt	2 tblsp. sugar
½ c. butter or regular margarine	1 tblsp. ground cinnamon

Sift together flour, cream of tartar, baking soda and salt; set aside.

Cream together butter and ¾ c. sugar in bowl until light and fluffy, using electric mixer at medium speed. Add egg and vanilla, beating well.

Gradually stir dry ingredients into creamed mixture, blending well. Shape dough into 1" balls. Combine 2 tblsp. sugar and cinnamon. Roll balls in sugar-cinnamon mixture. Arrange 6 balls in ring, equally spaced, on 10" round of cardboard covered with waxed paper. Place in microwave oven on an inverted saucer.

Microwave (high setting) 1 minute 15 seconds, or until set, giving cardboard one-quarter turn once. Slide waxed paper from cardboard to wooden board or heat-proof counter. Cool. Makes 2½ dozen.

Chocolate Snow Cookies

These cookies have the same round shape and crunchy texture as Swedish Tea Cakes, but they're flavored with cocoa.

1¾ c. sifted flour	½ c. sugar
½ c. baking cocoa	½ tsp. vanilla
⅛ tsp. salt	1 c. chopped walnuts
¾ c. butter or regular margarine	Confectioners' sugar

Sift together flour, cocoa and salt; set aside.

Cream together butter and sugar in bowl until light and fluffy, using electric mixer at medium speed. Blend in vanilla.

Gradually stir dry ingredients into creamed mixture, blending well. Stir in walnuts. Shape dough into 1" balls. Arrange 9 balls in ring, equally spaced, on 10" round of cardboard covered with waxed paper. Place cardboard in microwave oven on inverted saucer.

Microwave (high setting) 2 minutes, or until set, giving cardboard one-quarter turn once. Let stand 2 minutes on cardboard. Slide waxed paper from cardboard to wooden board or heat-proof counter. When cool, sprinkle with confectioners' sugar. Makes 3 dozen.

Speedy Peanut Butter Cookies

Cookies microwave more quickly on the inside. Cooling them directly on the counter allows the outside to finish cooking.

1½ c. sifted flour	½ c. sugar
¼ tsp. baking soda	½ c. brown sugar, packed
¼ tsp. salt	1 egg
½ c. shortening	1 tsp. vanilla
½ c. peanut butter	

Sift together flour, baking soda and salt; set aside.

Cream together shortening, peanut butter, sugar and brown sugar in bowl until light and fluffy, using electric mixer at medium speed. Add egg and vanilla, beating well.

Gradually stir dry ingredients into creamed mixture, blending well. Shape mixture into 1" balls. Arrange 6 balls in ring, equally spaced, on 10" round of cardboard covered with waxed paper. Flatten each with a fork, making a crisscross pattern. Place cardboard in microwave oven on an inverted saucer.

Microwave (high setting) 1 minute 15 seconds, or until set, giving cardboard one-quarter turn once. Slide waxed paper from cardboard to wooden board or heat-proof counter. Cool. Makes 3 dozen.

Hurry-Up Brownies

There's only one dish to wash after making these brownies; the batter is mixed right in the baking dish.

1 c. sifted flour	1 c. sugar
½ tsp. baking powder	2 eggs
½ tsp. salt	1 tsp. vanilla
½ c. butter or regular	½ c. chopped walnuts
margarine	
2 (1-oz.) squares	
unsweetened chocolate	

Sift together flour, baking powder and salt; set aside.

Combine butter and chocolate in 8" square glass baking dish. Microwave (medium setting) 3 minutes, or until melted, stirring twice. Stir in sugar. Add eggs and vanilla, beating well with a spoon.

Gradually stir dry ingredients into chocolate mixture, blending well. Stir in walnuts.

Microwave (high setting) 5 minutes, or until top is no longer wet, giving dish one-quarter turn twice. Cool in dish on wooden board or heat-proof counter. Cut into 2" squares. Makes 16.

Microwaved Brownies

The chocolate for these frosted cake-like brownies melts in minutes in the microwave and is always velvety-smooth.

2 (1-oz.) squares unsweetened chocolate	1 c. brown sugar, packed
¾ c. unsifted flour	2 eggs
½ tsp. baking soda	1½ tsp. vanilla
⅛ tsp. salt	½ c. milk
½ c. soft butter or regular margarine	½ c. chopped walnuts
	Chocolate Frosting (recipe follows)

Place chocolate in 6-oz. glass custard cup. Microwave (medium setting) 3 to 3½ minutes, or until melted. Set aside to cool.

Stir together flour, baking soda and salt; set aside.

Combine butter, brown sugar, eggs, vanilla and cooled chocolate in mixing bowl. Beat until thoroughly combined, using electric mixer at medium speed. Blend in milk.

Gradually stir dry ingredients into chocolate mixture, mixing well. Stir in walnuts. Spread batter evenly in greased 12x8x2" (2-qt.) glass baking dish.

Microwave (high setting) 6 to 8 minutes, or until top springs back when touched lightly with finger, giving dish one-half turn once. Cool in dish on wooden board or heat-proof counter. Prepare Chocolate Frosting. Spread with frosting. Cut into 2" squares. Makes 24.

Chocolate Frosting: Place 1½ (1-oz.) squares unsweetened chocolate in 6-oz. custard cup. Microwave (medium setting) 3 minutes, or until melted. Cool. Beat 4 tblsp. soft butter or regular margarine and cooled chocolate in mixing bowl until smooth, using a spoon. Blend in 1½ c. sifted confectioners' sugar. Stir in 1 tsp. vanilla and 1 to 2 tblsp. milk. Beat until mixture is smooth and of spreading consistency, using a spoon.

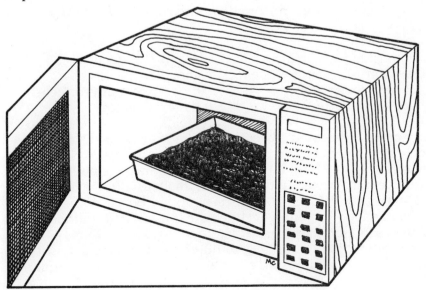

Cheesecake Bars

A buttery crust and a lemon-flavored cream cheese filling combine to make these cookies taste like miniature cheesecakes.

⅓ c. butter or regular margarine	¼ c. sugar
⅓ c. brown sugar, packed	1 egg
1 c. sifted flour	1 tblsp. milk
½ c. chopped walnuts	1 tblsp. lemon juice
1 (8-oz.) pkg. cream cheese, softened	½ tsp. vanilla

Cream together butter and brown sugar in bowl until light and fluffy, using electric mixer at medium speed. Stir in flour and walnuts. (Mixture will be crumbly.) Remove 1 c. crumb mixture and reserve for topping. Press remaining crumb mixture into bottom of 8″ square glass baking dish.

Microwave (high setting) 2 minutes, giving dish one-quarter turn once.

Beat cream cheese in bowl until smooth, using electric mixer at medium speed. Gradually add sugar, egg, milk, lemon juice and vanilla, beating well. Spread cream cheese mixture over crust. Sprinkle with reserved 1 c. crumb mixture.

Microwave (high setting) 6 minutes, or until set, giving dish one-quarter turn twice. Cool in dish on wooden board or heat-proof counter. Cut into 2″ squares. Makes 16.

Chocolate Scotcheroos

Morsels of chocolate and butterscotch are combined into a smooth icing for these crispy bar cookies.

6 c. toasted rice cereal	1 (6-oz.) pkg. semisweet chocolate pieces
1 c. sugar	1 (6-oz.) pkg. butterscotch-flavored pieces
1 c. light corn syrup	
1 c. peanut butter	

Arrange cereal in greased 13x9x2″ (3-qt.) glass baking dish.

Combine sugar and corn syrup in 3-qt. glass casserole.

Microwave (high setting) 4 minutes, or until mixture boils, stirring once. Add peanut butter and stir until melted. Pour evenly over cereal. (Do not stir.) Cool in dish on wooden board or heat-proof counter. When cool, combine chocolate pieces and butterscotch-flavored pieces in 1-qt. glass casserole.

Microwave (medium setting) 2 minutes, or until melted, stirring once. Spread over bars. Cool completely. Cut into 1½″ squares. Makes 48.

Caramel Cereal Confection

This candy-like cookie will appeal to your child's sweet tooth, but it contains protein-rich cereal and peanuts as well as caramel.

1 (14-oz.) bag caramels
¼ c. butter or regular
   margarine
¼ c. water
8 c. high-protein cereal flakes

1 (6½-oz.) can salted
   peanuts
1 (6-oz.) pkg. semisweet
   chocolate pieces

Arrange caramels in a single layer in bottom of 3-qt. glass casserole. Cut butter into 4 pieces and place on top of caramels. Pour water over all. Cover.

Microwave (high setting) 6 minutes, or until mixture can be stirred smooth. Add cereal flakes, one quarter at a time, stirring to coat well. Stir in peanuts and then chocolate pieces. Press mixture firmly into buttered 13x9x2" baking pan. Cover and chill in refrigerator until firm, about 1 hour. Cut into 3¼x1⅛" bars. Makes 32.

Crispy Peanut Bars

Cereal bars flavored with peanut butter become special with a brown sugar frosting and a sprinkle of chopped peanuts.

½ c. sugar
½ c. light corn syrup
⅛ tsp. salt
1 c. peanut butter
2 c. toasted rice cereal

Brown Sugar Frosting
   (recipe follows)
¼ c. chopped dry roasted
   peanuts

Combine sugar, corn syrup and salt in 2-qt. glass casserole.

Microwave (high setting) 3½ to 4½ minutes, or until sugar is dissolved. Blend in peanut butter. Gently stir in rice cereal.

Pat mixture evenly into aluminum foil-lined 8" square glass baking dish. Prepare Brown Sugar Frosting. Spread Brown Sugar Frosting on top. Sprinkle with peanuts. Cool completely. Remove from baking dish and peel off foil. Cut into 2x1" bars. Makes 32.

Brown Sugar Frosting: Combine ¼ c. butter or regular margarine and ¼ c. brown sugar (packed) in small glass bowl. Microwave (high setting) 2 to 2½ minutes, or until butter is melted and sugar is dissolved, stirring once. Stir in 1 tblsp. milk and ½ tsp. vanilla. Add ¼ c. sifted confectioners' sugar; beat until smooth and of spreading consistency, using a spoon.

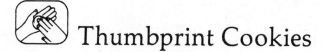 # Thumbprint Cookies

These cookies are rolled in finely chopped walnuts to give them both color and crunchiness.

2 c. sifted flour	2 egg yolks
¼ tsp. salt	½ tsp. vanilla
1 c. butter or regular margarine	1¼ c. finely chopped walnuts
½ c. brown sugar, packed	½ c. red currant jelly

Sift together flour and salt; set aside.

Cream together butter and brown sugar in bowl until light and fluffy, using electric mixer at medium speed. Add egg yolks and vanilla, beating well.

Gradually stir dry ingredients into creamed mixture, blending well. Shape mixture into 1" balls. Roll balls in walnuts. Arrange 9 balls in ring, equally spaced, on 10" round of cardboard covered with waxed paper. Place cardboard in microwave oven on inverted saucer.

Microwave (high setting) 45 seconds. Press thumb into center of each ball, making an indentation. Give cardboard one-quarter turn. Microwave (high setting) 55 seconds more, or until set. Slide waxed paper from cardboard to wooden board or heat-proof counter. When cool, place 1 heaping measuring teaspoon jelly in indentation in each cookie. Makes 3½ dozen.

4 | Especially for Kids

Most children love cookies, and what could be more fun than baking homemade cookies as a family? Your kitchen is an ideal learning center, not only for teaching youngsters how to bake cookies, but also as a place to share feelings and thoughts.

Many of the cookies in this chapter can be prepared by a 10-year-old without assistance, and depending on the age of your child, the only help needed may be with the oven or the electric mixer. Even the youngest child can break up nuts, measure ingredients, cut out cookies and decorate them with colored sugar or silver dragées.

This chapter includes every child's favorite flavors. For example, the Jumbo Oatmeal-Peanut Butter Cookies contain three: peanut butter, oatmeal and raisins. Our Double

Treat Cookies are a variation of the basic chocolate chip, to which peanut butter and chopped peanuts have been added. Since chocolate is by far the favorite flavor, we've included several choices: Chocolate-Marshmallow Cookies are soft chocolate drops topped with marshmallow halves and thin chocolate icing; Chocolate Brownie Bars have all the flavor of traditionally made brownies, but they can be easily prepared because they're made with chocolate-flavored syrup.

The chapter begins with the easiest recipes. Six-Layer Cookies don't even require an electric mixer; just layer the ingredients into the pan and bake. Some of the other cookies are made with cake or pudding mixes for extra-easy preparation: Banana-Fudge Cookies start with chocolate cake mix and are flavored with bananas and chocolate chips. Chocolate Chip Brownies are a snap to make because the batter is made with a yellow cake mix and just spread in a pan—no shaping needed. Two brownies that are sure to make a hit are made with a pudding mix: Pudding Brownies and Chewy Chocolate Squares.

You can teach your child to enjoy making nutritious cookies, too. Golden Carrot Cookies are cake-like drop cookies loaded with shredded carrots and flavored with a dash of lemon extract. Protein-rich oatmeal cookies are also good choices—there are five versions in this chapter, each one sure to appeal to a youngster's sweet tooth.

Some of the cookies are especially fun to shape. Your child will like shaping Pretzel Cookies, vanilla-flavored twists which resemble pretzels topped with finely chopped walnuts. Mexican Cookie Rings are doughnut-shaped cookies formed by pushing a thumb through the center of each ball of dough. If you're looking for a rolled sugar cookie, the dough for German Sugar Cookies is easy to work with and doesn't need chilling before rolling out—a great cookie dough for easily frustrated youngsters.

The times shared in the kitchen with a child are cherished times. The mess in your kitchen—the spilled sugar or dropped egg—won't seem to matter once you see the pride in your child's face when the family cookie plate is passed.

Six-Layer Cookies

A simple six-ingredient cookie made with graham cracker crumbs layered into a pan before baking. Easy enough for preschoolers.

½ c. butter or regular
   margarine
2 c. graham cracker crumbs
1⅓ c. flaked coconut
1 (6-oz.) pkg. semisweet
   chocolate pieces

1 (14-oz.) can sweetened
   condensed milk (not
   evaporated)
1 c. chopped pecans

Melt butter in 13x9x2" baking pan over low heat. Remove from heat; sprinkle graham cracker crumbs evenly over melted butter.

Then sprinkle with coconut and an even layer of chocolate pieces. Pour sweetened condensed milk evenly over layers. Top with pecans. Do not stir.

Bake in 350° oven 35 minutes, or until mixture is set. Cool in pan on rack. Cut into 2¼x1" bars. Makes 52.

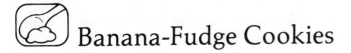

Banana-Fudge Cookies

Because these drop cookies are made from a cake mix, they're extra easy—a good choice for a child's first cookies.

1 (18½-oz.) pkg. chocolate
   cake mix
⅓ c. mashed ripe bananas
1 egg

2 tblsp. water
1 (6-oz.) pkg. semisweet
   chocolate pieces

Combine cake mix, bananas, egg and water in bowl. Beat until smooth, using electric mixer at medium speed. Stir in chocolate pieces. Drop mixture by rounded teaspoonfuls, about 2" apart, on greased baking sheets.

Bake in 350° oven 8 minutes, or until no imprint remains when touched lightly with finger. Remove from baking sheets; cool on racks. Makes 3½ dozen.

Peanut Butter-Fudge Bars

This cake-mix cookie is flavored with protein-rich peanut butter, chocolate chips, coconut and walnuts. A real child-pleaser!

1 (18½-oz.) pkg. yellow cake mix	2 tblsp. butter or regular margarine, melted
1 c. peanut butter	2 tsp. vanilla
½ c. butter or regular margarine, melted	½ tsp. salt
2 eggs	1 (12-oz.) pkg. semisweet chocolate pieces
1 (14-oz.) can sweetened condensed milk (not evaporated)	1 c. flaked coconut
	1 c. chopped walnuts

Combine cake mix, peanut butter, ½ c. melted butter and eggs in bowl. Stir until well mixed. Press two thirds of mixture in bottom of ungreased 13x9x2" baking pan. Reserve remaining dough for topping.

Combine sweetened condensed milk, 2 tblsp. melted butter, vanilla and salt in another bowl; mix well. Stir in chocolate pieces, coconut and walnuts. Spread over first layer. Crumble reserved dough evenly over filling.

Bake in 350° oven 25 to 30 minutes, or until golden brown. Cool in pan on rack. Cut into 2¼x1" bars. Makes 52.

Chocolate Chip Brownies

Another quickly prepared cookie that's just right for a young child—a chewy chocolate chip-studded cookie in bar form.

1 (18½-oz.) pkg. yellow cake mix	¼ c. brown sugar, packed
2 eggs	½ c. semisweet chocolate pieces
¼ c. water	¼ c. chopped walnuts
¼ c. butter or regular margarine	

Combine cake mix, eggs, water, butter and brown sugar in bowl. Beat until smooth, using wooden spoon. Stir in chocolate pieces and walnuts. Spread mixture in greased 15½x10½x1" jelly roll pan.

Bake in 350° oven 25 minutes, or until top springs back when touched lightly with finger. Cool in pan on rack. Cut into 2" squares. Makes 35.

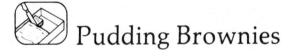Homemade Brownie Mix

You don't need to rely on commercial mixes to turn out brownies in a hurry. Make your own mix for last-minute desserts or snacks.

4 c. sifted flour	1½ c. nonfat dry milk
4½ c. sugar	1½ tblsp. baking powder
1 c. baking cocoa	1½ tsp. salt

Sift together flour, sugar, cocoa, dry milk, baking powder and salt three times. Store in airtight container. Makes about 11 cups.

To make brownies: Combine 1¾ c. Homemade Brownie Mix, 1 egg, ¼ c. warm water, ¼ c. cooking oil and 1 tsp. vanilla in bowl. Beat 1 minute, using electric mixer at medium speed. Stir in ¼ c. chopped walnuts. Pour mixture into greased 9" square baking pan.

Bake in 350° oven 20 minutes, or until no imprint remains when touched lightly with finger. Cool in pan on rack. Cut into 2¼" squares. Makes 16.

Pudding Brownies

Simply prepared brownies flavored with a chocolate pudding mix. They're even better dusted with confectioners' sugar.

½ c. sifted flour	2 eggs
¼ tsp. baking powder	⅔ c. sugar
1 (3⅝-oz.) pkg. chocolate pudding and pie filling	1 tsp. vanilla
	½ c. chopped walnuts
⅓ c. butter or regular margarine, melted	

Sift together flour and baking powder; set aside.

Combine pudding mix and melted butter in bowl. Add eggs, sugar and vanilla; beat until blended, using electric mixer at medium speed.

Stir dry ingredients into chocolate mixture, mixing well. Stir in walnuts. Spread mixture in greased 8" square baking pan.

Bake in 350° oven 40 minutes, or until no imprint remains when touched lightly with finger. Cool in pan on rack. Cut into 2" squares. Makes 16.

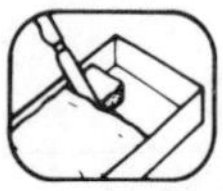

Chewy Chocolate Squares

This pudding-mix cookie has a butter-crumb bottom layer and a chocolate-flavored topping rich in raisins, pecans and coconuts.

1 c. unsifted flour	1 (3⅝-oz.) pkg. chocolate
¼ c. sifted confectioners'	pudding and pie filling
sugar	½ tsp. baking powder
½ c. butter or regular	⅔ c. evaporated milk
margarine	1⅔ c. flaked coconut
¼ c. sugar	½ c. chopped pecans
1 egg	½ c. raisins

Combine flour and confectioners' sugar in bowl. Cut in butter until crumbs form, using pastry blender. Mix until mixture holds together, using hands. Press mixture into ungreased 8″ square baking pan.

Bake in 350° oven 10 minutes. Place on rack. Prepare filling.

Combine sugar and egg in another bowl. Beat until light, using electric mixer at medium speed. Stir in pudding mix, baking powder and evaporated milk. Add coconut, pecans and raisins; mix well. Pour over baked crust.

Bake in 350° oven 30 minutes, or until set. Cool in pan on rack. Cut into 2″ squares. Makes 16.

Refrigerator Butterscotch Wafers

An Oregon farm woman recalls that when she was a child, a neighbor woman gave her these cookies for picking up her mail.

1¼ c. sifted flour	1 c. brown sugar, packed
½ tsp. baking soda	1 egg
¼ tsp. cream of tartar	½ tsp. vanilla
¼ tsp. salt	½ c. chopped pecans
½ c. butter or regular	
margarine	

Sift together flour, baking soda, cream of tartar and salt; set aside.

Cream together butter and brown sugar in bowl until light and fluffy, using electric mixer at medium speed. Add egg and vanilla, blending well.

Gradually stir dry ingredients into creamed mixture, blending well. Stir in pecans. (Dough will be soft.) Shape dough into 12″ roll on waxed paper. Roll up in waxed paper. Refrigerate overnight.

Cut roll into 48 slices, about ¼″ thick. Place slices, about 2″ apart, on greased baking sheets.

Bake in 375° oven 6 minutes, or until golden brown. Remove from baking sheets; cool on racks. Makes 4 dozen.

Toasted Marshmallow Brownies

A Nebraska family calls these "moon brownies" because the baked marshmallow top looks a little like the surface of the moon.

1 c. sifted flour	2 tsp. vanilla
½ c. baking cocoa	1 c. chopped walnuts
1 c. butter or regular margarine	2 c. miniature marshmallows
2 c. sugar	¾ c. semisweet chocolate pieces
4 eggs	

Sift together flour and cocoa; set aside.

Cream together butter and sugar in bowl until light and fluffy, using electric mixer at medium speed. Add eggs, one at a time, beating well after each addition. Blend in vanilla.

Stir dry ingredients into creamed mixture, mixing well. Add walnuts. Spread mixture in 13x9x2" baking pan. Sprinkle with marsh-mallows and chocolate pieces.

Bake in 325° oven 55 minutes, or until toothpick inserted in center of brownies comes out clean. Cool in pan on rack. Cut into 2¼" squares. Makes 24.

Chocolate Brownie Bars

Chocolate-flavored syrup is used for these speedy brownies. They're super-easy because there's no need to melt chocolate.

1 c. sifted flour	4 eggs
½ tsp. baking powder	1 (16-oz.) can chocolate-flavored syrup
½ c. butter or regular margarine	Chocolate Frosting (recipe follows)
1 c. sugar	

Sift together flour and baking powder; set aside.

Cream together butter and sugar in bowl until light and fluffy, using electric mixer at medium speed. Add eggs, one at a time, beating well after each addition.

Gradually stir dry ingredients into creamed mixture, mixing well. Blend in chocolate-flavored syrup. Pour mixture into greased and floured 9" square baking pan.

Bake in 350° oven 35 minutes, or until top springs back when touched lightly with finger. Cool in pan on rack. Prepare Chocolate Frosting. Frost bars with Chocolate Frosting. Cut into 3x1" bars. Makes 27.

Chocolate Frosting: Combine 2 c. sifted confectioners' sugar, 1 tblsp. butter or regular margarine, ½ tsp. vanilla and 1 (1-oz.) square unsweetened chocolate (melted and cooled) in bowl. Add enough milk (about 2 tblsp.) to make a frosting of spreading consistency. Beat until smooth, using a spoon.

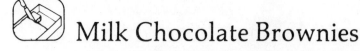

Milk Chocolate Brownies

No frosting is needed for these bar cookies—instead, a layer of walnuts and chocolate chips is baked right on top.

1½ c. sifted flour	2 tsp. vanilla
½ c. baking cocoa	1 c. flaked coconut
½ tsp. salt	½ c. semisweet chocolate
½ c. butter or regular	pieces
margarine	½ c. chopped walnuts
2 c. sugar	2 tblsp. sugar
4 eggs	

Sift together flour, cocoa and salt; set aside.

Melt butter in saucepan over low heat. Remove from heat. Add 2 c. sugar; beat well, using a spoon. Mix in eggs and vanilla; blend well.

Stir dry ingredients into saucepan, mixing thoroughly. Stir in coconut. Spread mixture in greased 13x9x2" baking pan.

Combine chocolate pieces, walnuts and 2 tblsp. sugar; sprinkle evenly over batter.

Bake in 350° oven 25 minutes, or until top springs back when touched lightly with finger. Cool in pan on rack. Cut into 2¼x 1" bars. Makes 52.

Chocolate Vanilla-Layered Bars

These scrumptious bar cookies are made by flavoring a third of the batter with chocolate. The texture is soft and cake-like.

1½ c. sifted flour	3 eggs
¼ tsp. salt	1 tsp. vanilla
¾ c. butter or regular	1½ (1-oz.) squares
margarine	unsweetened chocolate,
1½ c. sugar	melted and cooled

Sift together flour and salt; set aside.

Cream together butter and sugar in bowl until light and fluffy, using electric mixer at medium speed. Add eggs, one at a time, beating well after each addition. Beat in vanilla.

Gradually stir dry ingredients into creamed mixture, blending well. Spread two thirds of the batter in greased 9" square baking pan.

Stir melted chocolate into remaining batter. Spread chocolate batter evenly over vanilla batter in pan.

Bake in 350° oven 35 minutes, or until top springs back when touched lightly with finger. Cool in pan on rack. Cut into 3x1" bars. Makes 27.

Raisin-Chocolate Chip Cookies

Lots of iron-rich raisins are stirred into this basic chocolate chip cookie dough. Children are sure to like this combination.

2½ c. sifted flour	2 eggs
1 tsp. baking soda	2 tblsp. milk
¼ tsp. salt	2 tsp. vanilla
1 c. butter or regular	2 c. raisins
margarine	1 (6-oz.) pkg. semisweet
¾ c. sugar	chocolate pieces
¾ c. brown sugar, packed	1 c. chopped walnuts

Sift together flour, baking soda and salt into large mixing bowl. Add butter, sugar, brown sugar, eggs, milk and vanilla. Beat until blended, using electric mixer at low speed. Then beat at medium speed until fluffy.

Stir in raisins, chocolate pieces and walnuts. Drop mixture by heaping teaspoonfuls, about 2" apart, on greased baking sheets.

Bake in 375° oven 9 minutes, or until golden brown. Remove from baking sheets; cool on racks. Makes 4½ dozen.

Choco-Mint Snaps

These cookies resemble chocolate gingersnaps—all crackly on top. Peppermint extract and cinnamon make them different.

1¾ c. unsifted flour	1 (6-oz.) pkg. semisweet
2 tsp. baking soda	chocolate pieces, melted
1 tsp. ground cinnamon	and cooled
¼ tsp. salt	¼ c. light corn syrup
⅔ c. shortening	¼ tsp. peppermint extract
½ c. sugar	Sugar
1 egg	

Stir together flour, baking soda, cinnamon and salt; set aside.

Cream together shortening and ½ c. sugar in bowl until light and fluffy, using electric mixer at medium speed. Add egg, cooled chocolate, corn syrup and peppermint extract; blend well.

Stir dry ingredients into chocolate mixture, mixing well. Shape mixture into balls, using 1 tblsp. dough for each. Roll in sugar. Place balls, about 2" apart, on ungreased baking sheets.

Bake in 350° oven 10 minutes, or until no imprint remains when touched lightly with finger. Remove from baking sheets; cool on racks. Makes 2½ dozen.

Chocolate Fair Cookies

Although most cookies are made with all-purpose flour, this one features cake flour. It's also lightly spiced with cinnamon.

2 c. sifted cake flour
1½ tsp. baking powder
½ tsp. baking soda
½ tsp. ground cinnamon
½ tsp. salt
½ c. shortening
1 c. sugar

1 egg
3 (1-oz.) squares
   unsweetened chocolate,
   melted and cooled
2 tblsp. milk
Sugar

Sift together cake flour, baking powder, baking soda, cinnamon and salt; set aside.

Cream together shortening and 1 c. sugar in bowl until light and fluffy, using electric mixer at medium speed. Add egg and melted chocolate; beat well.

Gradually stir dry ingredients into chocolate mixture, mixing well. Blend in milk. Cover and chill in refrigerator 8 hours or overnight.

Divide dough in half. Roll out each half on lightly floured surface to ⅛" thickness. Cut with floured 2½" round cookie cutter. Place, about 2" apart, on ungreased baking sheets. Sprinkle each with sugar.

Bake in 350° oven 9 minutes, or until no imprint remains when touched lightly with finger. Remove from baking sheets; cool on racks. Makes about 4 dozen.

Chocolate Chip-Cherry Drops

A Texas woman developed this recipe for chocolate chip cookies dotted with red maraschino cherries. Her grandchildren love them.

2 c. unsifted flour
½ tsp. baking soda
½ tsp. salt
⅓ c. butter or regular
   margarine
⅓ c. cooking oil
½ c. sugar
½ c. brown sugar, packed

1 egg
1 tblsp. vanilla
1 (6-oz.) pkg. semisweet
   chocolate pieces
½ c. chopped walnuts
½ c. chopped red
   maraschino cherries,
   well drained

Stir together flour, baking soda and salt; set aside.

Cream together butter, oil, sugar and brown sugar in bowl until light and fluffy, using electric mixer at medium speed. Add egg and vanilla, beating well.

Add dry ingredients to creamed mixture, mixing well with a spoon. Stir in chocolate pieces, walnuts and cherries. Drop mixture by teaspoonfuls, about 2" apart, on ungreased baking sheets.

Bake in 375° oven 10 to 12 minutes, or until golden brown. Remove from baking sheets; cool on racks. Makes 4 dozen.

 Chocolate Chip Pizza

When these cookies come out of the oven, they look like sweet pizzas—the dough is baked in pie plates and then cut into wedges.

1 c. sifted flour	1 egg
½ tsp. baking powder	1 tblsp. hot water
½ tsp. salt	1 tsp. vanilla
⅛ tsp. baking soda	½ c. chopped walnuts
⅓ c. butter or regular margarine, melted	1 (6-oz.) pkg. semisweet chocolate pieces
1 c. brown sugar, packed	1 c. miniature marshmallows

Sift together flour, baking powder, salt and baking soda; set aside.

Combine melted butter and brown sugar in mixing bowl. Beat until blended, using electric mixer at medium speed. Add egg, hot water and vanilla; mix well.

Stir dry ingredients into egg mixture, mixing well. Stir in walnuts. Spread dough in 2 greased 9″ glass pie plates. Sprinkle each with one half of chocolate pieces and one half of marshmallows.

Bake in 350° oven 20 minutes, or until golden brown. Cool in pans on racks. Cut each pie into 8 wedges. Makes 16.

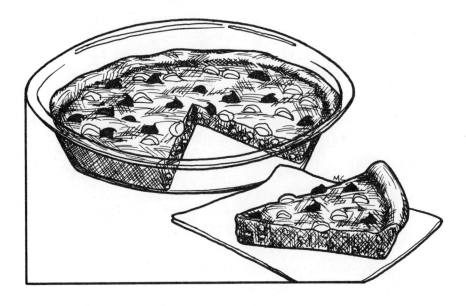

Chocolate-Marshmallow Cookies

This mild chocolate cookie features a marshmallow layer topped with a thin chocolate icing. Doubly good with a cup of cocoa.

1¾ c. unsifted flour	1 tsp. vanilla
½ c. baking cocoa	½ c. milk
½ tsp. baking soda	½ c. chopped walnuts
½ tsp. salt	18 regular marshmallows,
½ c. shortening	cut into halves
1 c. sugar	Cocoa Frosting (recipe
1 egg	follows)

Sift together flour, cocoa, baking soda and salt; set aside.

Cream together shortening and sugar in bowl until light and fluffy, using electric mixer at medium speed. Add egg and vanilla, beating well.

Add dry ingredients alternately with milk to creamed mixture, beating well after each addition, using a spoon. Stir in walnuts. Drop mixture by teaspoonfuls, about 2" apart, on ungreased baking sheets.

Bake in 350° oven 8 to 10 minutes, or until no imprint remains when touched lightly with finger. Top each with a marshmallow half, cut side down. Return to oven and bake 2 more minutes. Remove from baking sheets; cool on racks. Prepare Cocoa Frosting. Frost each with Cocoa Frosting. Makes 3 dozen.

Cocoa Frosting: Sift together 2 c. sifted confectioners' sugar, ⅓ c. baking cocoa and dash of salt into mixing bowl. Add 3 tblsp. melted butter or regular margarine, 4 tblsp. light cream and ½ tsp. vanilla. Mix until smooth and creamy, using a spoon.

Golden Carrot Cookies

If you're looking for a cookie recipe featuring a healthful ingredient, try this one. Nutritious and good-tasting, too.

2 c. sifted flour	1 egg
2 tsp. baking powder	1 tsp. vanilla
½ tsp. salt	½ tsp. lemon extract
¾ c. butter or regular	1¼ c. finely shredded
margarine	pared carrots
¾ c. sugar	

Sift together flour, baking powder and salt; set aside.

Cream together butter and sugar in bowl until light and fluffy, using electric mixer at medium speed. Add egg; beat well. Blend in vanilla and lemon extract.

Gradually stir dry ingredients into creamed mixture, mixing well. Stir in carrots. Drop mixture by teaspoonfuls, about 2" apart, on greased baking sheets.

Bake in 375° oven 15 minutes, or until golden brown. Remove from baking sheets; cool on racks. Makes 4 dozen.

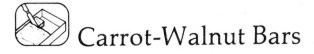 Carrot-Walnut Bars

Here's another yummy carrot cookie. This one's made with strained carrots and iced with cream cheese frosting.

2 c. sifted flour	1 c. cooking oil
2 c. sugar	3 (4½-oz.) jars baby food
2 tsp. baking soda	strained carrots
2 tsp. ground cinnamon	½ c. chopped walnuts
¼ tsp. salt	Cream Cheese Frosting
4 eggs	(recipe follows)

Sift together flour, sugar, baking soda, cinnamon and salt into mixing bowl. Add eggs, oil and carrots. Beat 3 minutes, using electric mixer at medium speed and scraping bowl occasionally. Stir in walnuts. Pour mixture into 2 greased and floured 13x9x2" baking pans.

Bake in 350° oven 30 minutes, or until top springs back when touched lightly with finger. Cool in pans on racks. Prepare Cream Cheese Frosting. Frost bars with Cream Cheese Frosting. Cut into 3x1" bars. Makes 78.

Cream Cheese Frosting: Combine 2 c. sifted confectioners' sugar, 1 (8-oz.) pkg. softened cream cheese, ¼ c. soft butter or regular margarine and 1 tsp. vanilla in bowl. Beat until light and fluffy, using electric mixer at medium speed.

Crisp Oatmeal Cookies

Oatmeal cookies are traditional favorites of children, and for good reason. These also contain flaked coconut and rice cereal.

1½ c. sifted flour	2 eggs
1 tsp. baking powder	2 tsp. vanilla
1 tsp. baking soda	2½ c. oven-toasted rice
1 c. butter or regular	cereal
margarine	2 c. quick-cooking oats
1 c. brown sugar, packed	1 c. flaked coconut
1 c. sugar	

Sift together flour, baking powder and baking soda; set aside.

Cream together butter, brown sugar and sugar in bowl until light and fluffy, using electric mixer at medium speed. Add eggs, one at a time, beating well after each addition. Blend in vanilla.

Gradually stir dry ingredients into creamed mixture, mixing well. Stir in rice cereal, oats and coconut. Drop mixture by teaspoonfuls, about 2" apart, on greased baking sheets.

Bake in 325° oven 12 to 15 minutes, or until golden brown. Cool slightly on baking sheets. Remove from baking sheets; cool completely on racks. Makes about 5½ dozen.

Ranger Oatmeal Cookies

Another version of a coconut-oatmeal cookie—this one made with shortening instead of butter to cut costs.

2 c. sifted flour	2 eggs
1½ tsp. baking soda	1 tsp. vanilla
1 tsp. baking powder	1 c. quick-cooking oats
½ tsp. salt	1 c. chopped walnuts
1 c. shortening	1 c. flaked coconut
1 c. sugar	1 c. oven-toasted rice cereal
1 c. brown sugar, packed	

Sift together flour, baking soda, baking powder and salt; set aside.

Cream together shortening, sugar and brown sugar in bowl until light and fluffy, using electric mixer at medium speed. Add eggs, one at a time, beating well after each addition. Beat in vanilla.

Gradually stir dry ingredients into creamed mixture, mixing well. Stir in oats, walnuts, coconut and rice cereal. Shape mixture into 1" balls. Place balls, about 2" apart, on greased baking sheets.

Bake in 350° oven 15 minutes, or until golden brown. Remove from baking sheets; cool on racks. Makes 6 dozen.

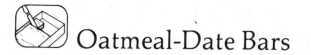

Oatmeal-Date Bars

Since the date filling is cooked on the range, this recipe is recommended for an older child. It features iron-rich oatmeal.

3 c. cut-up pitted dates	½ c. shortening
¼ c. sugar	¼ c. butter or regular
1 c. water	margarine
1¾ c. sifted flour	1 c. brown sugar, packed
1 tsp. salt	1 c. quick-cooking oats
½ tsp. baking soda	

Combine dates, sugar and water in small saucepan. Cook over low heat, stirring constantly, 10 minutes or until mixture is thick. Remove from heat. Cool completely.

Sift together flour, salt and baking soda; set aside.

Cream together shortening, butter and brown sugar in bowl until light and fluffy, using electric mixer at medium speed.

Gradually stir dry ingredients into creamed mixture, mixing well. Stir in oats. Press one half of mixture into greased and floured 13x9x2" baking pan. Spread with cooled date filling. Carefully top with remaining half of crumb mixture, patting lightly.

Bake in 400° oven 25 to 30 minutes, or until golden brown. Cool in pan on rack. Cut into 3x1" bars. Makes 39.

Refrigerator Oatmeal Chippers

Cookies made with large amounts of oatmeal are rich in protein, thiamine, iron and phosphorus. Nutritious and good.

1½ c. sifted flour	1 c. sugar
1 tsp. baking soda	2 eggs
½ tsp. salt	1 tsp. vanilla
1 c. butter or regular	3 c. quick-cooking oats
margarine	¼ c. semisweet chocolate
1 c. brown sugar, packed	pieces

Sift together flour, baking soda and salt; set aside.

Cream together butter, brown sugar and sugar in bowl until light and fluffy, using electric mixer at medium speed. Add eggs, one at a time, beating well after each addition. Blend in vanilla.

Gradually stir dry ingredients into creamed mixture, blending well. Stir in oats. Divide dough in half. Shape each half into a 12" roll. Wrap each in waxed paper and chill in refrigerator overnight.

Cut each roll into 36 slices, about ⅓" thick. Place slices, about 2" apart, on greased baking sheets. Place 6 chocolate pieces on top of each slice.

Bake in 350° oven 10 minutes, or until golden brown. Remove from baking sheets; cool on racks. Makes 6 dozen.

Jumbo Oatmeal-Peanut Butter Cookies

An iron-rich cookie containing peanut butter, oatmeal and raisins—a flavor combination that can't be beat.

2 c. sifted flour	1 c. sugar
1 tsp. baking soda	1 c. brown sugar, packed
1 tsp. salt	2 eggs
1 tsp. ground cinnamon	1 tsp. vanilla
¾ c. butter or regular	¼ c. milk
margarine	1½ c. quick-cooking oats
½ c. peanut butter	1 c. raisins

Sift together flour, baking soda, salt and cinnamon; set aside.

Cream together butter, peanut butter, sugar and brown sugar in bowl until light and fluffy, using electric mixer at medium speed. Add eggs, one at a time, beating well after each addition. Blend in vanilla and milk.

Gradually stir dry ingredients into creamed mixture, blending well. Stir in oats and raisins. Drop mixture by tablespoonfuls, about 2" apart, on greased baking sheets.

Bake in 350° oven 15 minutes, or until golden brown. Remove from baking sheets; cool on racks. Makes 3 dozen.

Peanut Butter Bars

A child of seven or younger could help make this cookie. These bars were prize-winners at an Indiana fair.

1 c. sifted flour
1 tsp. baking powder
¼ tsp. salt
⅓ c. shortening
½ c. peanut butter
1 c. sugar
¼ c. brown sugar, packed

2 eggs
1 tsp. vanilla
1⅓ c. flaked coconut
Confectioners' Sugar
   Frosting (recipe follows)
Chopped peanuts

Sift together flour, baking powder and salt; set aside.

Cream together shortening, peanut butter, sugar and brown sugar in bowl until light and fluffy, using electric mixer at medium speed. Add eggs, one at a time, beating well after each addition. Blend in vanilla.

Stir dry ingredients into creamed mixture, mixing thoroughly. Stir in coconut. Spread batter in greased 13x9x2" baking pan.

Bake in 350° oven 25 minutes, or until top springs back when touched lightly with finger. Cool in pan on rack. Prepare Confectioners' Sugar Frosting. Spread bars with Confectioners' Sugar Frosting. Sprinkle with peanuts. Cut into 3x1" bars. Makes 39.

Confectioners' Sugar Frosting: Combine 2 c. sifted confectioners' sugar, ¼ c. soft butter or regular margarine, 1 tsp. vanilla, ⅛ tsp. salt and 3 tblsp. light cream in bowl; beat until smooth, using a spoon.

Gumdrop Jewels

You don't need to be an accomplished baker to turn out attractive cookies; tiny hands can easily decorate these drop cookies.

2 c. sifted flour
½ tsp. baking powder
¼ tsp. salt
½ c. butter or regular
   margarine
¾ c. brown sugar, packed

1 egg
¾ tsp. vanilla
¾ c. chopped walnuts
Assorted small gumdrops,
   cut into slices

Sift together flour, baking powder and salt; set aside.

Cream together butter and brown sugar in bowl until light and fluffy, using electric mixer at medium speed. Add egg and vanilla; blend well.

Gradually stir dry ingredients into creamed mixture, mixing well. Stir in walnuts. Drop mixture by teaspoonfuls, about 2" apart, on lightly greased baking sheets. Decorate tops with gumdrop slices.

Bake in 350° oven 12 to 15 minutes, or until golden brown. Remove from baking sheets; cool on racks. Makes 3½ dozen.

Double Treat Cookies

Two favorite cookies in one: chocolate chip and peanut butter. Crunchy cookies like these are terrific after-school treats.

2 c. sifted flour
2 tsp. baking soda
½ tsp. salt
1 c. shortening
1 c. sugar
1 c. brown sugar, packed
2 eggs

1 tsp. vanilla
1 c. peanut butter
1 c. chopped, salted peanuts
1 (6-oz.) pkg. semisweet
   chocolate pieces
Sugar

Sift together flour, baking soda and salt; set aside.

Cream together shortening, 1 c. sugar and brown sugar in bowl until light and fluffy, using electric mixer at medium speed. Add eggs, one at a time, beating well after each addition. Beat in vanilla and peanut butter.

Gradually stir dry ingredients into creamed mixture, mixing well. Stir in peanuts and chocolate pieces.

Shape mixture into 1" balls. Place balls, about 2" apart, on ungreased baking sheets. Flatten each with bottom of a glass dipped in sugar.

Bake in 350° oven 8 minutes, or until golden brown. Remove from baking sheets; cool on racks. Makes 7 dozen.

Mexican Cookie Rings

Children will enjoy rolling the dough into balls and punching out the centers with their thumbs to form ring shapes.

1½ c. sifted flour
½ tsp. baking powder
½ tsp. salt
½ c. butter or regular
   margarine

⅔ c. sugar
3 egg yolks
1 tsp. vanilla
Multicolored decorating
   candies

Sift together flour, baking powder and salt; set aside.

Cream together butter and sugar in bowl until light and fluffy, using electric mixer at medium speed. Add egg yolks and vanilla; beat well.

Gradually stir dry ingredients into creamed mixture, mixing well. Shape mixture into 1" balls. Push your thumb through center of each ball and shape dough into a ring. Dip top of each ring in decorating candies. Place rings, about 2" apart, on lightly greased baking sheets.

Bake in 375° oven 10 to 12 minutes, or until golden brown. Remove from baking sheets; cool on racks. Makes 2 dozen.

Butterscotch Bars

These candy-like brown sugar bars are swirled with melted butterscotch morsels, then frosted with a butter icing.

2 c. sifted flour
1 tsp. baking soda
½ tsp. salt
1 c. butter or regular
    margarine
⅔ c. brown sugar, packed
⅔ c. sugar
2 eggs

1 tsp. vanilla
½ tsp. water
1 c. chopped walnuts
1 (12-oz.) pkg. butterscotch-
    flavored pieces
Butter Cream Frosting
    (recipe follows)

Sift together flour, baking soda and salt; set aside.

Cream together butter, brown sugar and sugar in bowl until light and fluffy, using electric mixer at medium speed. Add eggs, one at a time, beating well after each addition. Blend in vanilla and water.

Gradually stir dry ingredients into creamed mixture, blending well. Stir in walnuts. Spread mixture in greased 15½x10½x1″ jelly roll pan. Sprinkle butterscotch-flavored pieces over top.

Bake in 375° oven 2 minutes. Remove from oven; cut through batter with metal spatula to marbleize melted butterscotch and batter. Return to oven and bake 12 more minutes, or until top springs back when touched lightly with finger. Cool slightly in pan on rack. Prepare Butter Cream Frosting. While bars are still warm, spread with Butter Cream Frosting. Cool completely. Cut into 2½x1½″ bars. Makes 48.

Butter Cream Frosting: Combine 2 c. sifted confectioners' sugar, ¼ c. butter or regular margarine, 2 tblsp. milk and ½ tsp. vanilla in bowl; beat until smooth, using a spoon.

 Pretzel Cookies

This dough also can be formed into other shapes, such as initials, hearts, rings or other simple designs.

3 c. sifted flour	3 eggs
1/8 tsp. salt	1/2 tsp. vanilla
2/3 c. butter or regular margarine	1/2 c. sugar
1/2 c. sugar	1/2 c. finely chopped walnuts

Sift together flour and salt; set aside.

Cream together butter and 1/2 c. sugar in bowl until light and fluffy, using electric mixer at medium speed. Add 2 of the eggs, one at a time, beating well after each addition. Beat in vanilla.

Gradually stir dry ingredients into creamed mixture, mixing well. Knead dough until smooth. Cover and let stand 1 hour at room temperature. Combine 1/2 c. sugar and walnuts; set aside.

Pinch off small portions of dough about the size of a walnut. Roll each on floured surface to form pencil-shaped rope. Form into a pretzel shape. Beat remaining egg slightly. Brush tops of each cookie with beaten egg and sprinkle with walnut mixture. Place, about 1" apart, on ungreased baking sheets.

Bake in 325° oven 25 minutes, or until very lightly browned. Remove from baking sheets; cool on racks. Makes about 3½ dozen.

Danish Sugar Cookies

Decorate with plain sugar as directed, or roll balls of dough in chocolate jimmies, crushed cornflakes or colored sugar.

2 c. sifted flour	1/2 c. shortening
1/2 tsp. baking soda	1 c. sugar
1/2 tsp. cream of tartar	1 egg
1/8 tsp. salt	1/2 tsp. vanilla
1/2 c. butter or regular margarine	1/2 tsp. lemon extract
	Sugar

Sift together flour, baking soda, cream of tartar and salt; set aside.

Cream together butter, shortening and 1 c. sugar in bowl until light and fluffy, using electric mixer at medium speed. Add egg, vanilla and lemon extract; beat well.

Gradually stir dry ingredients into creamed mixture, mix well. Cover and chill in refrigerator 2 hours.

Shape dough into 1" balls and roll in sugar. Place balls, about 1" apart, on greased baking sheets. Flatten each by pressing with bottom of drinking glass.

Bake in 350° oven 8 minutes, or until golden brown. Remove from baking sheets; cool on racks. Makes about 5 dozen.

German Sugar Cookies

This basic dough is easy to work with and doesn't need to be chilled before rolling. A good choice for elementary school children.

3 c. sifted flour	1 c. sugar
½ tsp. baking powder	2 eggs
½ tsp. baking soda	1 tsp. vanilla
¼ tsp. salt	
1 c. butter or regular margarine	

Sift together flour, baking powder, baking soda and salt; set aside.

Cream together butter and sugar in bowl until light and fluffy, using electric mixer at medium speed. Add eggs, one at a time, beating well after each addition. Blend in vanilla.

Gradually stir dry ingredients into creamed mixture, blending well.

Divide dough in half. Roll out each half on lightly floured surface to ¼" thickness. Cut with floured 2" cookie cutters. Place, about 2" apart, on greased baking sheets.

Bake in 350° oven 10 to 12 minutes, or until golden brown. Remove from baking sheets; cool on racks. Makes 6 dozen.

Sugar and Spice Cookies

Children like to make molded cookies because it's fun to shape the dough into balls. These cookies are crunchy and extra-spicy.

2 c. sifted flour	¾ c. shortening
2 tsp. baking soda	1 c. sugar
1 tsp. ground cinnamon	1 egg
¾ tsp. ground ginger	¼ c. molasses
½ tsp. ground cloves	2 tsp. sugar
¼ tsp. salt	1 tsp. ground cinnamon

Sift together flour, baking soda, 1 tsp. cinnamon, ginger, cloves and salt; set aside.

Cream together shortening and 1 c. sugar in bowl until light and fluffy, using electric mixer at medium speed. Add egg and molasses, blending well.

Gradually stir dry ingredients into creamed mixture, mixing well. Shape mixture into balls, using 1 tsp. dough for each. Roll in a mixture of 2 tsp. sugar and 1 tsp. cinnamon. Place balls, about 2" apart, on greased baking sheets.

Bake in 375° oven 10 minutes, or until golden brown. Remove from baking sheets; cool on racks. Makes about 3 dozen.

5 | Super-Nutritious Treats

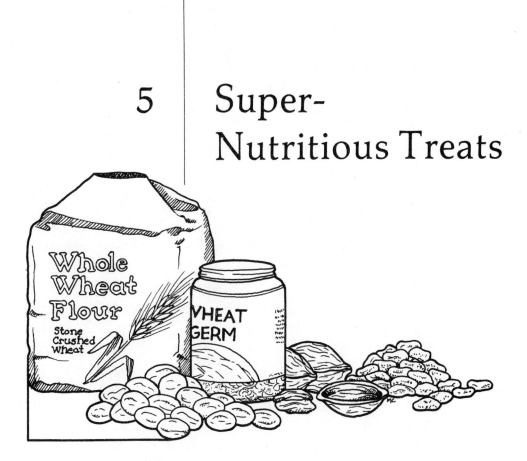

Each and every cookie in this chapter has been specially selected for both flavor and wholesomeness, from the Crisp Peanut Butter Cookies right down to the Fudge Walnut and Super Chocolate Chip Cookies. If you're concerned about nutrition for yourself and your family, here are 33 ways to satisfy a craving for sweets without sacrificing wholesome ingredients.

Farm and ranch women have always added healthful ingredients to plain cookie dough for extra nutrition and flavor—it's almost a tradition. You, too, can boost the nutritional value of cookies in many ways.

By substituting whole-wheat flour for all or part of the white flour, you'll add both fiber and B vitamins. Our energy-packed Whole-Wheat Brownies are just as flavorful as regular brownies, but they have added nutrition as well as the traditional fudgy brownie texture.

Any basic cookie dough can be enriched with extra protein by adding nonfat dry milk to the dry ingredients, as we did in recipes for the yummy Molasses Whole-Wheat Cookies, Raisin-Carrot Oatmeals and Oatmeal-Fruit Cookies. Add whole-wheat flour, wheat germ, nonfat dry milk, sunflower seeds and peanuts to a basic chocolate chip dough—and you've transformed it into a protein-rich Super Chocolate Chip. Although this cookie usually is made with chocolate chips, you also can substitute carob chips, often available in health food stores.

Since so many of us don't get enough iron in our daily diets, you may want to add iron-rich ingredients as well as wheat germ to your cookies. Both oatmeal and wheat germ are found in Wheat-Oat Crisps, and extra wheat germ is used to give Honeyed Raisin Cookies a golden brown crust.

Don't count out dried fruits—they add both iron and vitamins. Good Health Bars are generously laden with raisins, apricots and sunflower seeds; our Date and Apricot Bars are made by sandwiching a luscious date-apricot filling between a rich crumb crust. People of all ages are sure to appreciate our unusual Family Cookies—soft drop cookies mildly spiced with four different spices and chock-full of bits of oranges, apples, dates, carrots and raisins.

We've also included two cookies made with granola, crunchy Granola Cookies and Granola-Chocolate Chip Cookies. The first is made with packaged granola, and the other uses Country-Style Granola that you make yourself. This homemade granola also makes a fine cereal or snack.

Once you've made a batch of these super cookies, you won't need to sell your family and friends on them—they're so good, they'll sell themselves!

Good Health Bars

These soft bar cookies deserve their name—they're rich in iron, Vitamin A and all the B vitamins. So delicious, too.

3 c. stirred whole-wheat flour	2 c. milk
¾ c. unsifted flour	¾ c. cooking oil
½ c. wheat germ	½ c. honey
1 c. sugar	½ c. dark corn syrup
1 c. nonfat dry milk	2 c. raisins
2 tsp. baking powder	1⅓ c. snipped dried apricots (6 oz.)
1 tsp. salt	1 c. roasted, salted sunflower seeds
1 tsp. ground cinnamon	
4 eggs	

Stir together whole-wheat flour, flour, wheat germ, sugar, dry milk, baking powder, salt and cinnamon in large bowl.

Slightly beat eggs in another bowl, using a rotary beater. Blend in milk, oil, honey and corn syrup. Add to dry ingredients, stirring just until moistened. Stir in raisins, apricots and sunflower seeds. Spread mixture in greased 15½x10½x1" jelly roll pan.

Bake in 350° oven 45 minutes, or until top springs back when touched lightly with finger. Cool in pan on rack. Cut into 4x1" bars. Makes 40.

Honeyed Raisin Cookies

Wheat germ adds both iron and B vitamins to these country-style cookies. Honey, lemon rind and raisins add lots of flavor.

2 c. sifted flour	½ c. honey
1 tsp. baking powder	1 tsp. grated lemon rind
¼ tsp. salt	1 egg
½ c. butter or regular margarine	½ c. wheat germ
½ c. sugar	1 c. raisins
	⅓ c. wheat germ

Sift together flour, baking powder and salt; set aside.

Cream together butter, sugar and honey in bowl until light and fluffy, using electric mixer at medium speed. Add lemon rind and egg, beating thoroughly.

Stir dry ingredients into creamed mixture, mixing well. Stir in ½ c. wheat germ and raisins. Cover and chill in refrigerator at least 1 hour.

Shape dough into 1" balls. Roll each in ⅓ c. wheat germ. Place balls, about 2" apart, on greased baking sheets. Flatten each slightly with fingers.

Bake in 400° oven 8 to 10 minutes, or until lightly browned. Remove from baking sheets; cool on racks. Makes about 3 dozen.

Super Chocolate Chip Cookies

These flavorful cookies contain whole-wheat flour, wheat germ, non-fat dry milk, sunflower seeds and peanuts. So good!

½ c. stirred whole-wheat
    flour
½ c. wheat germ
2 tblsp. nonfat dry milk
½ tsp. baking soda
½ c. butter or regular
    margarine
½ c. brown sugar, packed

1 egg
½ tsp. vanilla
1 (6-oz.) pkg. semisweet
    chocolate pieces
½ c. dry-roasted sunflower
    seeds
½ c. chopped peanuts

Stir together whole-wheat flour, wheat germ, dry milk and baking soda; set aside.

Cream together butter and brown sugar in bowl until light and fluffy, using electric mixer at medium speed. Add egg and vanilla; beat well.

Stir dry ingredients into creamed mixture, mixing well. Stir in chocolate pieces, sunflower seeds and peanuts. Drop mixture by rounded teaspoonfuls, about 2" apart, on greased baking sheets.

Bake in 350° oven 10 to 12 minutes, or until lightly browned. Remove from baking sheets; cool on racks. Makes 3 dozen.

Molasses Whole-Wheat Cookies

There's no sugar in these old-fashioned soft drop cookies—molasses is the sweetener. Raisins add flavor and iron.

½ c. nonfat dry milk
2 tsp. baking powder
½ tsp. baking soda
½ tsp. salt
⅓ c. shortening
¾ c. molasses

1 tsp. vanilla
2 eggs
1 c. plus 2 tblsp. stirred
    whole-wheat flour
½ c. raisins

Sift together nonfat dry milk, baking powder, baking soda and salt; set aside.

Beat together shortening, molasses and vanilla in bowl until smooth, using electric mixer at medium speed. Add eggs, one at a time, beating well after each addition.

Gradually stir dry ingredients and whole-wheat flour into creamed mixture, mixing well. Stir in raisins. Drop mixture by teaspoonfuls, about 2" apart, on lightly greased baking sheets.

Bake in 350° oven 10 to 12 minutes, or until lightly browned. Remove from baking sheets; cool on racks. Makes 4 dozen.

Whole-Wheat Raisin Cookies

Because the recipe calls for whole-wheat flour and lots of raisins, these big chocolate chip cookies are more nutritious than most.

2½ c. sifted flour	4 eggs
2½ c. stirred whole-wheat flour	2 tsp. vanilla
½ tsp. salt	2 tsp. baking soda
1 c. butter or regular margarine	2 tblsp. hot water
½ c. shortening	1 (12-oz.) pkg. semisweet chocolate pieces
1½ c. brown sugar, packed	1 c. raisins
1½ c. sugar	1 c. chopped walnuts
	Sugar

Stir together flour, whole-wheat flour and salt; set aside.

Cream together butter, shortening, brown sugar and 1½ c. sugar in bowl until light and fluffy, using electric mixer at medium speed. Add eggs, one at a time, beating well after each addition. Blend in vanilla.

Dissolve baking soda in hot water. Add to creamed mixture with dry ingredients, mixing well. Stir in chocolate pieces, raisins and walnuts. Drop mixture by heaping tablespoonfuls or small ice cream scoop, about 3" apart, on greased baking sheets. Flatten each to make 2½" circle, using bottom of drinking glass dipped in sugar.

Bake in 350° oven 12 minutes, or until golden brown. Remove from baking sheets; cool on racks. Makes 4 dozen.

Whole-Wheat Brownies

Mild chocolate brownies made with baking cocoa and studded with walnuts. Whole-wheat flour adds a nutty flavor.

½ c. butter or regular margarine	¼ tsp. salt
1 c. brown sugar, packed	6 tblsp. baking cocoa
2 eggs	2 tblsp. butter or regular margarine, melted
½ tsp. vanilla	1 c. chopped walnuts
½ c. stirred whole-wheat flour	

Cream together ½ c. butter and brown sugar in bowl until light and fluffy, using electric mixer at medium speed. Add eggs, one at a time, beating well after each addition. Beat in vanilla.

Gradually stir whole-wheat flour and salt into creamed mixture, mixing well. Combine cocoa and 2 tblsp. melted butter. Add cocoa mixture and walnuts; mix well. Spread mixture in greased 9" square baking pan.

Bake in 325° oven 45 minutes, or until no imprint remains when touched lightly with finger. Cool in pan on rack. Cut into 3x1" bars. Makes 27.

Sunflower Refrigerator Cookies

Crisp, thin whole-grained cookies, served with a fresh pear, make quite a nutritious after-school snack.

1½ c. quick-cooking oats	½ c. sugar
¾ c. stirred whole-wheat flour	½ c. brown sugar, packed
¼ c. wheat germ	1 egg
½ tsp. baking soda	1 tsp. vanilla
¼ tsp. salt	¾ c. dry-roasted sunflower seeds
½ c. butter or regular margarine	

Stir together oats, whole-wheat flour, wheat germ, baking soda and salt; set aside.

Cream together butter, sugar and brown sugar in bowl until light and fluffy, using electric mixer at medium speed. Add egg and vanilla; beat thoroughly.

Stir dry ingredients into creamed mixture, mixing well. Stir in sunflower seeds.

Divide dough in half and form each into a roll, about 2" in diameter. Wrap each tightly in waxed paper and chill in refrigerator at least 4 hours.

Cut rolls into ¼" slices. Place slices, about 2" apart, on ungreased baking sheets.

Bake in 375° oven 10 to 12 minutes, or until lightly browned. Remove from baking sheets; cool on racks. Makes about 4 dozen.

Applesauce Oatmeal Cookies

Puffy cake-like cookies flavored with applesauce and spiced with cinnamon and cloves. They keep well in the cookie jar.

1¾ c. sifted flour	1 c. sugar
1 tsp. baking soda	1 egg
1 tsp. ground cinnamon	1 c. applesauce
½ tsp. baking powder	½ c. raisins
½ tsp. salt	1 c. quick-cooking oats
½ tsp. ground cloves	
½ c. butter or regular margarine	

Sift together flour, baking soda, cinnamon, baking powder, salt and cloves; set aside.

Cream together butter and sugar in bowl until light and fluffy, using electric mixer at medium speed. Add egg and applesauce, beating well.

Gradually stir dry ingredients into creamed mixture, blending well. Stir in raisins and oats. Drop mixture by teaspoonfuls, about 3" apart, on greased baking sheets.

Bake in 375° oven 15 minutes, or until golden brown. Remove from baking sheets; cool on racks. Makes 4 dozen.

Wheat-Oat Crisps

Carob chips can be used instead of chocolate in these protein-rich oatmeal cookies flavored with coconut and walnuts.

1 c. stirred whole-wheat
   flour
1 tsp. salt
½ tsp. baking soda
¾ c. shortening
1 c. brown sugar, packed
½ c. sugar
1 egg

¼ c. water
1 tsp. vanilla
3 c. quick-cooking oats
2 tblsp. wheat germ
½ c. flaked coconut
½ c. chopped walnuts
¼ c. semisweet chocolate
   pieces

Stir together whole-wheat flour, salt and baking soda; set aside.

Cream together shortening, brown sugar and sugar in bowl until light and fluffy, using electric mixer at medium speed. Add egg, water and vanilla; beat well.

Gradually stir dry ingredients into creamed mixture, mixing well. Stir in oats, wheat germ, coconut and walnuts. Drop mixture by tea-spoonfuls, about 2″ apart, on lightly greased baking sheets. Top each with one chocolate piece.

Bake in 350° oven 12 to 15 minutes, or until golden brown. Remove from baking sheets; cool on racks. Makes 5 dozen.

Peanut-Oat Bars

Bars can be prepared in almost no time: Heat four ingredients, add to the rest and stir. They bake in just 20 minutes.

3½ c. quick-cooking oats
1 c. flaked coconut
⅔ c. butter or regular
   margarine
⅓ c. peanut butter

½ c. brown sugar, packed
⅓ c. light corn syrup
¾ c. chopped, salted peanuts
1 egg, beaten

Toast oats in shallow baking pan in 350° oven 8 minutes. Add coconut; toast 5 more minutes, stirring frequently. Remove from oven.

Combine butter, peanut butter, brown sugar and corn syrup in 2-qt. saucepan; mix well. Cook over low heat until mixture is smooth. Remove from heat.

Add peanut butter mixture to oat mixture, peanuts and egg in bowl; blend well. Press mixture firmly into well-greased 15½x10½ x1″ jelly roll pan.

Bake in 350° oven 20 minutes, or until golden brown. Cool in pan on rack. Cut into 2½x1½″ bars. Makes 48.

Mincemeat-Filled Oatsies

Country-style oatmeals featuring a mincemeat filling. The dough is refrigerated, so you may want to make it a day in advance.

1 c. sifted flour	¾ c. sugar
1 tsp. baking soda	5 c. quick-cooking oats
¼ tsp. salt	1 c. prepared mincemeat
1 tsp. vinegar	1 tsp. lemon juice
½ c. milk	¼ c. water
½ c. butter or regular margarine	6 tblsp. sugar

Sift together flour, baking soda and salt; set aside. Combine vinegar and milk; stir to mix and set aside.

Cream together butter and ¾ c. sugar in bowl until light and fluffy, using electric mixer at medium speed.

Add dry ingredients alternately with soured milk to creamed mixture, beating well after each addition, using electric mixer at low speed. Stir in oats. Cover and chill in refrigerator 4 hours or longer.

Meanwhile, combine mincemeat, lemon juice, water and 6 tblsp. sugar in saucepan. Cook over medium heat until mixture comes to a boil, stirring constantly. Remove from heat and cool well.

Divide dough into thirds. Use one third at a time, leaving remaining dough in refrigerator. Roll out dough on floured surface to ⅛" thickness. Cut with floured 2½" round cookie cutter. Place 1 tsp. mincemeat filling in center of one round. Top with another round and press edges together to seal. Place filled rounds, about 2" apart, on ungreased baking sheets.

Bake in 350° oven 10 minutes, or until golden brown. Remove from baking sheets; cool on racks. Makes 3½ dozen.

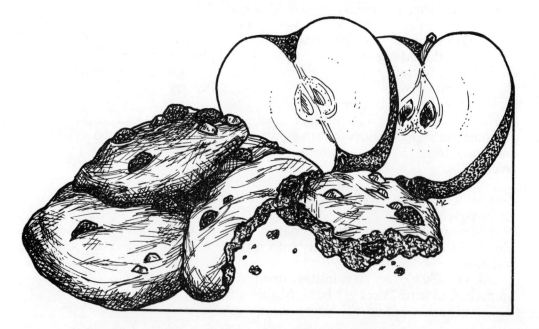

Oatmeal-Fruit Cookies

Dates, raisins, walnuts and coconut make these oatmeals extra-good. Grated orange rind adds a delicate flavor note.

1 c. sifted flour
¼ c. nonfat dry milk
½ tsp. baking powder
½ tsp. baking soda
¼ tsp. salt
½ c. butter or regular
   margarine
½ c. sugar
½ c. brown sugar, packed

1 egg
½ tsp. vanilla
1 tblsp. water
¾ c. quick-cooking oats
½ c. chopped pitted dates
½ c. raisins
½ c. chopped walnuts
½ c. flaked coconut
1½ tsp. grated orange rind

Sift together flour, dry milk, baking powder, baking soda and salt; set aside.

Cream together butter, sugar and brown sugar in bowl until light and fluffy, using electric mixer at medium speed. Beat in egg and vanilla.

Stir dry ingredients into creamed mixture, mixing well. Blend in water. Stir in oats, dates, raisins, walnuts, coconut and orange rind. Shape level tablespoonfuls of mixture into balls. Place balls, about 2" apart, on greased baking sheets.

Bake in 375° oven 10 to 12 minutes, or until lightly browned. Remove from baking sheets; cool on racks. Makes 3 dozen.

Crisp Peanut Butter Cookies

A Vermont homemaker sent us this recipe for drop cookies made with high-protein cereal. Your favorite flaked cereal also can be used.

2 c. sifted flour
2 tsp. baking soda
¼ tsp. salt
1 c. butter or regular
   margarine
1 c. peanut butter

¾ c. sugar
¾ c. brown sugar, packed
2 eggs
1 tsp. vanilla
3 c. crushed Product 19
   cereal

Sift together flour, baking soda and salt; set aside.

Cream together butter, peanut butter, sugar and brown sugar in bowl until light and fluffy, using electric mixer at medium speed. Add eggs, one at a time, beating well after each addition. Blend in vanilla.

Gradually stir dry ingredients into creamed mixture, blending well. Stir in cereal. Drop mixture by rounded teaspoonfuls, about 3" apart, on ungreased baking sheets. Flatten each with floured tines of fork, making crisscross pattern.

Bake in 350° oven 8 to 10 minutes, or until golden brown. Remove from baking sheets; cool on racks. Makes about 6 dozen.

Multi-Fruited Drops

Each chewy bite of this unusual oatmeal cookie is loaded with dates, raisins, walnuts and coconut. This recipe makes eight dozen.

2 c. sifted flour	1 tsp. vanilla
1 tsp. baking powder	1½ c. quick-cooking oats
½ tsp. baking soda	1 tblsp. grated orange rind
½ tsp. salt	1 tblsp. grated lemon rind
1 c. butter or regular	1 c. chopped pitted dates
margarine	1 c. raisins
1 c. sugar	1 c. chopped walnuts
1 c. brown sugar, packed	1 c. flaked coconut
2 eggs	

Sift together flour, baking powder, baking soda and salt; set aside.

Cream together butter, sugar and brown sugar in bowl until light and fluffy, using electric mixer at medium speed. Add eggs, one at a time, beating well after each addition. Beat in vanilla.

Gradually stir dry ingredients into creamed mixture, mixing well. Stir in oats, orange rind, lemon rind, dates, raisins, walnuts and coconut. Drop mixture by teaspoonfuls, about 2" apart, on greased baking sheets.

Bake in 375° oven 12 minutes, or until golden brown. Remove from baking sheets; cool on racks. Makes about 8 dozen.

Peanut-Molasses Cookies

Prunes are the surprise ingredient in these molasses-peanut butter gems. They add a great fruity flavor as well as nutrition.

1 c. sifted flour	½ c. molasses
1 tsp. baking powder	½ c. peanut butter
½ tsp. salt	½ tsp. vanilla
¼ tsp. baking soda	1 egg
¼ c. shortening	2 tblsp. milk
¼ c. brown sugar, packed	1 c. chopped pitted prunes

Sift together flour, baking powder, salt and baking soda; set aside.

Cream together shortening, brown sugar, molasses, peanut butter and vanilla in bowl until light and fluffy, using electric mixer at medium speed. Add egg and milk; beat well.

Gradually stir dry ingredients into creamed mixture, mixing well. Stir in prunes. Drop mixture by teaspoonfuls, about 2" apart, on greased baking sheets.

Bake in 375° oven 10 to 15 minutes, or until golden brown. Remove from baking sheets; cool on racks. Makes 5 dozen.

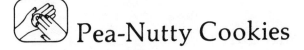

Pea-Nutty Cookies

Doubly-good peanut butter cookies coated with crunchy peanuts. These crispy cookies are rich in protein and several B vitamins.

1¼ c. sifted flour	½ c. peanut butter
¾ tsp. baking soda	½ c. sugar
½ tsp. baking powder	½ c. brown sugar, packed
¼ tsp. salt	1 egg
½ c. butter or regular	1 tsp. vanilla
margarine	1 c. finely chopped peanuts

Sift together flour, baking soda, baking powder and salt; set aside.

Cream together butter, peanut butter, sugar and brown sugar in bowl until light and fluffy, using electric mixer at medium speed. Add egg and vanilla; beat thoroughly.

Stir dry ingredients into creamed mixture, mixing well. Cover and chill in refrigerator at least 1 hour.

Shape dough into 1" balls. Roll each in chopped peanuts. Place balls, about 3" apart, on greased baking sheets. Flatten each with bottom of drinking glass.

Bake in 375° oven 10 to 12 minutes, or until lightly browned. Remove from baking sheets; cool on racks. Makes about 3 dozen.

Date and Apricot Bars

Flavorful fruited bars featuring a crumb crust made with oatmeal. These cookies are as rich in taste as they are nutritious.

1½ c. cut-up dried apricots	2 c. sifted flour
2 c. water	2 c. quick-cooking oats
1 c. cut-up pitted dates	1 c. brown sugar, packed
½ c. sugar	¾ c. butter or regular
1 tsp. grated lemon rind	margarine, melted
½ c. chopped pecans	1 tsp. baking soda
1/16 tsp. salt	1 tsp. vanilla

Cook apricots in water in saucepan over medium heat until tender. Drain, reserving 3 tblsp. cooking liquid. Combine cooked apricots, dates, sugar and reserved 3 tblsp. cooking liquid in saucepan. Simmer over medium heat for 3 minutes. Stir in lemon rind, pecans and salt. Remove from heat. Cool well.

Combine flour, oats, brown sugar, butter, baking soda and vanilla in bowl; mix well. Press one half of crumb mixture in greased 13x9x2" baking pan. Spread with cooled filling. Top with remaining crumb mixture.

Bake in 375° oven 35 minutes, or until golden brown. Cool in pan on rack. Cut into 3x1" bars. Makes 39.

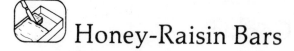

Honey-Raisin Bars

A party-sized recipe—it makes 96 extra-spicy bars. For a special touch, glaze bars with your favorite confectioners' sugar icing.

3½ c. sifted flour	1 c. brown sugar, packed
3 tsp. ground cinnamon	1 c. honey
2 tsp. baking soda	3 eggs
2 tsp. salt	2 tsp. vanilla
1 tsp. ground cardamom	1½ c. quick-cooking oats
1 tsp. ground nutmeg	2 c. raisins
1 tsp. ground allspice	1 c. chopped walnuts
1½ c. shortening	Confectioners' sugar
1 c. sugar	

Sift together flour, cinnamon, baking soda, salt, cardamom, nutmeg and allspice; set aside.

Cream together shortening, sugar and brown sugar in bowl until light and fluffy, using electric mixer at medium speed. Beat in honey, eggs and vanilla; blend well.

Gradually add dry ingredients to creamed mixture, mixing well with spoon. Stir in oats, raisins and walnuts. Spread mixture in 2 greased 15½x10½x1" jelly roll pans.

Bake in 375° oven 18 minutes, or until no imprint remains when touched lightly with finger. Cool in pans on racks. Cut into 2½ x1½" bars. Roll in confectioners' sugar. Makes 96.

Raisin-Carrot Oatmeals

This small-batch cookie recipe turns out 30 cinnamon-spiced oatmeals chock-full of shredded carrots and plump raisins.

1 c. sifted flour	⅓ c. brown sugar, packed
¼ c. nonfat dry milk	⅓ c. light molasses
1 tsp. salt	1 egg
½ tsp. baking powder	1½ c. quick-cooking oats
½ tsp. baking soda	1 c. grated, pared carrots
½ tsp. ground cinnamon	¾ c. raisins
⅓ c. cooking oil	

Sift together flour, dry milk, salt, baking powder, baking soda and cinnamon; set aside.

Beat together oil, brown sugar, molasses and egg in bowl until blended, using electric mixer at medium speed.

Stir dry ingredients into oil mixture, mixing until blended. Stir in oats, carrots and raisins. Drop mixture by heaping teaspoonfuls, about 2" apart, on greased baking sheets.

Bake in 375° oven 10 minutes, or until lightly browned. Remove from baking sheets; cool on racks. Makes about 2½ dozen.

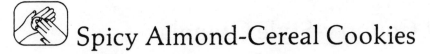 Spicy Almond-Cereal Cookies

These rich almond cookies are spiced with cinnamon and cloves and rolled in a crunchy whole-grain cereal before baking.

2 c. sifted flour	1 egg yolk
1 tsp. ground cinnamon	2 tblsp. milk
½ tsp. ground cloves	2 c. ground blanched
¼ tsp. salt	almonds
1 c. butter or regular	1½ c. Grape-Nuts cereal
margarine	
2 c. sifted confectioners'	
sugar	

Sift together flour, cinnamon, cloves and salt; set aside.

Cream together butter and confectioners' sugar in bowl until light and fluffy, using electric mixer at medium speed. Beat in egg yolk and milk.

Gradually stir dry ingredients into creamed mixture, blending well. Stir in almonds. Shape dough into 1" balls. Roll balls in cereal. Place balls, about 3" apart, on greased baking sheets. Flatten each with bottom of drinking glass.

Bake in 350° oven 10 minutes, or until no imprint remains when cookies are lightly touched with finger. Remove from baking sheets; cool on racks. Makes about 5 dozen.

Granola Cookies

Protein-rich cookies made with packaged granola, raisins and peanuts— a rich, crunchy combination.

1¾ c. packaged regular	1 tsp. salt
granola	1 tsp. baking soda
1½ c. sifted flour	½ tsp. ground cinnamon
¾ c. sugar	1 tsp. vanilla
¾ c. brown sugar, packed	1 egg
½ c. butter or regular	1 c. raisins
margarine	¾ c. coarsely chopped
½ c. shortening	peanuts

Combine all ingredients except raisins and peanuts in large bowl. Beat just until mixed, using electric mixer at low speed and scraping bowl constantly. Increase speed to medium. Beat 2 minutes more, scraping sides of bowl occasionally.

Stir in raisins and peanuts. Drop mixture by heaping teaspoonfuls, about 2" apart, on greased baking sheets.

Bake in 375° oven 10 to 12 minutes, or until lightly browned. Remove from baking sheets; cool on racks. Makes 5½ dozen.

Country-Style Granola

This homemade granola can be used as a cereal, a snack or as an ingredient in Granola-Chocolate Chip Cookies (recipe follows).

5 c. old-fashioned rolled oats	½ c. brown sugar, packed
1½ c. wheat germ	½ c. cooking oil
1 c. shredded coconut	⅓ c. water
1 c. chopped peanuts	2 tsp. vanilla
½ c. whole-bran cereal (not flakes)	

Combine oats, wheat germ, coconut, peanuts, bran cereal and brown sugar in large bowl; mix well. Combine oil, water and vanilla; pour over cereal mixture. Mix thoroughly, using a spoon. Turn mixture into 15½x10½x1″ jelly roll pan or shallow roasting pan.

Bake in 350° oven 1 hour, stirring every 15 minutes. Cool and store in covered containers. Makes about 10 cups.

Granola-Chocolate Chip Cookies

Homemade granola is the basis for this extra-flavorful, extra-nutritious and extra-crunchy version of a chocolate chip cookie.

¾ c. sifted flour	½ c. sugar
½ tsp. baking soda	1 egg
½ tsp. salt	1 tsp. vanilla
½ c. butter or regular margarine	2 c. Country-Style Granola
½ c. brown sugar, packed	1 (6-oz.) pkg. semisweet chocolate pieces

Sift together flour, baking soda and salt; set aside.

Cream together butter, brown sugar and sugar in bowl until light and fluffy, using electric mixer at medium speed. Beat in egg and vanilla.

Stir dry ingredients into creamed mixture, mixing well. Add Country-Style Granola and chocolate pieces; mix well. Drop mixture by teaspoonfuls, about 2″ apart, on greased baking sheets.

Bake in 350° oven 10 to 12 minutes, or until lightly browned. Remove from baking sheets; cool on racks. Makes about 4 dozen.

Nutritious Chocolate Drops

One Texas farm woman bakes these favorites to welcome her children home from school. They're extra-good with a cup of hot cocoa.

2 (1-oz.) squares unsweetened chocolate	½ c. milk
¼ c. butter or regular margarine	1 tsp. vanilla
	1 c. flaked coconut
1½ c. buttermilk baking mix	1 c. whole-bran cereal (not flakes)
¾ c. sugar	1 c. chopped pecans
1 egg	

Melt chocolate and butter in saucepan over low heat. Remove from heat; cool to room temperature.

Combine baking mix, sugar, egg, milk, vanilla and cooled chocolate mixture in bowl. Beat until light and fluffy, using electric mixer at medium speed.

Stir in coconut, bran cereal and pecans. Drop mixture by heaping teaspoonfuls, about 2" apart, on ungreased baking sheets.

Bake in 375° oven 8 minutes, or until a slight imprint remains when touched lightly with finger. Remove from baking sheets; cool on racks. Makes 4 dozen.

Banana Drop Cookies

Soft, cake-like banana cookies coated with crunchy bran cereal before baking. The cereal adds color, flavor and nutrition.

1 c. whole-bran cereal (not flakes)	¼ c. butter or regular margarine
6 tblsp. sugar	1 c. sugar
½ tsp. ground cinnamon	2 eggs
2½ c. sifted flour	1½ tsp. vanilla
3 tsp. baking powder	1 c. mashed ripe bananas (3 medium)
1 tsp. salt	
½ c. shortening	

Crush bran cereal until fine crumbs form, using a rolling pin. Combine crushed cereal with 6 tblsp. sugar and cinnamon; set aside.

Sift together flour, baking powder and salt; set aside.

Cream together shortening, butter and 1 c. sugar in bowl until light and fluffy, using electric mixer at medium speed. Add eggs, one at a time, beating well after each addition. Beat in vanilla and bananas.

Stir dry ingredients into creamed mixture, mixing well. Drop mixture by teaspoonfuls into bran mixture. Roll gently until coated. Place, about 2" apart, on greased baking sheets.

Bake in 400° oven 10 minutes, or until golden brown. Remove from baking sheets; cool on racks. Makes 4½ dozen.

Banana Cookies

Soy flour and walnuts add extra protein to these soft banana drops. If you wish, dust baked cookies with confectioners' sugar.

2½ c. sifted flour	1 c. mashed ripe bananas
1 c. sugar	(about 3 medium)
¼ c. stirred soy flour	½ c. buttermilk
1½ tsp. baking soda	2 eggs
½ tsp. salt	1 tsp. vanilla
¼ tsp. ground cinnamon	1 c. chopped walnuts
½ c. butter or regular	
margarine	

Combine all ingredients except walnuts in large bowl. Beat 3 minutes, using electric mixer at low speed, scraping bowl occasionally. Stir in walnuts. Drop mixture by heaping teaspoonfuls, about 2" apart, on greased baking sheets.

Bake in 375° oven 9 to 11 minutes, or until lightly browned. Remove from baking sheets; cool on racks. Makes 5½ dozen.

Family Cookies

The flavorful combination of carrots, fruits and walnuts in this lightly spiced cookie makes it absolutely scrumptious.

1 c. cut-up, pared carrots	½ tsp. salt
1 large apple, cored and cut	½ tsp. ground nutmeg
into wedges	¼ tsp. ground allspice
1 large orange, cut into	¼ tsp. ground cloves
wedges (not peeled)	1 c. butter or regular
1 c. cut-up pitted dates	margarine
1 c. raisins	2 c. sugar
4½ c. sifted flour	3 eggs
1 tsp. baking soda	1 c. chopped walnuts
1 tsp. ground cinnamon	

Grind carrots, apple, orange, dates and raisins in food grinder, using medium blade. Set aside.

Sift together flour, baking soda, cinnamon, salt, nutmeg, allspice and cloves; set aside.

Cream together butter and sugar in bowl until light and fluffy, using electric mixer at medium speed. Add eggs, one at a time, beating well after each addition.

Gradually stir dry ingredients into creamed mixture, mixing well. Stir in ground fruit mixture and walnuts. Drop mixture by teaspoonfuls, about 2" apart, on greased baking sheets.

Bake in 350° oven 10 to 12 minutes, or until golden brown. Remove from baking sheets; cool on racks. Makes 7½ dozen.

Rolled Spicy Fruit Cookies

Big three-inch spice cookies flavored with molasses, brown sugar, raisins and currants. They make great dunkers with milk or coffee.

4 c. sifted flour	¼ tsp. ground cloves
1 tsp. baking powder	1 c. shortening
1 tsp. baking soda	1½ c. brown sugar, packed
½ tsp. salt	3 eggs
1 tsp. ground cinnamon	½ c. molasses
½ tsp. ground ginger	1 c. dried currants
¼ tsp. ground allspice	1 c. raisins

Sift together flour, baking powder, baking soda, salt, cinnamon, ginger, allspice and cloves; set aside.

Cream together shortening and brown sugar in bowl until light and fluffy, using electric mixer at medium speed. Add eggs, one at a time, beating well after each addition. Blend in molasses.

Gradually stir dry ingredients into creamed mixture, mixing well. Stir in currants and raisins. Cover and chill in refrigerator overnight.

Divide dough into fourths. Use one fourth of the dough at a time, keeping remaining dough in refrigerator. Roll out each fourth on floured surface to ¼" thickness. Cut with floured 3" round cookie cutter. Place rounds, about 2" apart, on ungreased baking sheets.

Bake in 375° oven 10 minutes, or until golden brown. Remove from baking sheets; cool on racks. Makes 4 dozen.

Cashew-Date Drops

Active people will appreciate these cookies for a between-meal snack. Perfect for backpackers and hikers as well as field crews.

1½ c. unsifted flour	¼ c. honey
½ tsp. baking powder	1 egg
½ tsp. salt	1 tsp. vanilla
½ c. butter or regular margarine	1 c. chopped pitted dates
½ c. brown sugar, packed	1⅓ c. chopped cashew nuts

Stir together flour, baking powder and salt; set aside.

Cream together butter and brown sugar in bowl until light and fluffy, using electric mixer at medium speed. Add honey, egg and vanilla, beating until blended.

Stir dry ingredients into creamed mixture, mixing well. Stir in dates. Cover and chill in refrigerator at least 1 hour.

Drop mixture by heaping teaspoonfuls into chopped cashews. Roll lightly to coat. Place, about 2" apart, on greased baking sheets. Flatten each with bottom of drinking glass to ½" thickness.

Bake in 400° oven 9 to 11 minutes, or until lightly browned. Remove from baking sheets; cool on racks. Makes about 3 dozen.

Pumpkin Cookies

If your family likes pumpkin tea bread, they'll like these spicy drops filled with raisins and walnuts. Add a lemon icing if you wish.

2½ c. sifted flour	2 eggs
4 tsp. baking powder	1 tsp. vanilla
½ tsp. salt	1½ c. mashed pumpkin,
½ tsp. ground cinnamon	cooked or canned
½ tsp. ground nutmeg	1 c. raisins
½ c. shortening	1 c. chopped walnuts
1¼ c. brown sugar, packed	

Sift together flour, baking powder, salt, cinnamon and nutmeg; set aside.

Cream together shortening and brown sugar in bowl until light and fluffy, using electric mixer at medium speed. Add eggs, one at a time, beating well after each addition. Beat in vanilla and pumpkin.

Gradually stir dry ingredients into creamed mixture, mixing well. Stir in raisins and walnuts. Drop mixture by heaping teaspoonfuls, about 2″ apart, on greased baking sheets.

Bake in 375° oven 15 minutes, or until lightly browned. Remove from baking sheets; cool on racks. Makes 5 dozen.

Fudge Walnut Cookies

Both cottage cheese and eggs add protein to this big-batch recipe. Store in freezer and defrost for spur-of-the-moment entertaining.

5½ c. sifted flour	2 c. cream-style cottage
1 c. baking cocoa	cheese
2 tsp. baking powder	4 tsp. vanilla
1 tsp. baking soda	1 c. chopped walnuts
1 tsp. salt	1 (6-oz.) pkg. semisweet
1½ c. shortening	chocolate pieces
3⅓ c. sugar	Confectioners' sugar
4 eggs	

Sift together flour, cocoa, baking powder, soda and salt; set aside.

Cream together shortening and sugar in bowl until light and fluffy, using electric mixer at medium speed. Add eggs, one at a time, beating well after each addition. Blend in cottage cheese and vanilla.

Gradually add dry ingredients to creamed mixture, mixing well with spoon. Stir in walnuts and chocolate pieces. Drop mixture by teaspoonfuls, about 2″ apart, on greased baking sheets.

Bake in 350° oven 12 to 15 minutes, or until a slight imprint remains when touched lightly with finger. Remove from baking sheets. While still warm, roll cookies in confectioners' sugar. Cool completely on racks. Makes about 11 dozen.

Cottage Cheese Brownies

For brownie fans, here's an Ohio farm woman's recipe, an interesting variation made with a cinnamon-spiced cottage cheese filling.

1 c. sifted flour	1 tblsp. cornstarch
⅔ c. sugar	½ tsp. ground cinnamon
½ c. baking cocoa	¼ tsp. salt
¾ tsp. baking powder	1 tsp. vanilla
¼ tsp. salt	¼ c. butter or regular
1 c. cream-style cottage	margarine, melted
cheese, sieved	2 eggs
¼ c. sugar	¼ c. milk
1 egg, well beaten	1 tsp. vanilla

Sift together flour, ⅔ c. sugar, cocoa, baking powder and ¼ tsp. salt into large bowl; set aside.

Mix together cottage cheese, ¼ c. sugar, 1 egg, cornstarch, cinnamon, ¼ tsp. salt and 1 tsp. vanilla in another bowl; set aside.

Combine butter, 2 eggs, milk and 1 tsp. vanilla in small bowl; mix well. Add egg mixture to dry ingredients. Beat 2 minutes, using electric mixer at medium speed. Spread half of batter in greased 8″ square baking pan. Top with cottage cheese mixture. Spread with remaining batter.

Bake in 350° oven 40 minutes, or until no imprint remains when touched lightly with finger. Cool in pan on rack. Cut into 2x1″ bars. Makes 32.

Super Molasses-Ginger Cookies

These old-fashioned ginger cookies taste just like Grandmom's, but they've been enriched by the addition of soy flour.

1 c. unsifted flour
1 c. stirred soy flour
1½ tsp. ground ginger
1 tsp. baking soda
1 tsp. ground cinnamon
½ tsp. salt
½ c. butter or regular
   margarine

¼ c. shortening
1 c. sugar
1 egg
⅓ c. light molasses
Sugar

Stir together flour, soy flour, ginger, baking soda, cinnamon and salt; set aside.

Cream together butter, shortening and 1 c. sugar in bowl until light and fluffy, using electric mixer at medium speed. Beat in egg and molasses.

Stir dry ingredients into creamed mixture, mixing well. Cover and chill in refrigerator at least 1 hour.

Shape dough into 1" balls. Roll each in sugar. Place balls, about 2" apart, on greased baking sheets.

Bake in 375° oven 10 to 12 minutes, or until lightly browned. Remove from baking sheets; cool on racks. Makes 4 dozen.

6 | To Tuck in a Lunch Box

Homemade cookies make a sandwich lunch seem special, and any one of the recipes in this chapter will produce a delicious addition to a lunch box or camping kit. We've given you a diverse assortment of 37 cookies to choose from, and every one of them will travel to your lunch site without crumbling.

If you like chewy cookies, try the Texas Ranger Cookies: These brown sugary treats are chock-full of flaked coconut and nuggets of pecans. Graham Cracker Chews are another good choice because these quickly prepared cookies don't even require an electric mixer.

For cookies with a crunchy texture, there are recipes for plain home-style treats such as rolled Corn Meal Cookies and crispy Lemon Thins. Both are perfect dessert partners with fresh fruit.

There are fruited cookies, too, full of flavor and nutrition. When you bite into a Date-Filled Oatmeal Cookie, you'll discover a luscious dark date filling. The tangy Apricot Bars are soft and cake-like, flecked with bits of apricot, topped with a light orange icing and sprinkled with chopped walnuts. Near the end of this chapter, there's a recipe for making scrumptious Fig Bars that closely resemble the popular store-bought treats.

Chocolate-lovers will find their favorites here, too—15 in all. Two of these are mixed right in the saucepan to save on cleanup time—Chocolate Saucepan Cookies, crunchy with walnuts and topped with a coffee-flavored chocolate icing, and Chocolate Fudge Squares, simply delicious served plain. Other fudgy brownies include Honey Brownies (honey is substituted for part of the sugar) and 1949 Brownies—classic brownies that have been a favorite of one Missouri farmer for more than 30 years.

All the cookies in this chapter freeze well, so you can keep serving-size packages ready in your freezer. Either plastic wrap or aluminum foil will keep in the freshly baked flavor for as long as one year. When you're ready to assemble a meal that's meant to travel, tuck a packet of frozen cookies in your lunch box or bag—the cookies will easily thaw to room temperature by lunchtime.

Whether you're packing a working lunch or a picnic basket, you're sure to find in the pages that follow just the right cookies to add a touch of home to your meal.

Extra-Crisp Rolled Cookies

This easily handled dough is perfect for the novice cookie baker. For a homey touch, sprinkle rounds with sugar before baking.

2 c. sifted flour	1 c. sugar
½ tsp. baking powder	1 egg
½ tsp. baking soda	2 tblsp. milk
½ tsp. salt	1 tsp. vanilla
⅔ c. butter or regular margarine	

Sift together flour, baking powder, baking soda and salt; set aside.

Cream together butter and sugar in bowl until light and fluffy, using electric mixer at medium speed. Add egg, milk and vanilla; beat 2 more minutes.

Gradually stir dry ingredients into creamed mixture, blending well. Cover and chill dough in refrigerator 2 hours.

Divide dough in half. Use one half of dough first, keeping remaining dough in refrigerator. Roll out each half of dough on floured surface to ⅛" thickness. Cut with floured 2½" round cookie cutter. Place rounds, about 2" apart, on greased baking sheets.

Bake in 375° oven 5 to 7 minutes, or until golden brown. Remove from baking sheets; cool on racks. Makes 3½ dozen.

Refrigerator Cinnamon-Almond Cookies

Toasted chopped almonds and cinnamon make these simple cookies distinctive. They keep well in the cookie jar, too.

1 c. chopped, blanched almonds	1 c. butter or regular margarine
2 c. sifted flour	1 c. sugar
1 tsp. ground cinnamon	1 egg
½ tsp. salt	

To toast almonds, spread in 13x9x2" baking pan. Bake in 350° oven 15 minutes, stirring every 5 minutes. Remove; cool completely.

Sift together flour, cinnamon and salt; set aside.

Cream together butter and sugar in bowl until light and fluffy, using electric mixer at medium speed. Beat in egg.

Gradually stir dry ingredients into creamed mixture, blending well. Stir in toasted almonds. Divide dough in half. Shape each half into 6" roll, about 1½" in diameter. Wrap each roll in waxed paper and chill in refrigerator overnight.

Cut each roll into 24 slices, about ¼" thick. Place slices, about 2" apart, on greased baking sheets.

Bake in 350° oven 8 minutes, or until golden brown. Remove from baking sheets; cool on racks. Makes 4 dozen.

Crunchy Butterscotch Cookies

Here's another version of a brown sugary refrigerator cookie—a top favorite in the Midwest. Tuck into a lunch box with a crisp apple.

2 c. sifted flour	1 c. brown sugar, packed
½ tsp. cream of tartar	1 egg
½ tsp. baking soda	1 tsp. vanilla
½ tsp. salt	1 c. chopped walnuts
¾ c. butter or regular margarine	

Sift together flour, cream of tartar, baking soda and salt; set aside.

Cream together butter and brown sugar in bowl until light and fluffy, using electric mixer at medium speed. Add egg and vanilla; beat well.

Gradually stir dry ingredients into creamed mixture, mixing well. Stir in walnuts. Shape dough into a roll, 1½" in diameter. Wrap tightly in plastic wrap or waxed paper. Chill in refrigerator several hours or overnight.

Cut roll into ¼" thick slices. Place slices, about 1½" apart, on greased baking sheets.

Bake in 400° oven 10 minutes, or until golden brown. Remove from baking sheets; cool on racks. Makes 4½ dozen.

Blonde Brownies

A butterscotch-flavored brownie generously studded with chocolate morsels. If you wish, sprinkle with confectioners' sugar after baking.

2 c. sifted flour	1 c. brown sugar, packed
1 tsp. baking powder	2 eggs
1 tsp. salt	1 tsp. vanilla
¼ tsp. baking soda	1 (6-oz.) pkg. semisweet
½ c. shortening	chocolate pieces

Sift together flour, baking powder, salt and baking soda; set aside.

Cream together shortening and brown sugar in bowl until light and fluffy, using electric mixer at medium speed. Add eggs, one at a time, beating well after each addition. Blend in vanilla.

Gradually stir dry ingredients into creamed mixture, mixing well. Stir in chocolate pieces. (Batter will be very stiff.) Spread mixture in greased 8" square glass baking dish.

Bake in 325° oven 35 minutes, or until no imprint remains when touched lightly with finger. Cool in dish on rack. Cut into 2" squares. Makes 16.

Lemon Thins

These thin, buttery rounds have an unforgettable crunchy texture plus the tang of fresh lemon juice and lemon rind.

2 c. sifted flour
½ tsp. baking powder
⅛ tsp. salt
1 c. butter or regular
    margarine

½ c. sugar
1 egg
1 tblsp. lemon juice
½ tsp. grated lemon rind

Sift together flour, baking powder and salt; set aside.

Cream together butter and sugar in bowl until light and fluffy, using electric mixer at medium speed. Add egg, lemon juice and lemon rind; beat well.

Gradually stir dry ingredients into creamed mixture, mixing well. Divide dough in half. Shape each half into a 6" roll. Wrap each roll in waxed paper. Chill in refrigerator overnight.

Cut each roll into ⅛" thick slices. Place slices, about 2" apart, on ungreased baking sheets.

Bake in 375° oven 8 to 10 minutes, or until golden brown. Remove from baking sheets; cool on racks. Makes 5 dozen.

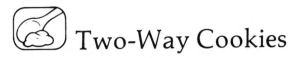

Two-Way Cookies

You make two different cookies at once when you use this unusual recipe: orange-flavored chocolate chips and coconut chews.

4 c. sifted flour
1 tsp. baking soda
1 tsp. salt
1 c. butter or regular
    margarine
1 c. sugar
1¼ c. brown sugar, packed

3 eggs
1 tsp. vanilla
½ tsp. orange extract
1 (6-oz.) pkg. semisweet
    chocolate pieces
1⅓ c. flaked coconut

Sift together flour, baking soda and salt; set aside.

Cream together butter, sugar and brown sugar in bowl until light and fluffy, using electric mixer at medium speed. Add eggs, one at a time, beating well after each addition. Beat in vanilla.

Gradually add dry ingredients to creamed mixture, beating well after each addition, using electric mixer at low speed. Divide dough in half.

Stir orange extract and chocolate pieces into one half. Stir coconut into other half. Drop mixtures separately by rounded teaspoonfuls, about 2" apart, on greased baking sheets, starting with chocolate chip-flavored dough.

Bake in 350° oven 12 to 15 minutes, or until golden brown. Remove from baking sheets; cool on racks. Makes about 6 dozen.

Texas Ranger Cookies

After just one bite of these pecan-studded coconut cookies, you'll know why they won a blue ribbon for a Texas farm woman.

2 c. sifted flour	1 c. brown sugar, packed
1 tsp. baking soda	2 eggs
½ tsp. baking powder	1 tsp. vanilla
½ tsp. salt	1 c. flaked coconut
1 c. shortening	1 c. chopped pecans
1 c. sugar	

Sift together flour, baking soda, baking powder and salt; set aside.

Cream together shortening, sugar and brown sugar in bowl until light and fluffy, using electric mixer at medium speed. Add eggs, one at a time, beating well after each addition. Blend in vanilla.

Gradually stir dry ingredients into creamed mixture, blending well. Stir in coconut and pecans. Drop mixture by rounded teaspoonfuls, about 3" apart, on ungreased baking sheets.

Bake in 375° oven 10 minutes, or until golden brown. Remove from baking sheets; cool on racks. Makes 6 dozen.

Corn Meal Cookies

These crispy corn meal cookies are a little bit different, and they won't crumble when packed in an active child's school lunch box.

3 c. sifted flour	1½ c. sugar
1 c. yellow corn meal	3 eggs
1½ tsp. baking powder	1 tsp. lemon extract
1 tsp. ground nutmeg	½ tsp. vanilla
½ tsp. salt	½ c. raisins
1 c. shortening	Sugar

Sift together flour, corn meal, baking powder, nutmeg and salt; set aside.

Cream together shortening and 1½ c. sugar in bowl until light and fluffy, using electric mixer at medium speed. Add eggs, one at a time, beating well after each addition. Add lemon extract and vanilla.

Gradually stir dry ingredients into creamed mixture, mixing well. Stir in raisins.

Divide dough in half. Roll out each half of dough on floured surface to ⅛" thickness. Cut with floured 2½" round cookie cutter. Place rounds, about 2" apart, on greased baking sheets. Sprinkle each with sugar.

Bake in 400° oven 10 minutes, or until golden brown. Remove from baking sheets; cool on racks. Makes 7 dozen.

Chocolate Chip-Peanut Cookies

We've combined chocolate pieces and salted peanuts in this family-style cookie. Makes a welcome treat in any packed lunch.

1 c. sifted flour
½ tsp. salt
½ tsp. baking soda
½ c. butter or regular
   margarine
½ c. sugar
¼ c. brown sugar, packed

1 egg
1 tsp. vanilla
1 (6-oz.) pkg. semisweet
   chocolate pieces
½ c. coarsely chopped salted
   peanuts

Sift together flour, salt and baking soda; set aside.

Cream together butter, sugar and brown sugar in bowl until light and fluffy, using electric mixer at medium speed. Add egg and vanilla; beat well.

Gradually stir dry ingredients into creamed mixture, blending well. Stir in chocolate pieces and peanuts. Drop mixture by teaspoonfuls, about 2" apart, on greased baking sheets.

Bake in 375° oven 10 to 12 minutes, or until golden brown. Remove from baking sheets; cool on racks. Makes 3 dozen.

Brazil Nut Bars

Bar cookies are the easiest to prepare because you needn't drop or roll out the dough. These have a rich, nutty flavor.

2 c. sifted flour
2 tsp. baking powder
¾ tsp. salt
½ tsp. ground cinnamon
½ c. shortening
⅓ c. butter or regular
   margarine

1 c. brown sugar, packed
2 eggs, beaten
1 tsp. vanilla
1 c. thinly sliced or chopped
   Brazil nuts
1 egg white

Sift together flour, baking powder, salt and cinnamon; set aside.

Cream together shortening, butter and brown sugar in bowl until light and fluffy, using electric mixer at medium speed. Add eggs and vanilla; beat well.

Gradually stir dry ingredients into creamed mixture, mixing well. Stir in half of the Brazil nuts. Spread mixture in greased 15½x10½x1" jelly roll pan. Beat egg white slightly. Brush over dough; sprinkle with remaining nuts.

Bake in 350° oven 25 minutes, or until no imprint remains when touched lightly with finger. Cool slightly in pan on rack. While still warm, cut into 2½x1½" bars. Cool completely. Makes 48.

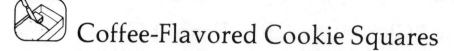 # Coffee-Flavored Cookie Squares

Old-fashioned bar cookies, flavored with coffee and dotted with raisins, make an energy-packed field snack with iced lemonade.

1½ c. sifted flour
½ tsp. baking powder
½ tsp. baking soda
½ tsp. ground cinnamon
¼ tsp. salt
½ c. butter or regular
   margarine
1 c. brown sugar, packed

1 egg
½ c. hot coffee
½ c. raisins
½ c. chopped walnuts
1 tblsp. flour
Thin Vanilla Glaze
   (recipe follows)

Sift together 1½ c. flour, baking powder, baking soda, cinnamon and salt; set aside.

Cream together butter and brown sugar in bowl until light and fluffy, using electric mixer at medium speed. Add egg; beat well.

Gradually add dry ingredients alternately with coffee to creamed mixture, mixing well after each addition, using electric mixer at low speed. Combine raisins, walnuts and 1 tblsp. flour; stir into dough. Spread mixture in greased 13x9x2" baking pan.

Bake in 350° oven 20 minutes, or until top springs back when touched lightly with finger. Cool slightly in pan on rack. Prepare Thin Vanilla Glaze. While bars are still warm, spread with Thin Vanilla Glaze. Cool completely. Cut into 2¼" squares. Makes 24.

Thin Vanilla Glaze: Combine 1 c. sifted confectioners' sugar, 1 tblsp. soft butter or regular margarine, 1 tsp. vanilla and 2½ tblsp. milk in bowl. Mix until smooth, using a spoon. Add more milk, if necessary, to make a thin glaze.

Graham Cracker Chews

These bar cookies are best made the day before you serve them. The extra time gives them a chance to develop their full flavor.

1⅔ c. graham cracker crumbs	2 eggs, well beaten
2 tblsp. flour	1 tsp. vanilla
½ c. butter or regular margarine	1½ c. brown sugar, packed
	¼ tsp. baking powder
	½ c. chopped walnuts

Combine 1⅓ c. of the graham cracker crumbs and flour in bowl. Cut in butter until mixture is crumbly, using pastry blender. Press crumb mixture into greased 9" square baking pan. Bake in 350° oven 20 minutes.

Meanwhile, mix together eggs and vanilla in bowl.

Blend together ⅓ c. graham cracker crumbs, brown sugar, baking powder and walnuts; stir into eggs. Pour mixture over baked crust.

Bake in 350° oven 20 minutes, or until mixture is set. Cool in pan on rack. Cut into 3x1" bars. Makes 27.

Chocolate Saucepan Cookies

You'll save on cleanup time with these cookies because the batter's mixed in the same saucepan you use to melt the butter.

2 c. unsifted flour	1½ tsp. vanilla
½ tsp. baking powder	2 (1-oz.) squares unsweetened chocolate, melted and cooled
½ tsp. baking soda	
½ tsp. salt	½ c. milk
½ c. butter or regular margarine	½ c. chopped walnuts
1 c. brown sugar, packed	Coffee Chocolate Icing (recipe follows)
1 egg	

Stir together flour, baking powder, baking soda and salt; set aside.

Melt butter in 2-qt. saucepan over low heat. Remove from heat. Stir in brown sugar; mix well. Add egg and vanilla; blend well. Stir in cooled chocolate.

Add dry ingredients alternately with milk to chocolate mixture, stirring well after each addition. Stir in walnuts. Drop mixture by rounded teaspoonfuls, about 2" apart, on ungreased baking sheets.

Bake in 350° oven 8 minutes, or until no imprint remains when touched lightly with finger. Remove from baking sheets; cool on racks. Prepare Coffee Chocolate Icing. Frost cookies with Coffee Chocolate Icing. Makes 5 dozen.

Coffee Chocolate Icing: Melt 1 (1-oz.) square unsweetened chocolate and 1 tblsp. butter or regular margarine in saucepan over low heat. Remove from heat. Add ½ tsp. instant coffee powder, 3 tblsp. hot water, ½ tsp. vanilla and 2 c. sifted confectioners' sugar. Beat until smooth and creamy, using a spoon.

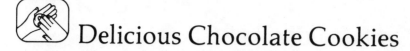

Delicious Chocolate Cookies

These chewy, crackle-top chocolate cookies are rolled in confectioners' sugar before baking. They're reliably good every time.

2 c. sifted flour	2 c. sugar
2 tsp. baking powder	2 tsp. vanilla
¼ tsp. salt	4 eggs
½ c. butter or regular margarine	½ c. chopped walnuts
4 (1-oz.) squares unsweetened chocolate	Confectioners' sugar

Sift together flour, baking powder and salt; set aside.

Melt together butter and chocolate in small saucepan over low heat. Combine chocolate mixture, sugar and vanilla; blend well. Add eggs, one at a time, beating well after each addition, using a spoon.

Gradually stir dry ingredients into chocolate mixture, mixing well. Stir in walnuts. Cover and chill dough in refrigerator several hours.

Shape dough into 1" balls. Roll in confectioners' sugar. Place balls, about 2" apart, on greased baking sheets.

Bake in 350° oven 15 minutes, or until no imprint remains when touched lightly with finger. Remove from baking sheets; cool on racks. Makes 6 dozen.

Chocolate Chip Drops

Half the chocolate pieces are melted and stirred into the batter; the other half are added whole along with the chopped walnuts.

1 (12-oz.) pkg. semisweet chocolate pieces	½ c. butter or regular margarine
1 c. sifted flour	½ c. sugar
½ tsp. baking soda	1 egg
½ tsp. salt	½ c. chopped walnuts

Melt 1 c. of the semisweet chocolate pieces in small saucepan over low heat. Remove from heat. Set aside to cool.

Sift together flour, baking soda and salt; set aside.

Cream together butter and sugar in bowl until light and fluffy, using electric mixer at medium speed. Add egg; beat well. Gradually add melted chocolate, beating well.

Gradually stir dry ingredients into creamed mixture, mixing well with spoon. Stir in walnuts and remaining chocolate pieces. Drop by teaspoonfuls, about 2" apart, on greased baking sheets.

Bake in 350° oven 12 to 15 minutes, or until no imprint remains when touched lightly with finger. Remove from baking sheets; cool on racks. Makes 4 dozen.

Devil's Food Cookies

A Nebraska farm woman told us that she has packed these frosted chocolate cookies in lunch boxes for years.

2 c. sifted flour	2 (1-oz.) squares
½ tsp. baking soda	unsweetened chocolate,
¼ tsp. salt	melted and cooled
½ c. butter or regular	¾ c. dairy sour cream
margarine	½ c. chopped walnuts
1 c. brown sugar, packed	Chocolate Icing
1 egg	(recipe follows)
1 tsp. vanilla	

Sift together flour, baking soda and salt; set aside.

Cream together butter and brown sugar in bowl until light and fluffy, using electric mixer at medium speed. Add egg; beat well. Blend in vanilla and cooled chocolate.

Add dry ingredients alternately with sour cream to chocolate mixture, beating well after each addition, using electric mixer at low speed. Stir in walnuts. Drop mixture by heaping teaspoonfuls, about 2" apart, on greased baking sheets.

Bake in 350° oven 10 minutes, or until no imprint remains when touched lightly with finger. Remove from baking sheets; cool on racks. Prepare Chocolate Icing. Frost cookies with Chocolate Icing. Makes 4½ dozen.

Chocolate Icing: Melt 2 (1-oz.) squares unsweetened chocolate and 2 tblsp. butter or regular margarine in saucepan over low heat. Remove from heat. Stir in 2 c. sifted confectioners' sugar, 2 tblsp. water and 1 tsp. vanilla. Beat until smooth, using a spoon.

Frosted Chocolate Drop Cookies

A delightful variation of a good basic chocolate cookie, containing raisins and walnuts and iced with a glossy chocolate frosting.

1¾ c. unsifted flour	1 tsp. vanilla
½ c. baking cocoa	¾ c. buttermilk
½ tsp. baking soda	½ c. chopped raisins
½ tsp. salt	½ c. chopped walnuts
½ c. shortening	Chocolate Frosting
1 c. sugar	(recipe follows)
1 egg	

Stir together flour, cocoa, baking soda and salt; set aside.

Cream together shortening and sugar in bowl until light and fluffy, using electric mixer at medium speed. Add egg and vanilla, beating well.

Add dry ingredients alternately with buttermilk to creamed mixture, beating well after each addition, using electric mixer at low speed. Stir in raisins and walnuts. Drop mixture by teaspoonfuls, about 2" apart, on ungreased baking sheets.

Bake in 350° oven 10 minutes, or until no imprint remains when touched lightly with finger. Remove from baking sheets; cool on racks. Prepare Chocolate Frosting. Frost cookies with Chocolate Frosting. Makes 4 dozen.

Chocolate Frosting: Combine 1 c. sugar, 1 (1-oz.) square unsweetened chocolate, ¼ c. butter or regular margarine and ⅓ c. milk in saucepan. Cook over medium heat, stirring constantly, until mixture boils. Boil 1½ minutes. Remove from heat. Place saucepan in bowl of cold water. Beat until frosting begins to hold its shape, using electric mixer at high speed.

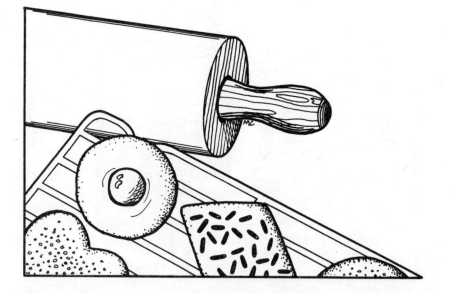

Black Walnut-Chocolate Cookies

One Kansas farm woman tells us she has been baking these extra-crisp cookies for 25 years, and they're still her favorite with coffee.

2½ c. unsifted flour	½ tsp. black walnut
2 tsp. baking powder	flavoring
½ tsp. salt	2 (1-oz.) squares
½ c. shortening	unsweetened chocolate,
1½ c. sugar	melted and cooled
1 egg	¼ c. milk
1 tsp. vanilla	½ c. chopped black walnuts

Stir together flour, baking powder and salt; set aside.

Cream together shortening and sugar in bowl until light and fluffy, using electric mixer at medium speed. Add egg, vanilla, walnut flavoring and cooled chocolate; blend well.

Add dry ingredients alternately with milk to creamed mixture, beating well after each addition, using electric mixer at low speed. Stir in black walnuts. Form dough into 2 rolls, 8" long and 2" in diameter. Wrap each in waxed paper or plastic wrap. Chill in refrigerator several hours.

Cut each roll into ¼" thick slices. Place slices, about 2" apart, on lightly greased baking sheets.

Bake in 350° oven 10 minutes, or until no imprint remains when touched lightly with finger. Immediately remove from baking sheets; cool on racks. Makes 5 dozen.

Chocolate Fudge Squares

No need to get out your electric mixer for these quick and easy brownies; all the ingredients are mixed right in the saucepan.

2 (1-oz.) squares	1 c. sugar
unsweetened chocolate	2 eggs
½ c. shortening	1 tsp. vanilla
½ c. sifted flour	½ c. coarsely chopped
¼ tsp. salt	walnuts

Melt chocolate and shortening in small saucepan over low heat; stir until smooth. Remove from heat and cool to room temperature.

Sift together flour and salt; set aside.

Add sugar to chocolate mixture, mixing thoroughly with spoon. Add eggs, one at a time, mixing well with spoon. Stir in vanilla.

Gradually stir dry ingredients into chocolate mixture, blending well. Spread in greased 9" square baking pan. Sprinkle with walnuts.

Bake in 400° oven 18 minutes, or until a slight imprint remains when touched lightly with finger. Cool in pan on rack. Cut into 1½" squares. Makes 36.

Chocolate-Almond Bars

Unusual bar cookie with yellow cake-like bottom and chocolate cream cheese filling, topped with sprinkle of golden crumbs.

1 (6-oz.) pkg. semisweet chocolate pieces	½ tsp. baking powder
1 (3-oz.) pkg. cream cheese	¼ tsp. salt
⅓ c. evaporated milk	½ c. butter or regular margarine
½ c. chopped walnuts	¾ c. sugar
2 tblsp. sesame seeds	1 egg
¼ tsp. almond extract	¼ tsp. almond extract
1½ c. sifted flour	

Combine chocolate pieces, cream cheese and evaporated milk in 2-qt. saucepan. Cook over medium heat, stirring constantly, until mixture is melted and thick. Remove from heat. Stir in walnuts, sesame seeds and ¼ tsp. almond extract; set aside.

Sift together flour, baking powder and salt; set aside.

Cream together butter and sugar in bowl until light and fluffy, using electric mixer at medium speed. Add egg and ¼ tsp. almond extract.

Gradually stir dry ingredients into creamed mixture, blending well. Press one half of the dough in greased 12x8x2" (2-qt.) glass baking dish. Top with chocolate mixture. Crumble remaining dough on top.

Bake in 375° oven 25 minutes, or until top is lightly browned. Cool in pan on rack. Cut into 3x1" bars. Makes 32.

Delectable Chocolate Brownies

These moist brownies are made with baking cocoa—a little less expensive than chocolate—but they're rich-tasting all the same.

¾ c. sifted flour	1½ c. sugar
½ c. baking cocoa	2 eggs
¼ tsp. salt	½ tsp. vanilla
¾ c. butter or regular margarine	¾ c. chopped walnuts

Sift together flour, cocoa and salt; set aside.

Cream together butter and sugar in bowl until light and fluffy, using electric mixer at medium speed. Add eggs, one at a time, beating well after each addition. Beat in vanilla.

Gradually stir dry ingredients into creamed mixture, blending well. Stir in walnuts. Spread mixture in greased 9" square baking pan.

Bake in 350° oven 35 minutes, or until a slight imprint remains when touched lightly with finger. Cool in pan on rack. Cut into 3x1" bars. Makes 27.

1949 Brownies

This classic fudge brownie has been a favorite of one Missouri farmer for 30 years. So rich that it needs no icing.

½ c. butter or regular margarine	¾ tsp. salt
2 (1-oz.) squares unsweetened chocolate	2 eggs
¾ c. sifted flour	1 c. sugar
½ tsp. baking powder	1 tsp. vanilla
	1 c. chopped walnuts

Combine butter and chocolate in saucepan. Place over low heat until melted, stirring until smooth. Remove from heat; cool well.

Sift together flour, baking powder and salt; set aside.

Beat together eggs and sugar in bowl until thick and lemon-colored, using electric mixer at high speed. Blend in cooled chocolate mixture and vanilla.

Add dry ingredients to chocolate mixture, mixing well with spoon. Stir in walnuts. Pour mixture into greased 8" square baking pan.

Bake in 350° oven 30 minutes, or until a slight imprint remains when touched lightly with finger. Cool in pan on rack. Cut into 2" squares. Makes 16.

Honey Brownies

Honey is substituted for part of the sugar in this fudge brownie. These deliciously rich bars are a treat at any meal.

2 (1-oz.) squares unsweetened chocolate	2 eggs
⅓ c. butter or regular margarine	½ c. honey
¾ c. sifted flour	½ c. sugar
½ tsp. baking powder	1 tsp. vanilla
¼ tsp. salt	½ c. chopped walnuts
	Confectioners' sugar

Melt chocolate and butter in small saucepan over low heat; stir until smooth. Remove from heat and cool to room temperature.

Sift together flour, baking powder and salt; set aside.

Beat eggs slightly in bowl, using electric mixer at medium speed. Add honey, sugar and vanilla; beat well. Beat in cooled chocolate mixture.

Gradually add dry ingredients to chocolate mixture, beating well after each addition, using electric mixer at low speed. Stir in walnuts. Spread batter in greased and floured 9" square baking pan.

Bake in 350° oven 25 minutes, or until a slight imprint remains when touched lightly with finger. Cool in pan on rack. Cut into 3x1" bars. Roll in confectioners' sugar. Makes 27.

Pumpkin Drop Cookies

Tuck these spicy pumpkin gems alongside a banana in your child's lunch box—they're sure to become a school favorite.

2¼ c. unsifted flour	1 c. mashed pumpkin,
2 tsp. baking powder	cooked or canned
1 tsp. ground cinnamon	2 eggs
1 tsp. ground allspice	1 tsp. lemon juice
½ tsp. salt	1 tsp. vanilla
¼ tsp. ground ginger	1 c. raisins
⅓ c. shortening	½ c. flaked coconut
1 c. sugar	½ c. chopped walnuts

Stir together flour, baking powder, cinnamon, allspice, salt and ginger; set aside.

Cream together shortening and sugar in bowl until light and fluffy, using electric mixer at medium speed. Beat in pumpkin, eggs, lemon juice and vanilla; blend well.

Gradually stir dry ingredients into creamed mixture, mixing well. Stir in raisins, coconut and walnuts. Drop mixture by heaping teaspoonfuls, about 2" apart, on greased baking sheets.

Bake in 350° oven 10 to 12 minutes, or until golden brown. Remove from baking sheets; cool on racks. Makes about 4 dozen.

Peanut Butter Pressed Cookies

If you don't have time to make molded peanut butter cookies, try this version. The cookie press cuts preparation time in half.

1¾ c. sifted flour	½ c. sugar
¼ tsp. salt	1 egg yolk
¾ c. butter or regular	½ tsp. vanilla
margarine	⅓ c. semisweet chocolate
3 tblsp. creamy	pieces
peanut butter	

Sift together flour and salt; set aside.

Cream together butter, peanut butter and sugar in bowl until light and fluffy, using electric mixer at medium speed. Add egg yolk and vanilla, blending well.

Gradually stir dry ingredients into creamed mixture, mixing well.

Fit flower or crown design into cookie press. Placing one half of the dough in cookie press at a time, force dough through press, about 1" apart, on ungreased baking sheets. Place one chocolate piece in center of each.

Bake in 375° oven 6 to 8 minutes, or until delicately browned. Remove from baking sheets; cool on racks. Makes about 5 dozen.

Spicy Raisin-Molasses Cookies

Here's a mini-batch gingery cookie recipe for small families. One batch makes just enough to fill the average cookie jar.

2 c. sifted flour	½ c. shortening
1½ tsp. baking powder	¼ c. sugar
1 tsp. ground cinnamon	1 egg
1 tsp. ground ginger	¾ c. molasses
½ tsp. salt	1 c. golden raisins
¼ tsp. baking soda	

Sift together flour, baking powder, cinnamon, ginger, salt and baking soda; set aside.

Cream together shortening and sugar in bowl until light and fluffy, using electric mixer at medium speed. Add egg and molasses, beating well.

Gradually stir dry ingredients into creamed mixture, blending well. Stir in raisins. Drop mixture by teaspoonfuls, about 3" apart, on greased baking sheets.

Bake in 350° oven 12 to 14 minutes, or until no imprint remains when touched lightly with finger. Remove from baking sheets; cool on racks. Makes 3 dozen.

Hampshire Hermits

Cape Cod women packed unglazed hermits like these for their husbands when they went to sea because these cookies keep so well.

1¾ c. sifted flour	1 c. brown sugar, packed
1¾ tsp. ground cinnamon	2 eggs
¼ tsp. ground ginger	2 tblsp. dairy sour cream
¼ tsp. ground cloves	1 c. chopped walnuts
¼ tsp. baking soda	½ c. chopped raisins or
⅛ tsp. salt	currants
⅔ c. butter or regular	½ c. finely chopped citron
margarine	Lemon Glaze (recipe follows)

Sift together flour, cinnamon, ginger, cloves, baking soda and salt; set aside.

Cream together butter and brown sugar in bowl until light and fluffy, using electric mixer at medium speed. Add eggs, one at a time, beating well after each addition. Blend in sour cream.

Add dry ingredients to creamed mixture, beating well after each addition, using electric mixer at low speed. Stir in walnuts, raisins and citron. Drop mixture by tablespoonfuls, about 2" apart, on greased baking sheets.

Bake in 350° oven 12 to 15 minutes, or until golden brown. Remove from baking sheets; cool slightly on racks. Prepare Lemon Glaze. While cookies are still warm, brush with Lemon Glaze, using a pastry brush. Cool completely. Makes about 3 dozen.

Lemon Glaze: Combine 1 c. sifted confectioners' sugar and 2 tblsp. lemon juice in bowl. Stir until smooth.

Chocolate-Raisin Oat Cookies

Here's another variation of the oatmeal cookie. Raisins and semisweet chocolate morsels make it deliciously different.

1 c. sifted flour	1 egg
¾ tsp. baking powder	¾ c. quick-cooking oats
½ c. butter or regular	½ c. raisins
margarine	½ c. semisweet chocolate
¾ c. brown sugar, packed	pieces

Sift together flour and baking powder; set aside.

Cream together butter and brown sugar in bowl until light and fluffy, using electric mixer at medium speed. Beat in egg.

Gradually stir dry ingredients into creamed mixture, blending well. Stir in oats, raisins and chocolate pieces. (Dough will be stiff.) Drop by rounded teaspoonfuls, about 2" apart, on greased baking sheets.

Bake in 375° oven 8 to 10 minutes, or until golden brown. Remove from baking sheets; cool on racks. Makes 3½ dozen.

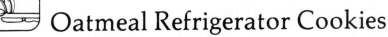 Oatmeal Refrigerator Cookies

If your family likes oatmeal cookies, try this refrigerator recipe. The prepared dough can be refrigerated for up to three weeks.

1½ c. sifted flour	1 c. brown sugar, packed
1 tsp. baking soda	2 eggs
½ tsp. salt	2 tsp. vanilla
1 c. shortening	3 c. quick-cooking oats
1 c. sugar	

Sift together flour, baking soda and salt; set aside.

Cream together shortening, sugar and brown sugar in bowl until light and fluffy, using electric mixer at medium speed. Add eggs, one at a time, beating well after each addition. Blend in vanilla.

Gradually add dry ingredients to creamed mixture; mix well with spoon. Stir in oats.

Divide dough into thirds. Shape each third into 10″ roll, 1¼″ in diameter. Wrap tightly in plastic wrap or waxed paper. Chill several hours or overnight.

Cut rolls into ⅛″ thick slices. Place slices, about 1½″ apart, on ungreased baking sheets.

Bake in 400° oven 6 to 8 minutes, or until golden brown. Remove from baking sheets; cool on racks. Makes about 8 dozen.

Coconut-Date Cookies

Plenty of chopped dates, walnuts and flaked coconut make these oatmeal cookies a favorite among the menfolk.

2 c. sifted flour	1 c. brown sugar, packed
1 tsp. baking powder	2 eggs
1 tsp. baking soda	1 tsp. vanilla
1 tsp. salt	2 c. quick-cooking oats
1 c. butter or regular	1 c. finely chopped dates
margarine	1 c. broken walnuts
1 c. sugar	1 c. flaked coconut

Sift together flour, baking powder, baking soda and salt; set aside.

Cream together butter, sugar and brown sugar in bowl until light and fluffy, using electric mixer at medium speed. Add eggs, one at a time, beating well after each addition. Blend in vanilla.

Gradually add dry ingredients to creamed mixture; mix well with spoon. Stir in oats, dates, walnuts and coconut. Chill dough in refrigerator 1 hour.

Drop mixture by teaspoonfuls, about 2″ apart, on greased baking sheets.

Bake in 350° oven 12 to 15 minutes, or until golden brown. Remove from baking sheets; cool on racks. Makes about 6 dozen.

Date-Filled Oatmeal Cookies

The recipe for these luscious date-filled oatmeal cookies is a treasured heirloom sent to us by a North Dakota farm woman.

Date Filling (recipe follows)	2 eggs
2½ c. sifted flour	1 tsp. vanilla
1½ tsp. cream of tartar	1 tsp. baking soda
1 c. shortening	1 tsp. hot water
1½ c. brown sugar, packed	1½ c. quick-cooking oats

Prepare Date Filling; set aside.

Sift together flour and cream of tartar; set aside.

Cream together shortening and brown sugar in bowl until light and fluffy, using electric mixer at medium speed. Add eggs, one at a time, beating well after each addition. Beat in vanilla.

Gradually stir dry ingredients into creamed mixture, mixing well. Dissolve baking soda in hot water. Stir baking soda mixture into mixture. Stir in oats.

Divide dough in half. Roll out each half of dough on floured surface to ³⁄₈" thickness. Cut with floured 2½" round cookie cutter. Place half of the rounds, about 2" apart, on greased baking sheets. Spoon some date filling on each. Top with another round and press edges together to seal, using a fork.

Bake in 350° oven 10 to 12 minutes, or until golden brown. Remove from baking sheets; cool on racks. Makes about 3½ dozen.

Date Filling: Snip 1 (8-oz.) pkg. pitted dates into small pieces, using scissors. Combine dates, 1 c. sugar, 1 c. water and ¹⁄₈ tsp. salt in small saucepan. Cook over medium heat 4 minutes, or until thick. Remove from heat and cool to room temperature.

Grape Swirl Cookies

A refrigerator cookie swirled with an old-fashioned grape filling made by combining grape jam, chopped walnuts and raisins.

Grape Filling (recipe follows)	1 c. brown sugar, packed
3½ c. sifted flour	²⁄₃ c. sugar
1 tsp. baking powder	2 eggs
1 tsp. salt	1 tsp. vanilla
¼ tsp. baking soda	
1 c. butter or regular margarine	

Prepare Grape Filling; set aside.

Sift together flour, baking powder, salt and baking soda; set aside.

Cream together butter, brown sugar and sugar in bowl until light and fluffy, using electric mixer at medium speed. Add eggs, one at a time, beating well after each addition. Beat in vanilla.

Gradually stir dry ingredients into creamed mixture, mixing well. Divide dough in half. Roll out each half on lightly floured surface to 13x9" rectangle. Spread each rectangle with one half of Grape Filling. Roll up like a jelly roll, starting at long side. Wrap tightly in plastic wrap or waxed paper. Chill in refrigerator 8 hours or overnight.

Cut rolls into ¼" thick slices, dipping knife frequently into warm water. Place slices, about 2" apart, on well-greased baking sheets.

Bake in 400° oven 12 minutes, or until golden brown. Remove from baking sheets; cool on racks. Makes about 8½ dozen.

Note: Be sure to work quickly when cutting rolls into slices because dough softens quickly at room temperature. Return remaining roll to refrigerator while first batch bakes.

Grape Filling: Combine ¾ c. grape jam, 1 c. chopped walnuts and 1½ c. chopped raisins in bowl; mix well.

Applesauce Roll-Up Cookies

You can bake one of these rolls now and freeze the other to be baked next month. For full flavor, freeze no longer than four weeks.

Applesauce Date Filling (recipe follows)	¼ tsp. salt
4 c. sifted flour	1 c. shortening
½ tsp. baking soda	2 c. brown sugar, packed
	3 eggs

Prepare Applesauce Date Filling. Cool to room temperature.

Meanwhile, sift together flour, baking soda and salt; set aside.

Cream together shortening and brown sugar in bowl until light and fluffy, using electric mixer at medium speed. Add eggs, one at a time, beating well after each addition.

Gradually stir dry ingredients into creamed mixture, mixing well. Divide dough in half. Roll out each half on waxed paper to 15x12" rectangle. Spread each rectangle with one half of Applesauce Date Filling. Roll up like a jelly roll. Wrap tightly in waxed paper. Chill in refrigerator overnight.

Cut each roll into ¼" thick slices. Place slices, about 2" apart, on lightly greased baking sheets.

Bake in 350° oven 12 minutes, or until golden brown. Remove from baking sheets; cool on racks. Makes about 10 dozen.

Applesauce Date Filling: Combine 1¾ c. applesauce, ¾ c. cut-up pitted dates and ½ c. sugar in small saucepan. Cook over low heat, stirring constantly, 12 minutes or until thick. Remove from heat. Stir in 1 tblsp. grated orange rind and 1 c. chopped walnuts.

Raisin-Chocolate Bars

For those who like extra-rich sweets: a crumbly bar cookie with an interesting filling of chocolate and raisins.

1 (14-oz.) can sweetened condensed milk (not evaporated)	¾ tsp. salt
	½ tsp. baking powder
	1 c. butter or regular margarine
2 (1-oz.) squares unsweetened chocolate	1⅓ c. brown sugar, packed
2 c. raisins	½ tsp. vanilla
1¾ c. sifted flour	2 c. quick-cooking oats

Combine sweetened condensed milk and chocolate in top of double boiler. Heat over hot water until chocolate melts. Stir in raisins; cool slightly.

Sift together flour, salt and baking powder; set aside.

Cream together butter and brown sugar in bowl until light and fluffy, using electric mixer at medium speed. Add vanilla; beat well.

Gradually stir dry ingredients into creamed mixture, mixing well. Add oats; mix until crumbly.

Press half of crumb mixture in greased 13x9x2" baking pan. Spread with chocolate mixture. Sprinkle with remaining crumbs.

Bake in 350° oven 30 to 35 minutes, or until golden brown. Cool in pan on rack. Cut into 3x1" bars. Makes 39.

Fig Bars

Luscious fig bars that resemble the popular store-bought fig cookies, but these taste even better because they're homemade.

4 c. sifted flour	2 c. brown sugar, packed
1 tsp. baking powder	3 eggs
1 tsp. baking soda	1 tsp. vanilla
1 tsp. salt	1 tblsp. lemon juice
1 c. butter or regular margarine	Fig Walnut Filling (recipe follows)

Sift together flour, baking powder, baking soda and salt; set aside.

Cream together butter and brown sugar in bowl until light and fluffy, using electric mixer at medium speed. Add eggs, one at a time, beating well after each addition. Beat in vanilla and lemon juice.

Gradually stir dry ingredients into creamed mixture, mixing well. Cover and chill in refrigerator 2 hours.

Meanwhile, prepare Fig Walnut Filling.

Divide dough in half. Roll out each half on floured surface to 18x12" rectangle. Cut into 4 (3") wide strips. Place Fig Walnut Filling down center of strips. Using a metal spatula, fold each side of dough lengthwise over filling. Cut each in half, making 9" strips. Transfer strips, seam side down, to ungreased baking sheets, about 2" apart.

Bake in 375° oven 15 minutes, or until golden brown. Remove from baking sheets; cool on racks. Cut into 2" bars. Makes about 5 dozen.

Fig Walnut Filling: Combine 1½ c. ground dried figs and 1 c. water in small saucepan. Cook over medium heat, stirring constantly, until mixture comes to a boil. Boil 5 minutes. Stir together ¾ c. sugar and 3 tblsp. flour. Stir sugar-flour mixture into figs. Cook over low heat, stirring frequently, until thick. Remove from heat. Stir in ¼ c. chopped walnuts and 2 tblsp. orange juice. Cool to room temperature.

 Apricot Bars

Tangy apricot bars with a taste of the tropics—the citrus-flavored icing is made with both lemon and orange.

1 c. boiling water	2 c. brown sugar, packed
1 c. dried apricots	2 eggs
1¾ c. sifted flour	1 tsp. vanilla
1 tsp. baking powder	1 tsp. grated orange rind
¾ tsp. salt	Orange Icing (recipe follows)
½ c. butter or regular margarine	½ c. chopped walnuts

Pour boiling water over apricots in bowl. Let stand 5 minutes. Drain apricots and cut into small pieces with scissors. Set aside.

Sift together flour, baking powder and salt; set aside.

Cream together butter and brown sugar in bowl until light and fluffy, using electric mixer at medium speed. Add eggs, one at a time, beating well after each addition. Beat in vanilla and orange rind.

Gradually stir dry ingredients into creamed mixture, mixing well. Stir in apricots. Spread batter in greased 15½x10½x1" jelly roll pan.

Bake in 350° oven 20 minutes, or until top springs back when touched lightly with finger. Cool in pan on rack 10 minutes. Meanwhile, prepare Orange Icing. Spread warm bars with Orange Icing. Sprinkle with walnuts, pressing them in lightly so they adhere to icing. Cool completely. Cut into 2½x1½" bars. Makes 48.

Orange Icing: Combine 1 c. sifted confectioners' sugar, 2 tsp. soft butter or regular margarine, 1 tsp. grated orange rind, 2 tsp. orange juice and 2 tsp. lemon juice in bowl. Stir until smooth.

California Fig Cookies

Country-style chewy drops that keep for weeks in the cookie jar—but these yummy treats probably won't last that long.

1 c. chopped dried figs	½ c. sugar
⅓ c. water	½ c. brown sugar, packed
2 c. sifted flour	1 egg
2 tsp. baking powder	1 tsp. vanilla
½ tsp. salt	48 walnut halves
1 c. butter or regular margarine	

Combine figs and water in small saucepan. Cook over medium heat 5 minutes, stirring frequently, until thickened. Remove from heat. Cool to room temperature.

Sift together flour, baking powder and salt; set aside.

Cream together butter, sugar and brown sugar in bowl until light and fluffy, using electric mixer at medium speed. Add egg and vanilla; beat well.

Gradually stir dry ingredients into creamed mixture, mixing well. Stir in fig mixture. Drop mixture by teaspoonfuls, about 2" apart, on greased baking sheets. Press a walnut half on top of each.

Bake in 375° oven 10 to 12 minutes, or until lightly browned. Remove from baking sheets; cool on racks. Makes 4 dozen.

7 | Bake Sale Sellouts

The most popular items at any country bake sale or bazaar are usually cookies. You'll often see children tugging at their mothers' sleeves begging for a fat sugar cookie or a crunchy molasses drop, and the grownups themselves find it hard to resist a homemade chocolate brownie.

It's the old-fashioned homey cookies that seem to disappear first. Big, firm-textured Farmhouse Walnut Cookies look as good as they taste with their sugary tops, and few can resist golden brown Cinnamon Jumbles, drop cookies sprinkled with a mixture of sugar and cinnamon.

Customers with a sweet tooth won't be able to walk by the sinfully Rich Butterscotch Cookies or Extra-Rich Two-Layer Bars. Both of these cookies will obtain a premium price at any sale, and the bar cookies are easy to make because they're layered into the pan—no need to drop batter or hand-form cookies.

More than half of these are big-batch recipes that make at least six dozen cookies. If you need dozens of picture-perfect buttery cookies that are a snap to prepare, try either the Pineapple Spritz or the almond-scented Chocolate Spritz. A cookie press will make short work of shaping the dough—you'll turn out between seven and nine dozen cookies in almost no time. If you want to decorate these, add silver dragées to the pineapple version before baking and sprinkle the baked chocolate spritz with sifted confectioners' sugar.

Since chocolate tends to be everyone's favorite flavor, we've included 14 recipes for chocolate cookies, including a basic soft Fudgy Chocolate Drop that's a popular addition to an annual bake sale in New York state. There's also a recipe for classic Tollhouse Bar Cookies—a version which saves a lot of time because the basic chocolate chip dough is spread in a pan rather than formed into drop cookies. Delectable Fudge Cinnamon Brownies are mildly flavored, swirled with a chocolate frosting and topped with a scattering of chopped pecans. If you keep a large canister of our Brownie Mix on hand during the fall fund-raising season, you'll be able to make the terrific Shortcut Brownies at a moment's notice.

Of course, we couldn't forget oatmeal and peanut butter cookies. The selection features Pride of Iowa Cookies, which are far and away FARM JOURNAL'S most popular oatmeal cookies—crunchy on the outside with chewy coconut and walnuts throughout. Our Peanut Butter Cookie Bars combine oats in a peanut-buttery dough. After baking, morsels of semisweet chocolate are melted on top; then the bars are drizzled with a peanut butter flavored icing.

Whether you bake these cookies for your next fund-raiser or just for yourself, they're sure to be a success.

Farmhouse Walnut Cookies

An Arkansas woman told us that these large crunchy cookies are best sellers in her area. They're flavored with sour cream.

5 c. sifted flour	2 c. sugar
4 tsp. baking powder	2 eggs
½ tsp. baking soda	1 c. dairy sour cream
½ tsp. salt	2 tsp. vanilla
1 c. butter or regular margarine	¾ c. chopped walnuts
	Sugar

Sift together flour, baking powder, baking soda and salt; set aside.

Cream together butter and 2 c. sugar in bowl until light and fluffy, using electric mixer at medium speed. Add eggs, one at a time, beating well after each addition. Blend in sour cream and vanilla.

Gradually stir dry ingredients into creamed mixture, blending well. Stir in walnuts. Drop mixture by rounded teaspoonfuls, about 3" apart, on greased baking sheets. Flatten each with greased bottom of drinking glass dipped in sugar to ¼" thickness.

Bake in 375° oven 12 minutes, or until golden brown. Remove from baking sheets; cool on racks. Makes about 6 dozen.

Cinnamon Jumbles

Buttermilk makes these cookies different; the dough is dropped by spoonfuls and sprinkled with cinnamon and sugar before baking.

4 c. sifted flour	2 eggs
1 tsp. baking soda	2 tsp. vanilla
1 tsp. salt	1½ c. buttermilk
1 c. butter or regular margarine	½ c. sugar
2 c. sugar	2 tsp. ground cinnamon

Sift together flour, baking soda and salt; set aside.

Cream together butter and 2 c. sugar in bowl until light and fluffy, using electric mixer at medium speed. Add eggs, one at a time, beating well after each addition. Beat in vanilla.

Add dry ingredients alternately with buttermilk to creamed mixture, beating well after each addition, using electric mixer at low speed. Cover and chill dough in refrigerator overnight.

Drop dough by rounded teaspoonfuls, about 2" apart, on greased baking sheets. Combine ½ c. sugar and cinnamon; sprinkle cinnamon-sugar mixture on each cookie.

Bake in 400° oven 8 to 10 minutes, or until golden brown. Remove from baking sheets; cool on racks. Makes about 5 dozen.

Crisp Rolled Sugar Cookies

Simply delicious rolled sugar cookies with a delicate nutmeg flavor: They're extra-crunchy, and so good with a glass of milk.

4½ c. sifted flour	1 c. butter or regular
2 tsp. baking powder	margarine
1 tsp. baking soda	2 c. sugar
1 tsp. salt	4 eggs
1 tsp. ground nutmeg	2 tblsp. milk

Sift together flour, baking powder, baking soda, salt and nutmeg; set aside.

Cream together butter and sugar in bowl until light and fluffy, using electric mixer at medium speed. Add eggs, one at a time, beating well after each addition.

Gradually add dry ingredients alternately with milk to creamed mixture; mix well with spoon. Cover and chill dough in refrigerator 2 to 3 hours.

Divide dough into fourths. Use one fourth of the dough at a time, keeping remaining dough in refrigerator. Roll out each fourth of dough on floured surface to ¼″ thickness. Cut with floured 2″ cookie cutter. Place, about 2″ apart, on greased baking sheets.

Bake in 425° oven 8 to 10 minutes, or until golden brown. Cool about 1 minute on baking sheets. Remove from baking sheets; cool on racks. Makes 6 dozen.

Brown Sugar Cookies

Butterscotch-flavored drop cookies loaded with chocolate morsels and chopped walnuts—a popular choice at any gathering.

2½ c. sifted flour	2 eggs
1 tsp. baking soda	2 tsp. vanilla
½ tsp. cream of tartar	½ c. chopped walnuts
1½ c. shortening	1 (6-oz.) pkg. semisweet
1½ c. brown sugar, packed	chocolate pieces

Sift together flour, baking soda and cream of tartar; set aside.

Cream together shortening and brown sugar in bowl until light and fluffy, using electric mixer at medium speed. Add eggs, one at a time, beating well after each addition. Blend in vanilla.

Gradually stir dry ingredients into creamed mixture, mixing well. Stir in walnuts and chocolate pieces. Drop mixture by teaspoonfuls, about 2″ apart, on greased baking sheets.

Bake in 350° oven 8 to 10 minutes, or until golden brown. Remove from baking sheets; cool on racks. Makes about 5 dozen.

Sesame Wafers

These dainty cookies have a crunchy texture and a nutlike flavor; toasted sesame seeds are stirred into the dough before baking.

1 c. sesame seeds	1½ c. brown sugar, packed
1¼ c. sifted flour	1 egg
¼ tsp. baking powder	1 tsp. vanilla
¼ tsp. salt	
¾ c. melted butter or regular margarine	

Spread sesame seeds in shallow baking pan.

Toast in 350° oven 20 minutes, or until they turn a pale brown, stirring occasionally. Remove from oven and cool well.

Sift together flour, baking powder and salt; set aside.

Beat together butter and brown sugar in bowl until well blended, using electric mixer at medium speed. Beat in egg and vanilla.

Gradually stir dry ingredients into sugar mixture, mixing well. Stir in sesame seeds. Drop mixture by half teaspoonfuls, about 2" apart, on lightly greased baking sheets.

Bake in 375° oven 5 to 6 minutes, or until edges are lightly browned. (Watch cookies carefully because bottoms burn easily.) Remove from baking sheets; cool on racks. Makes about 7 dozen.

Rich Butterscotch Cookies

This recipe calls for a whole pound of butter or margarine, but it yields eight dozen, and the cookies are worth it: They're sinfully rich.

4 c. sifted flour	1 c. plus 2 tblsp. brown sugar, packed
½ tsp. salt	1½ tsp. vanilla
2 c. butter or regular margarine	Sugar

Sift together flour and salt; set aside.

Cream together butter and brown sugar in bowl until light and fluffy, using electric mixer at medium speed. Blend in vanilla.

Gradually stir dry ingredients into creamed mixture, mixing well. Cover and chill dough in refrigerator 2 hours.

Shape dough into 1" balls. Place balls, about 2" apart, on greased baking sheets. Flatten each slightly with bottom of drinking glass dipped in sugar.

Bake in 350° oven 12 minutes, or until golden brown. Remove from baking sheets; cool on racks. Makes 8 dozen.

Pineapple Nut Cookies

A large-batch cookie recipe—makes nine dozen picture-perfect drop cookies featuring pineapple, walnuts and maraschino cherries.

4¼ c. sifted flour	1 tsp. vanilla
1 tsp. baking soda	1 (8½-oz.) can crushed
1 c. butter or regular	pineapple in juice
margarine	1 c. chopped walnuts
1 c. sugar	¼ c. chopped maraschino
1 c. brown sugar, packed	cherries
2 eggs	

Sift together flour and baking soda; set aside.

Cream together butter, sugar and brown sugar in bowl until light and fluffy, using electric mixer at medium speed. Add eggs, one at a time, beating well after each addition. Beat in vanilla.

Drain pineapple, reserving juice. Add dry ingredients alternately with pineapple juice to creamed mixture, beating well after each addition, using electric mixer at low speed. Stir in pineapple, walnuts and maraschino cherries. Drop mixture by teaspoonfuls, about 2″ apart, on greased baking sheets.

Bake in 350° oven 8 to 10 minutes, or until golden brown. Remove from baking sheets; cool on racks. Makes 9 dozen.

Pineapple Spritz

For special occasions, decorate these delicate buttery cookies with silver or gold dragées. This recipe also makes nine dozen.

4½ c. sifted flour	1 c. sugar
1 tsp. baking powder	1 egg
⅛ tsp. salt	2 tblsp. thawed frozen pine-
1½ c. butter or regular	apple juice concentrate
margarine	

Sift together flour, baking powder and salt; set aside.

Cream together butter and sugar in bowl until light and fluffy, using electric mixer at medium speed. Beat in egg and pineapple juice concentrate.

Gradually stir dry ingredients into creamed mixture, mixing well.

Fit flower or crown design into cookie press. Placing one half of the dough in cookie press at a time, force dough through press, about 1″ apart, on ungreased baking sheets.

Bake in 375° oven 8 to 10 minutes, or until set but not browned. Remove from baking sheets; cool on racks. Makes 9 dozen.

Coconut-Lemon Bars

These unforgettable bars feature a buttery crumb crust and a tangy lemon filling full of chewy coconut. A popular bake sale item.

1 c. sifted flour	1 tsp. baking powder
¼ c. sifted confectioners' sugar	6 tblsp. lemon juice
½ c. butter or regular margarine	1½ c. sugar
4 eggs	1 tsp. grated lemon rind
	3 c. flaked coconut

Sift together flour and confectioners' sugar into bowl. Cut in butter until mixture resembles coarse meal, using pastry blender. Press crumb mixture into bottom of greased 13x9x2" baking pan.

Bake in 350° oven 15 to 18 minutes, or until golden brown.

Meanwhile, combine eggs, baking powder, lemon juice, sugar and lemon rind in bowl. Beat until smooth, using electric mixer at medium speed. Stir in coconut. Pour mixture over baked crust.

Bake in 350° oven 30 minutes, or until golden brown. Cool in pan on rack. Cut into 3x1" bars. Makes 39.

Extra-Rich Two-Layer Bars

Good choice for a quick-energy snack, these double-rich bars have a layer of walnuts and coconut over a brown sugar crust.

1 c. butter or regular margarine	2 tblsp. flour
2 c. sifted flour	¾ tsp. baking soda
¼ c. sugar	1 tsp. vanilla
1 tsp. salt	1 c. chopped walnuts
2 eggs	1 c. flaked coconut
1½ c. brown sugar, packed	Confectioners' sugar

Beat butter in bowl until creamy, using electric mixer at medium speed. Stir in 2 c. flour, sugar and salt; mix well. Spread mixture in ungreased 13x9x2" baking pan.

Bake in 350° oven 10 minutes.

Meanwhile, beat eggs slightly in another bowl, using rotary beater. Add brown sugar, 2 tblsp. flour, baking soda and vanilla; beat until blended. Stir in walnuts and coconut. Spread mixture carefully over baked layer.

Bake in 350° oven 20 minutes, or until set. Cool in pan on rack. Sprinkle with confectioners' sugar. Cut into 2¼x1" bars. Makes 52.

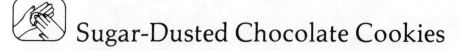 # Sugar-Dusted Chocolate Cookies

Crackling-crisp cookies have a robust chocolate flavor and light dusting of confectioners' sugar. Sure to be a moneymaker!

2 c. sifted flour	2 (1-oz.) squares
2 tsp. baking powder	unsweetened chocolate,
½ tsp. salt	melted and cooled
½ c. shortening	⅓ c. milk
1½ c. sugar	½ c. chopped pecans
2 eggs	Confectioners' sugar
2 tsp. vanilla	

Sift together flour, baking powder and salt; set aside.

Cream together shortening and sugar in bowl until light and fluffy, using electric mixer at medium speed. Add eggs, one at a time, beating well after each addition. Blend in vanilla and cooled chocolate.

Add dry ingredients alternately with milk to chocolate mixture, beating well after each addition, using electric mixer at low speed. Stir in pecans. Cover and chill in refrigerator 3 hours, or until mixture holds shape.

Shape mixture into 1" balls, using lightly greased hands. Roll in confectioners' sugar. Place balls, about 2" apart, on greased baking sheets.

Bake in 350° oven 14 minutes, or until a slight imprint remains when touched lightly with finger. Remove from baking sheets; cool on racks. Makes 6 dozen.

Chocolate Spritz

When you need lots of attractive cookies, turn to your cookie press. This recipe makes seven dozen beauties in a short time.

2½ c. sifted flour	1½ (1-oz.) squares
⅛ tsp. salt	unsweetened chocolate,
1 c. butter or regular	melted and cooled
margarine	3 egg yolks
⅔ c. sugar	¾ tsp. almond extract

Sift together flour and salt; set aside.

Cream together butter and sugar in bowl until light and fluffy, using electric mixer at medium speed. Beat in chocolate, egg yolks and almond extract.

Gradually stir dry ingredients into chocolate mixture, mixing well.

Fit flower or desired design into cookie press. Placing one half of the dough in cookie press at a time, force dough through press, about 1" apart, on ungreased baking sheets.

Bake in 400° oven 7 to 10 minutes, or until set. Remove from baking sheets; cool on racks. Makes about 7 dozen.

Coconut-Chocolate Nut Drops

Another version of the popular chocolate chip cookie, this one more chewy than most because of the addition of flaked coconut.

3 c. sifted flour	2 tsp. vanilla
1 tsp. baking soda	2 eggs
1 tsp. salt	1 tblsp. water
½ c. shortening	1 (12-oz.) pkg. semisweet
½ c. butter or regular	chocolate pieces
margarine	1 c. flaked coconut
1 c. sugar	1 c. chopped walnuts
1 c. brown sugar, packed	

Sift together flour, baking soda and salt; set aside.

Cream together shortening, butter, sugar and brown sugar in bowl until light and fluffy, using electric mixer at medium speed. Add vanilla, eggs and water; beat well.

Gradually stir dry ingredients into creamed mixture, mixing well. Stir in chocolate pieces, coconut and walnuts. Drop mixture by rounded teaspoonfuls, about 2″ apart, on greased baking sheets.

Bake in 350° oven 12 minutes, or until golden brown. Remove from baking sheets; cool on racks. Makes 6½ dozen.

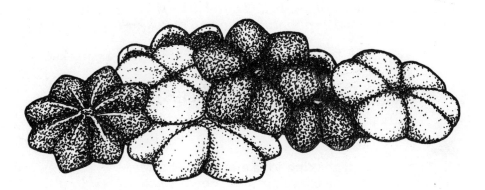

Fudgy Chocolate Drops

These soft, puffy chocolate drops are popular at an annual bake sale in New York state. They're also easy to prepare at the last minute.

2⅔ c. sifted flour
1 tsp. baking soda
½ tsp. salt
½ c. shortening
½ c. butter or regular
   margarine
1½ c. brown sugar, packed

2 eggs
2 tsp. vanilla
4 (1-oz.) squares
   unsweetened chocolate,
   melted and cooled
1 c. sour milk*

Sift together flour, baking soda and salt; set aside.

Cream together shortening, butter and brown sugar in bowl until light and fluffy, using electric mixer at medium speed. Add eggs, one at a time, beating well after each addition. Blend in vanilla and cooled chocolate.

Add dry ingredients alternately with sour milk to chocolate mixture, beating well after each addition, using electric mixer at low speed. Drop mixture by rounded teaspoonfuls, about 2" apart, on greased baking sheets.

Bake in 350° oven 8 minutes, or until no imprint remains when touched lightly with finger. Remove from baking sheets; cool on racks. Makes about 8 dozen.

*Note: To sour milk, place 1 tblsp. vinegar in measuring cup. Add enough milk to make 1 c.

Tollhouse Bar Cookies

Famous Tollhouse Cookies, baked into bars—saves fuss and bother of forming cookies by the spoonful when you're in a rush.

2⅓ c. sifted flour
1 tsp. baking soda
1 tsp. salt
1 c. butter or regular
   margarine
¾ c. sugar

¾ c. brown sugar, packed
2 eggs
1 tsp. vanilla
1 (12-oz.) pkg. semisweet
   chocolate pieces
1 c. chopped walnuts

Sift together flour, baking soda and salt; set aside.

Cream together butter, sugar and brown sugar in bowl until light and fluffy, using electric mixer at medium speed. Add eggs, one at a time, beating well after each addition. Beat in vanilla.

Gradually stir dry ingredients into creamed mixture, mixing well. Stir in chocolate pieces and walnuts. Spread in greased 15½x10½x1" jelly roll pan.

Bake in 375° oven 20 minutes, or until golden brown. Cool in pan on rack. Cut into 2" squares. Makes 35.

Chocolate Sandwich Treasures

You'll never miss store-bought chocolate sandwich cookies once you see how easy it is to make these from scratch.

4 c. sifted flour
2 tsp. baking soda
½ tsp. baking powder
½ tsp. salt
½ c. shortening
2 c. sugar
2 eggs

1 tsp. vanilla
1 c. buttermilk
¾ c. boiling water
½ c. baking cocoa
Creamy Vanilla Filling
   (recipe follows)

Sift together flour, baking soda, baking powder and salt; set aside.

Cream together shortening and sugar in bowl until light and fluffy, using electric mixer at medium speed. Add eggs, one at a time, beating well after each addition. Beat in vanilla.

Add dry ingredients alternately with buttermilk to creamed mixture, beating well after each addition, using electric mixer at low speed.

Combine boiling water and cocoa in small bowl; stir to mix. Cool slightly. Stir into batter. Drop mixture by teaspoonfuls, about 2" apart, on greased baking sheets.

Bake in 350° oven 8 minutes, or until no imprint remains when touched lightly with finger. Remove from baking sheets; cool on racks. Prepare Creamy Vanilla Filling. Spread Creamy Vanilla Filling on half of the cookies. Top each with another cookie to make a sandwich. Makes 5 dozen sandwich cookies.

Creamy Vanilla Filling: Combine 5 tblsp. flour and ½ c. milk in 2-qt. saucepan. Stir to form a smooth paste. Gradually stir in ½ c. milk. Cook over medium heat, stirring constantly, until mixture thickens. Remove from heat and cool completely. Cream together 1 c. shortening and 1 c. sifted confectioners' sugar in bowl until light and fluffy, using electric mixer at medium speed. Add ¼ tsp. salt and cooked mixture, beating until mixture is fluffy. Makes 2½ c. filling.

Chocolate-Banana Cookies

Flavorful, moist cookies that are best when made with very ripe bananas. The chocolate and banana flavors blend nicely.

2½ c. sifted flour	1 c. mashed ripe bananas
2 tsp. baking powder	(2½ medium)
¼ tsp. baking soda	1 (6-oz.) pkg. semisweet
¼ tsp. salt	chocolate pieces, melted
⅔ c. shortening	and cooled
1 c. sugar	Chocolate Frosting (recipe
2 eggs	follows)
1 tsp. vanilla	

Sift together flour, baking powder, baking soda and salt; set aside.

Cream together shortening and sugar in bowl until light and fluffy, using electric mixer at medium speed. Add eggs, one at a time, beating well after each addition. Beat in vanilla, bananas and cooled chocolate.

Gradually stir dry ingredients into chocolate mixture, mixing well. Drop mixture by teaspoonfuls, about 2" apart, on lightly greased baking sheets.

Bake in 350° oven 10 minutes, or until a slight imprint remains when touched lightly with finger. Remove from baking sheets; cool on racks. Prepare Chocolate Frosting. Frost cookies with Chocolate Frosting. Makes about 5 dozen.

Chocolate Frosting: Combine 2 tblsp. soft butter or regular margarine, 2 (1-oz.) squares unsweetened chocolate (melted and cooled), 3 tblsp. warm water and 2 c. sifted confectioners' sugar in bowl. Stir until smooth, using a spoon.

Brownie Mix

If you're often asked to bring items to bake sales, this mix is a real timesaver! Keep some on hand for a quick batch of brownies.

4 c. sifted flour	4 tsp. baking powder
8 c. sugar	4 tsp. salt
2½ c. baking cocoa	2 c. shortening

Sift together flour, sugar, cocoa, baking powder and salt into large bowl. Cut in shortening until well blended, using a pastry blender. Store in covered container in cool place or in refrigerator up to 3 months. Use mix to make Shortcut Brownies (recipe follows). Makes 16 cups.

Shortcut Brownies

These chocolate brownies are extra-yummy and extra-easy because they're made with your own homemade Brownie Mix. So fudgy, too.

2 c. Brownie Mix	1 tsp. vanilla
2 eggs, beaten	½ c. chopped walnuts

Combine Brownie Mix, eggs and vanilla in bowl; blend well, using a spoon. (Mixture will not be smooth.) Stir in walnuts. Spread mixture in greased 8″ square baking pan.

Bake in 350° oven 20 to 25 minutes, or until a slight imprint remains when touched lightly with finger. Cool in pan on rack. Cut into 2″ squares. Makes 16.

Fudge Cinnamon Brownies

If you like brownies with a mild chocolate flavor, try this cinnamon-spiced bar swirled with chocolate frosting and sprinkled with pecans.

2 c. sifted flour	2 eggs
2 c. sugar	1 tsp. vanilla
1 c. butter or regular	1 tsp. baking soda
margarine	1 tsp. ground cinnamon
7 tblsp. baking cocoa	Chocolate Fudge Frosting
1 c. water	(recipe follows)
½ c. buttermilk	1 c. chopped pecans

Sift together flour and sugar into bowl; set aside.

Mix together butter, cocoa and water in 2-qt. heavy saucepan. Cook over medium heat, stirring constantly, until mixture comes to a boil. Remove from heat. Slowly pour hot mixture over flour mixture, beating well after each addition, using electric mixer at low speed.

Add buttermilk, eggs, vanilla, baking soda and cinnamon. Beat well, using electric mixer at medium speed. Spread mixture in greased 15½x10½x1″ jelly roll pan.

Bake in 400° oven 20 minutes, or until top springs back when touched lightly with finger. Cool in pan on rack. Prepare Chocolate Fudge Frosting. Frost brownies with Chocolate Fudge Frosting. Sprinkle with pecans. Cut into 2″ squares. Makes 35.

Chocolate Fudge Frosting: Melt ½ c. butter or regular margarine in 2-qt. heavy saucepan over low heat. Stir in 5 tblsp. baking cocoa and 6 tblsp. milk; mix well. Cook over medium heat, stirring constantly, until mixture comes to a boil. Remove from heat. Gradually stir in 1 (1-lb.) pkg. confectioners' sugar (sifted), mixing well. Stir in 1 tsp. vanilla. Beat until smooth, using a spoon.

 Chocolate-Cream Cheese Bars

Two-tone brownie with a chocolaty, cake-like base topped with cream cheese mixture. Guaranteed to be a sellout.

½ c. butter or regular margarine	¾ c. chopped walnuts
1 (1-oz.) square unsweetened chocolate	1 (8-oz.) pkg. cream cheese, softened
1 c. sifted flour	¼ c. butter or regular margarine
1 c. sugar	½ c. sugar
1 tsp. baking powder	2 tblsp. flour
¼ tsp. salt	1 egg, beaten
2 eggs, beaten	½ tsp. vanilla
1 tsp. vanilla	¼ c. chopped walnuts

Combine ½ c. butter and chocolate in 2-qt. saucepan. Cook over low heat until butter and chocolate are melted. Stir until smooth. Remove from heat; cool to room temperature.

Sift together 1 c. flour, 1 c. sugar, baking powder and salt. Stir dry ingredients into cooled chocolate mixture; mix well. Add 2 eggs and 1 tsp. vanilla, blending well. Stir in ¾ c. walnuts. Spread batter in well-greased 13x9x2" baking pan.

Combine cream cheese and ¼ c. butter in bowl. Beat until smooth and creamy, using electric mixer at medium speed. Combine ½ c. sugar and 2 tblsp. flour. Gradually add to cheese mixture, beating well. Beat in 1 egg and ½ tsp. vanilla. Spread over chocolate batter. Sprinkle with ¼ c. walnuts.

Bake in 350° oven 30 to 35 minutes, or until no imprint remains when touched lightly with finger. Cool in pan on rack. Cut into 3x1" bars. Makes 39.

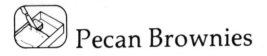

Semisweet Chocolate Brownies

Another mild-flavored brownie, this one made with melted semisweet chocolate. Dust lightly with confectioners' sugar if you wish.

1½ c. sifted flour
½ tsp. salt
1 c. butter or regular
    margarine
2 c. sugar
4 eggs

3 (1-oz.) squares
    semisweet chocolate,
    melted and cooled
2 tsp. vanilla
1 c. chopped walnuts

Sift together flour and salt; set aside.

Cream together butter and sugar in bowl until light and fluffy, using electric mixer at medium speed. Add eggs, one at a time, beating well after each addition. Blend in cooled chocolate and vanilla.

Gradually stir dry ingredients into chocolate mixture, mixing well. Stir in walnuts. Pour mixture into greased 13x9x2" baking pan.

Bake in 350° oven 35 minutes, or until top springs back when touched lightly with finger. Cool in pan on rack. Cut into 3x1" bars. Makes 39.

Pecan Brownies

This two-pan brownie recipe is a good choice for a bazaar because it makes 32 good-sized fudgy brownies topped with pecans.

2 c. sugar
1 c. brown sugar, packed
⅔ c. light corn syrup
1 c. butter or regular
    margarine
6 eggs

6 (1-oz.) squares
    unsweetened chocolate,
    melted and cooled
2 c. sifted flour
2 c. pecan halves

Combine sugar, brown sugar, corn syrup and butter in large bowl. Beat with electric mixer at medium speed for 2 minutes, or until smooth.

Add eggs; beat 2 more minutes. Blend in cooled chocolate.

Add flour; stir well. Reserve 32 pecan halves for decoration. Stir in remaining pecans. Spread batter evenly in 2 greased 9" square baking pans. Arrange 16 reserved pecan halves in rows on top in each pan.

Bake in 350° oven 40 minutes, or until no imprint remains when touched lightly with finger. Cool in pans on racks. Cut into 2¼" squares. Makes 32.

Double Boiler Brownies

"We like this recipe because it uses eggs from our farm, and it can be mixed right in the double boiler," says a Wisconsin farm woman.

1½ c. sifted flour	⅔ c. cooking oil
1 tsp. baking powder	2 c. sugar
1 tsp. salt	4 eggs
4 (1-oz.) squares	1 c. chopped walnuts
unsweetened chocolate	Sifted confectioners' sugar

Sift together flour, baking powder and salt; set aside.

Combine chocolate and oil in top of double boiler. Place over simmering water until chocolate is melted. Remove from heat and cool slightly.

Gradually add sugar to chocolate mixture, beating well after each addition, using electric mixer at medium speed. Add eggs; beat 2 minutes.

Gradually stir dry ingredients into chocolate mixture, mixing well. Stir in walnuts. (Batter will be stiff.) Spread mixture in greased 15½x10½x1" jelly roll pan.

Bake in 350° oven 25 minutes, or until no imprint remains when touched lightly with finger. Cool in pan on rack. Sprinkle with sifted confectioners' sugar. Cut into 4x1" bars. Makes 40.

Big-Batch Molasses Cookies

Recipe makes a gigantic batch of thin, old-fashioned spice cookies—15 dozen in all. Good choice for bake sale or bazaar.

5 c. sifted flour	1 c. shortening
1 tblsp. ground cinnamon	2 c. sugar
1 tblsp. ground ginger	2 eggs
1 tsp. salt	¾ c. dark molasses
1 tsp. baking powder	1½ tsp. lemon extract
1 tsp. baking soda	2 tblsp. vinegar

Sift together flour, cinnamon, ginger, salt, baking powder and baking soda; set aside.

Cream together shortening and sugar in bowl until light and fluffy, using electric mixer at medium speed. Add eggs, one at a time, beating well after each addition. Beat in molasses and lemon extract.

Gradually stir dry ingredients into creamed mixture with vinegar; mix well.

Roll dough out on floured surface to ⅛" thickness. Cut with floured 2" cookie cutter. Place, about 1½" apart, on greased baking sheets.

Bake in 350° oven 6 to 8 minutes, or until brown. Remove from baking sheets; cool on racks. Makes about 15 dozen.

Norwegian Molasses Cookies

If you like country-style lard cookies made with molasses, choose this recipe. The golden brown cookies are both crunchy and chewy.

5 c. sifted flour	2 c. sugar
3 tsp. baking soda	2 eggs
1/8 tsp. salt	1 c. molasses
1 c. lard	

Sift together flour, baking soda and salt; set aside.

Cream together lard and sugar in bowl until light and fluffy, using electric mixer at medium speed. Add eggs, one at a time, beating well after each addition. Beat in molasses.

Gradually stir dry ingredients into creamed mixture; mix well. Cover with plastic wrap. Chill 1 hour in refrigerator.

Shape dough into 1¼" balls. Place balls, about 2" apart, on greased baking sheets.

Bake in 350° oven 18 minutes, or until golden brown. Remove from baking sheets; cool on racks. Makes about 7 dozen.

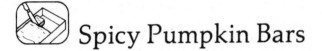

Spicy Pumpkin Bars

These cream cheese-frosted pumpkin bars are perfect for an autumn bazaar. Offer them along with apple cider.

2 c. sifted flour	1 c. brown sugar, packed
4 tsp. baking powder	¼ c. sugar
1¼ tsp. ground cinnamon	4 eggs
1 tsp. ground nutmeg	1 (16-oz.) can mashed
1 tsp. ground ginger	pumpkin (2 c.)
½ tsp. salt	Cream Cheese Icing (recipe
½ c. shortening	follows)

Sift together flour, baking powder, cinnamon, nutmeg, ginger and salt; set aside.

Cream together shortening, brown sugar and sugar in bowl until light and fluffy, using electric mixer at medium speed. Add eggs, one at a time, beating well after each addition. Beat in pumpkin.

Gradually stir dry ingredients into creamed mixture, mixing well. Spread mixture in greased 15½x10½x1" jelly roll pan.

Bake in 350° oven 30 minutes, or until top springs back when touched lightly with finger. Cool in pan on rack. Prepare Cream Cheese Icing. Frost bars with Cream Cheese Icing. If you wish, sprinkle with chopped walnuts. Cut into 4x1" bars. Makes 40.

Cream Cheese Icing: Combine 1 (3-oz.) pkg. softened cream cheese, 1 tblsp. butter or regular margarine, 2½ c. sifted confectioners' sugar, 1 tsp. grated lemon rind, pinch salt and 1 tblsp. milk in bowl. Stir until smooth, using a spoon.

Applesauce Oatmeal Drops

Applesauce and oatmeal are combined in this interesting cookie variation. It's lightly spiced and studded with raisins and nuts.

2½ c. sifted flour	2 c. brown sugar, packed
1 tsp. baking soda	2 eggs
1 tsp. salt	½ c. milk
1 tsp. ground cinnamon	2 c. applesauce
½ tsp. baking powder	1 c. quick-cooking oats
½ tsp. ground cloves	1 c. raisins
½ tsp. ground nutmeg	½ c. chopped walnuts
1 c. shortening	

Sift together flour, baking soda, salt, cinnamon, baking powder, cloves and nutmeg; set aside.

Cream together shortening and brown sugar in bowl until light and fluffy, using electric mixer at medium speed. Add eggs, one at a time, beating well after each addition. Stir in milk and applesauce.

Gradually stir dry ingredients into creamed mixture, mixing well. Stir in oats, raisins and walnuts. Cover and chill in refrigerator at least 2 hours. Drop mixture by heaping teaspoonfuls, about 2" apart, on greased baking sheets.

Bake in 400° oven 10 to 12 minutes, or until lightly browned. Remove from baking sheets; cool on racks. Makes 7 dozen cookies.

Refrigerator Chocolate Oatmeals

Instead of using chocolate jimmies, you can coat the roll of dough with chopped walnuts, flaked coconut or cinnamon and sugar.

1¼ c. sifted flour	2 tsp. vanilla
½ tsp. salt	1 c. quick-cooking oats
1 c. butter or regular margarine	⅓ c. chocolate jimmies
1 c. sifted confectioners' sugar	

Sift together flour and salt; set aside.

Cream together butter and confectioners' sugar in bowl until light and fluffy, using electric mixer at medium speed. Beat in vanilla.

Gradually stir dry ingredients into creamed mixture, mixing well. Stir in oats. Shape dough into roll, about 2" in diameter. Roll in chocolate jimmies. Wrap in plastic wrap and chill in refrigerator 1 hour.

Cut roll into ¼" thick slices. Place slices, about 2" apart, on greased baking sheets.

Bake in 325° oven 15 minutes, or until golden brown. Remove from baking sheets; cool on racks. Makes about 3 dozen.

Chocolate Chip-Oatmeal Cookies

These are 10 times better than regular oatmeals, in the opinion of one Michigan family: The special ingredient is chocolate chips.

2 c. sifted flour	2 eggs
1 tsp. baking powder	1 tsp. vanilla
1 tsp. baking soda	2 c. quick-cooking oats
½ tsp. salt	1 (12-oz.) pkg. semisweet
1 c. shortening	chocolate pieces
1 c. brown sugar, packed	½ c. chopped walnuts
1 c. sugar	

Sift together flour, baking powder, baking soda and salt; set aside.

Cream together shortening, brown sugar and sugar in bowl until light and fluffy, using electric mixer at medium speed. Add eggs, one at a time, beating well after each addition. Blend in vanilla.

Gradually stir dry ingredients into creamed mixture, blending well. Stir in oats, chocolate pieces and walnuts. Drop mixture by teaspoonfuls, about 2" apart, on greased baking sheets.

Bake in 350° oven 12 to 15 minutes, or until golden brown. Remove from baking sheets; cool on racks. Makes 6 dozen.

Coffee Oatmeal Cookies

Spicy oatmeal drop cookies, the flavor enhanced by coffee and light cream. They have raisins and nuts in every bite.

2 c. sifted flour	2 eggs
1 tsp. baking soda	⅓ c. cold coffee
1 tsp. ground cinnamon	¼ c. light cream
½ tsp. ground cloves	1 c. quick-cooking oats
¼ tsp. ground nutmeg	1 c. raisins
½ c. shortening	½ c. chopped walnuts
1 c. brown sugar, packed	

Sift together flour, baking soda, cinnamon, cloves and nutmeg; set aside.

Cream together shortening and brown sugar in bowl until light and fluffy, using electric mixer at medium speed. Add eggs, one at a time, beating well after each addition.

Add dry ingredients alternately with coffee and cream to creamed mixture, beating well after each addition, using electric mixer at low speed. Stir in oats, raisins and walnuts. Drop mixture by rounded teaspoonfuls, about 2" apart, on greased baking sheets. Flatten each with floured bottom of drinking glass.

Bake in 350° oven 8 to 10 minutes, or until lightly browned. Remove from baking sheets; cool on racks. Makes 6 dozen.

Cracked Coconut Oat Cookies

Since almost everyone likes oatmeal cookies, we've included this variation made with flaked coconut. It's sure to be popular.

2 c. sifted flour	1 c. sugar
1 tsp. baking powder	2 eggs
1 tsp. baking soda	2 tsp. vanilla
½ tsp. salt	2 c. quick-cooking oats
1 c. shortening	1 c. flaked coconut
1 c. brown sugar, packed	

Sift together flour, baking powder, baking soda and salt; set aside.

Cream together shortening, brown sugar and sugar in bowl until light and fluffy, using electric mixer at medium speed. Add eggs, one at a time, beating well after each addition. Blend in vanilla.

Gradually stir dry ingredients into creamed mixture; mix well. Stir in oats and coconut. (Dough will be very stiff.) Shape dough into 1" balls. Place balls, about 2" apart, on greased baking sheets. Flatten each with bottom of drinking glass dipped in water.

Bake in 350° oven about 15 minutes, or until golden brown. Remove from baking sheets; cool on racks. Makes 7 dozen.

Pride of Iowa Cookies

This oatmeal-coconut cookie recipe is requested again and again by farm women who have misplaced it. It's one of our best.

2 c. sifted flour	1 c. brown sugar, packed
1 tsp. baking powder	2 eggs
1 tsp. baking soda	2 tsp. vanilla
½ tsp. salt	3 c. quick-cooking oats
1 c. shortening	1 c. flaked coconut
1 c. sugar	½ c. chopped walnuts

Sift together flour, baking powder, baking soda and salt; set aside.

Cream together shortening, sugar and brown sugar in bowl until light and fluffy, using electric mixer at medium speed. Add eggs, one at a time, beating well after each addition. Beat in vanilla.

Gradually stir dry ingredients into creamed mixture, mixing well. Stir in oats, coconut and walnuts. Drop mixture by teaspoonfuls, about 2" apart, on greased baking sheets. Flatten each with floured tines of fork or bottom of drinking glass.

Bake in 350° oven 8 to 10 minutes, or until golden brown. Remove from baking sheets; cool on racks. Makes about 8 dozen.

Super Mix for Baking

Keep this mix handy for days when you don't have time to start peanut butter cookies from scratch. Enough for four big batches.

9 c. sifted flour	1 tblsp. salt
½ c. nonfat dry milk	2 c. shortening
⅓ c. baking powder	

Sift together flour, dry milk, baking powder and salt into large bowl. Cut in shortening until mixture resembles coarse cornmeal, using pastry blender. Store in covered container in cool place or refrigerator up to 3 months. Use mix to make Peanut Butter Cookies (recipe follows). Makes 12 cups.

Peanut Butter Cookies

These chocolate-kissed gems look extra-pretty, yet are easily prepared. Just shape dough into balls and top with candy kisses.

3 c. Super Mix for Baking	2 eggs, beaten
1 c. sugar	1 to 2 tblsp. milk
1 c. peanut butter	Chocolate candy kisses

Combine Super Mix for Baking and sugar in bowl. Stir in peanut butter and eggs; blend thoroughly with spoon. If dough seems dry, add milk. Shape mixture into 1" balls. Place balls, about 3" apart, on ungreased baking sheets. Press a candy kiss in each cookie.

Bake in 375° oven 15 to 20 minutes, or until golden brown. Remove from baking sheets; cool on racks. Makes 6 dozen.

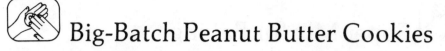

Big-Batch Peanut Butter Cookies

Classics like these peanut butter cookies make dependable sellers at bake sales. This recipe turns out 8½ dozen sweet treats.

2½ c. sifted flour	1 c. sugar
2 tsp. baking soda	1 c. brown sugar, packed
1 c. butter or regular	2 eggs
margarine	2 tsp. vanilla
1 c. peanut butter	

Sift together flour and baking soda; set aside.

Cream together butter, peanut butter, sugar and brown sugar in bowl until light and fluffy, using electric mixer at medium speed. Add eggs, one at a time, beating well after each addition. Blend in vanilla.

Gradually stir dry ingredients into creamed mixture, blending well. Shape dough into 1" balls. Place balls, about 2" apart, on greased baking sheets. Flatten each with floured tines of fork, making a crisscross pattern.

Bake in 350° oven 10 to 12 minutes, or until golden brown. Remove from baking sheets; cool on racks. Makes about 8½ dozen.

Peanut Butter Cookie Bars

A chewy oatmeal bottom layer topped with melted chocolate and drizzled with a smooth peanut butter icing.

1 c. sifted flour	⅓ c. peanut butter
¼ tsp. baking soda	½ tsp. vanilla
¼ tsp. salt	1 c. quick-cooking oats
½ c. butter or regular	1 (6-oz.) pkg. semisweet
margarine	chocolate pieces
½ c. sugar	Peanut Butter Icing (recipe
½ c. brown sugar, packed	follows)
1 egg	

Sift together flour, baking soda and salt; set aside.

Cream together butter, sugar and brown sugar in bowl until light and fluffy, using electric mixer at medium speed. Add egg, peanut butter and vanilla; beat well.

Gradually stir dry ingredients into creamed mixture, blending well. Stir in oats. Spread mixture in greased 13x9x2" baking pan.

Bake in 350° oven 25 minutes, or until no imprint remains when touched lightly with finger. Remove from oven; sprinkle top with chocolate pieces. Let stand 5 minutes so chocolate can melt. Spread melted chocolate evenly over top. Cool in pan on rack. Prepare Peanut Butter Icing. Drizzle bars with Peanut Butter Icing. Cut into 2¼x1" bars. Makes 52.

Peanut Butter Icing: Combine ½ c. sifted confectioners' sugar, ¼ c. creamy peanut butter and 3 tblsp. milk in bowl; beat until smooth, using a spoon. Add 1 more tblsp. milk, if necessary, to make an icing that can be drizzled.

 # Date Pinwheels

Classic cookies with a baked-in date and walnut filling. This big-yield recipe has been carefully handed down through several generations.

3 c. sifted flour	1 c. brown sugar, packed
1 tsp. baking powder	1 c. sugar
1 tsp. baking soda	3 eggs
¼ tsp. salt	1 tsp. vanilla
1 c. shortening	Date Filling (recipe follows)

Sift together flour, baking powder, baking soda and salt; set aside.

Cream together shortening, brown sugar and sugar in bowl until light and fluffy, using electric mixer at medium speed. Add eggs, one at a time, beating well after each addition. Beat in vanilla.

Gradually stir dry ingredients into creamed mixture, mixing well. Cover and chill dough in refrigerator 2 hours.

Meanwhile, prepare Date Filling.

Divide dough into fourths. Roll each fourth on floured surface into 10x6" rectangle. Spread each rectangle with one fourth of the Date Filling. Roll up like a jelly roll, starting from long side. Wrap in plastic wrap and chill in refrigerator overnight.

Cut each roll into ⅛" thick slices. Place slices, about 2" apart, on greased baking sheets.

Bake in 350° oven 10 to 12 minutes, or until golden brown. Remove from baking sheets; cool on racks. Makes 11 dozen.

Date Filling: Combine 1 c. cut-up pitted dates, 1 c. water and ½ c. sugar in small saucepan. Cook over medium heat, stirring constantly, until mixture thickens. Remove from heat. Stir in 1 c. chopped walnuts. Cool completely.

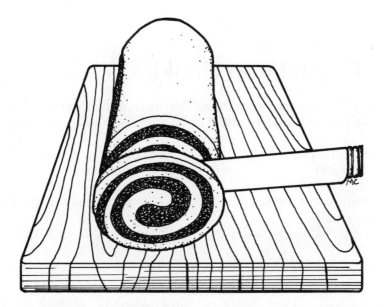

 Spicy Date Bars

The rich molasses 'n' spice flavor of these date bars makes them a necessary addition to this collection of favorite cookie recipes.

2 c. sifted flour	2 eggs
1 tsp. ground cinnamon	½ c. molasses
½ tsp. baking soda	1 tsp. vanilla
½ tsp. salt	1 c. finely chopped pitted
½ tsp. ground ginger	dates
½ tsp. ground nutmeg	1 c. chopped walnuts
⅔ c. butter or regular	Creamy Vanilla Frosting
margarine	(recipe follows)
1 c. brown sugar, packed	

Sift together flour, cinnamon, baking soda, salt, ginger and nutmeg. Reserve ¼ c. dry ingredients; set aside.

Cream together butter and brown sugar in bowl until light and fluffy, using electric mixer at medium speed. Add eggs, one at a time, beating well after each addition. Beat in molasses and vanilla.

Gradually stir dry ingredients into creamed mixture, mixing well. Combine reserved ¼ c. dry ingredients with dates and walnuts. Stir date-nut mixture into batter. Spread mixture in greased 15½x10½x1" jelly roll pan.

Bake in 375° oven 20 to 25 minutes, or until top springs back when touched lightly with finger. Cool slightly in pan on rack. Prepare Creamy Vanilla Frosting. While bars are still warm, spread with Creamy Vanilla Frosting. Cool completely. Cut into 2½x1½" bars. Makes 48.

Creamy Vanilla Frosting: Combine 1¼ c. sifted confectioners' sugar, 1 tblsp. soft butter or regular margarine, ½ tsp. vanilla, ⅛ tsp. almond extract and 1½ tsp. milk in bowl. Beat until smooth, using a spoon.

Raisin Drop Cookies

An Iowa farm woman welcomes her husband in from a hard day's work outdoors with coffee and a couple of these soft, chewy cookies.

1½ c. raisins	1 c. butter or regular
1 c. water	margarine
3 c. sifted flour	¾ c. sugar
1 tsp. baking soda	¾ c. brown sugar, packed
1 tsp. salt	2 eggs
¾ tsp. baking powder	1 tsp. vanilla

Combine raisins and water in small saucepan. Cook over medium heat until mixture comes to a boil. Reduce heat and simmer 10 minutes. Remove from heat; cool completely. Drain raisins, reserving ½ c. cooking liquid. Set aside.

Sift together flour, baking soda, salt and baking powder; set aside.

Cream together butter, sugar and brown sugar in bowl until light and fluffy, using electric mixer at medium speed. Add eggs, one at a time, beating well after each addition. Blend in vanilla.

Add dry ingredients alternately with reserved ½ c. cooking liquid to creamed mixture, beating well after each addition, using electric mixer at low speed. Stir in raisins. Drop mixture by rounded teaspoonfuls, about 3" apart, on greased baking sheets.

Bake in 375° oven 6 to 8 minutes, or until golden brown. Remove from baking sheets; cool on racks. Makes 5½ dozen.

Orange-Glazed Prune Cookies

These cinnamony drop cookies are soft and cake-like. Each is spread with a thin layer of orange glaze for an extra-tangy touch.

3½ c. sifted flour
1 tsp. baking powder
1 tsp. baking soda
1 tsp. ground cinnamon
½ tsp. salt
1 c. butter or regular
   margarine
2 c. brown sugar, packed

2 eggs
1 tsp. vanilla
½ c. milk
2 c. chopped cooked prunes
1 c. chopped walnuts
Orange Glaze (recipe
   follows)

Sift together flour, baking powder, baking soda, cinnamon and salt; set aside.

Cream together butter and brown sugar in bowl until light and fluffy, using electric mixer at medium speed. Add eggs, one at a time, beating well after each addition. Beat in vanilla.

Add dry ingredients alternately with milk to creamed mixture, mixing well with spoon. Stir in prunes and walnuts. Drop mixture by teaspoonfuls, about 2" apart, on greased baking sheets.

Bake in 350° oven 15 to 20 minutes, or until lightly browned. Remove from baking sheets; cool on racks. Prepare Orange Glaze. Ice cookies with a thin layer of Orange Glaze. Makes 8½ dozen.

Orange Glaze: Combine 3 c. sifted confectioners' sugar, 1 tsp. grated orange rind and ¼ c. orange juice in bowl. Beat until smooth, using a spoon.

Candied Fruit Bars

Richly fruited bars like these are popular at Christmas bazaars and bake sales. Orange frosting is the special topper.

1½ c. sifted flour	½ c. melted shortening
1¾ c. sugar	½ tsp. vanilla
1 tsp. baking powder	1½ c. mixed candied fruit
½ tsp. salt	Orange Frosting (recipe
4 eggs	follows)

Sift together flour, sugar, baking powder and salt. Reserve ¼ c. dry ingredients; set aside.

Combine eggs, shortening and vanilla in bowl. Beat until thick and lemon-colored, using electric mixer at high speed.

Gradually stir dry ingredients into egg mixture, mixing well. Mix reserved ¼ c. dry ingredients with candied fruit. Stir candied fruit into batter. Spread batter in greased 13x9x2" baking pan.

Bake in 350° oven 30 minutes, or until top springs back when touched lightly with finger. Cool slightly in pan on rack. Prepare Orange Frosting. While bars are still warm, frost with Orange Frosting. Cool completely. Cut into 3x1" bars. Makes 39.

Orange Frosting: Combine 1 c. sifted confectioners' sugar, 1½ tblsp. orange juice and ½ tsp. grated orange rind in bowl. Beat until smooth, using a spoon.

Crybaby Cookies

Large three-inch cookies chock-full of coconut, walnuts and raisins. Both molasses and raisins make these a good source of iron.

4¾ c. sifted flour	1½ c. raisins
3 tsp. baking powder	1 c. plus 2 tblsp. shortening
1½ tsp. baking soda	1 c. plus 2 tblsp. sugar
1 tsp. salt	2 eggs
2 c. shredded or flaked	1 c. light molasses
coconut	1 c. milk
2 c. chopped walnuts	

Sift together flour, baking powder, baking soda and salt. Combine dry ingredients with coconut, walnuts and raisins; set aside.

Cream together shortening and sugar in bowl until light and fluffy, using electric mixer at medium speed. Add eggs, one at a time, beating well after each addition. Beat in molasses.

Add coconut mixture alternately with milk, stirring well after each addition. Drop mixture by tablespoonfuls, about 2" apart, on greased baking sheets.

Bake in 375° oven 10 minutes, or until golden brown. Remove from baking sheets; cool on racks. Makes about 9½ dozen.

8 | Penny-Wise Treats

Cookies don't need to be chock-full of expensive ingredients to be rich and flavorful—you can indulge your taste for sugar and spice (and even chocolate) by turning to low-cost alternatives. All the cookies in this chapter are made without butter, and there are six chocolaty creations made with baking cocoa.

For a simple cookie that's just plain delicious, try a Midwestern favorite: Snickerdoodles. These extra-crunchy molded cookies feature a light cinnamon-and-sugar coating. Or bake the Chewy Honey Cookies, old-fashioned rounds of goodness with crackly sugar tops.

Coconut-Nutmeg Cookies are soft, cake-like morsels spiced with just a whisper of nutmeg. Since they're made with a yellow cake mix, these cookies are a great choice

when you want a few dozen homemade cookies in a jiffy—and they taste better and cost less than store-bought.

In this chapter there are recipes both for large groups and
small families. If you need lots of gingery spice cookies, stir
up Ginger Cookies for a Crowd; this time-tested recipe
yields 12 dozen mouth-watering treats. When you need just
a few cookies, turn to Coconut-Cornflake Crisps or
Coconut Bar Cookies. Each recipe makes just enough to fill
a family-sized cookie jar.

Our fruited cookies, such as Nut-Raisin Cookies and
Peanut Butter-Apple Cookies, are rich in nutrition, but at a
bargain price. The unusual Spicy Raisin Drops have a surprise ingredient—ketchup—which adds both color and
flavor; these puffy cookies are thinly iced with a tangy
lemon glaze to counterbalance the spicy flavor of the
cookies themselves.

You'll be proud to serve these cookies to company, too.
Friendship Brownies, lightly dusted with confectioners'
sugar, and Marshmallow-Fudge Squares, topped with a
layer of marshmallow creme, are especially good party
treats. For a more formal occasion, try Double Orange
Cookies, drop cookies thinly iced with an orange glaze, or
Lemon Snowballs, delicate puffs baked to a golden brown
and dusted with confectioners' sugar. Or serve elegant
Frosted Carrot Bars, moist, cake-like cookies laced with
walnuts and coconut and topped off by a cream cheese
frosting.

Whether you're baking cookies for an everyday treat or
planning to celebrate a special occasion, you can splurge on
flavor without straining your budget.

 # Snickerdoodles

This scrumptious cookie is made from everyday ingredients that you probably have on hand. It's economical, but so good.

2¾ c. sifted flour
2 tsp. cream of tartar
1 tsp. baking soda
¼ tsp. salt
½ c. regular margarine
½ c. shortening

1½ c. sugar
2 eggs
1 tsp. vanilla
3 tblsp. sugar
3 tblsp. ground cinnamon

Sift together flour, cream of tartar, baking soda and salt; set aside.

Cream together margarine, shortening and 1½ c. sugar in bowl until light and fluffy, using electric mixer at medium speed. Add eggs, one at a time, beating well after each addition. Blend in vanilla.

Gradually stir dry ingredients into creamed mixture, mixing well with spoon. Shape dough into 1" balls. Combine 3 tblsp. sugar and cinnamon. Roll each in sugar-cinnamon mixture. Place balls, about 2" apart, on ungreased baking sheets.

Bake in 400° oven 8 to 10 minutes, or until golden brown. Remove from baking sheets; cool on racks. Makes about 6 dozen.

 # Chewy Honey Cookies

Here's another basic cookie, this one made with honey. Its sparkling sugar topping gives it a home-style look.

4½ c. sifted flour
4 tsp. baking soda
½ tsp. salt
1½ c. shortening
2 c. sugar

½ c. honey
2 eggs
2 tsp. vanilla
Sugar

Sift together flour, baking soda and salt; set aside.

Cream together shortening and 2 c. sugar in bowl until light and fluffy, using electric mixer at medium speed. Blend in honey. Add eggs, one at a time, beating well after each addition. Blend in vanilla.

Gradually add dry ingredients to creamed mixture, mixing well with spoon. Shape dough into 1" balls. Place balls, about 2" apart, on greased baking sheets. Flatten each slightly with bottom of drinking glass dipped in sugar.

Bake in 350° oven 12 to 15 minutes, or until golden brown. Remove from baking sheets; cool on racks. Makes about 7 dozen.

Drop Sugar Cookies

Simply delicious sugar cookie featuring chopped walnuts. Great recipe for a small family because it makes just 30 cookies.

1¾ c. sifted flour	1 egg
½ tsp. baking powder	1 tsp. vanilla
½ tsp. baking soda	¼ c. milk
½ c. regular margarine	½ c. chopped walnuts
1 c. sugar	

Sift together flour, baking powder and baking soda; set aside.

Cream together margarine and sugar in bowl until light and fluffy, using electric mixer at medium speed. Add egg; beat well. Blend in vanilla.

Add dry ingredients alternately with milk, beating well after each addition, using electric mixer at low speed. Stir in walnuts. Drop mixture by teaspoonfuls, about 2" apart, on greased baking sheets. Flatten each with back of floured spoon.

Bake in 375° oven 8 to 10 minutes, or until golden brown. Remove from baking sheets; cool on racks. Makes about 2½ dozen.

Extra-Good Rolled Cookies

You don't need to chill the dough for these easy rolled cookies; just roll out immediately and cut into shapes.

3¼ c. sifted flour	1½ c. sugar
4 tsp. baking powder	1½ tsp. vanilla
1 tsp. salt	⅔ c. evaporated milk
½ c. shortening	Colored decorating sugar
½ c. regular margarine	

Sift together flour, baking powder and salt; set aside.

Cream together shortening, margarine and sugar in bowl until light and fluffy, using electric mixer at medium speed. Blend in vanilla.

Add dry ingredients alternately with evaporated milk to creamed mixture, beating well after each addition, using electric mixer at low speed.

Divide dough into thirds. Roll out each third on floured surface to ¼" thickness. Cut with floured 2½" round cookie cutter. Place rounds, about 1½" apart, on greased baking sheets. Sprinkle each with colored decorating sugar.

Bake in 375° oven 8 minutes, or until very lightly browned. Remove from baking sheets; cool on racks. Makes 4½ dozen.

Anise Drops

These unusual cookies are dropped onto baking sheets and left to dry overnight before baking. Very crisp and flavorful.

1¾ c. sifted flour	3 eggs
½ tsp. baking powder	1 c. plus 2 tblsp. sugar
½ tsp. salt	1 tsp. anise extract

Sift together flour, baking powder and salt; set aside.

Beat eggs in bowl until light and lemon-colored, using electric mixer at high speed. Gradually add sugar, beating well after each addition. Continue beating at medium speed for 20 minutes.

Gradually add dry ingredients to egg mixture, beating well after each addition, using electric mixer at low speed. Blend in anise extract. Drop dough by teaspoonfuls, about 1" apart, on well-greased baking sheets, swirling mixture to make cookies round. Let stand 8 hours or overnight to dry.

Bake in 325° oven 10 minutes, or until cookies are a creamy golden color, but not browned on bottom. Remove from baking sheets; cool on racks. Makes 4 dozen.

Buttermilk Cinnamon Bars

Three-layer bars featuring a brown sugary coconut-walnut crust, cinnamon-spiced cake center and thin vanilla glaze.

2 c. sifted flour	1 tsp. baking soda
1¼ c. sugar	¾ tsp. salt
¾ c. brown sugar, packed	1 tsp. ground cinnamon
½ c. regular margarine	1 c. buttermilk
½ c. chopped walnuts	1 tsp. vanilla
½ c. flaked coconut	Confectioners' Sugar Icing
1 egg	(recipe follows)

Combine flour, sugar and brown sugar in bowl. Cut in margarine until mixture forms coarse crumbs, using pastry blender. Combine 2 c. of the crumb mixture with walnuts and coconut. Press nut mixture into greased 13x9x2" baking pan.

Combine egg, baking soda, salt, cinnamon, buttermilk and vanilla in another bowl. Beat until smooth, using electric mixer at medium speed. Stir egg mixture into remaining crumb mixture, mixing just until moistened. Spread over crumb-nut layer.

Bake in 350° oven 35 minutes, or until golden brown. Cool in pan on rack 10 minutes. Prepare Confectioners' Sugar Icing. Frost slightly warm bars with Confectioners' Sugar Icing. Cool completely. Cut into 3¼x1⅛" bars. Makes 32.

Confectioners' Sugar Icing: Combine ¾ c. sifted confectioners' sugar, ½ tsp. vanilla and 4 tsp. milk in bowl; beat until smooth using a spoon.

Coconut-Nutmeg Cookies

When you want to mix up a batch of homemade cookies at the last minute, try this recipe. It's based on a yellow cake mix.

1 (18½-oz.) pkg. yellow cake mix	1 tsp. ground nutmeg
1 c. flaked coconut	1 egg
½ c. regular margarine	2 tblsp. water

Combine cake mix, coconut, margarine, nutmeg, egg and water in bowl. Mix well using a spoon. Drop mixture by teaspoonfuls, about 2" apart, on greased baking sheets.

Bake in 350° oven 12 to 15 minutes, or until golden brown. Remove from baking sheets; cool on racks. Makes 3½ dozen.

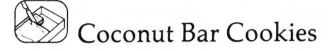 Coconut Bar Cookies

This prize-winning recipe is just the right size for small families. It turns out 16 extra-chewy bars in almost no time.

½ c. sifted flour
½ tsp. baking powder
½ tsp. salt
⅓ c. regular margarine

1 c. sugar
2 eggs
1 tsp. vanilla
1 c. flaked coconut

Sift together flour, baking powder and salt; set aside.

Cream together margarine and sugar in bowl until light and fluffy, using electric mixer at medium speed. Add eggs, one at a time, beating well after each addition. Blend in vanilla.

Gradually stir dry ingredients into creamed mixture, mixing well. Stir in coconut. Spread mixture in greased and floured 8" square baking pan.

Bake in 350° oven 30 minutes, or until no imprint remains when touched lightly with finger. Cool in pan on rack. Cut into 2" squares. Makes 16.

Ginger Cookies for a Crowd

These molasses 'n' spice cookies are extra-good, but so easy on the budget. This recipe makes 12 dozen gingery gems.

5½ c. sifted flour
3 tsp. baking soda
2 tsp. baking powder
1 tsp. salt
1 tsp. ground cinnamon
¾ tsp. ground ginger

1 c. shortening
1 c. sugar
1 egg, beaten
½ tsp. vanilla
1 c. dark molasses
½ c. strong coffee

Sift together flour, baking soda, baking powder, salt, cinnamon and ginger; set aside.

Cream together shortening and sugar in bowl until light and fluffy, using electric mixer at medium speed. Add egg and vanilla; blend well.

Beat in molasses and coffee; blend well. Gradually stir in dry ingredients, mixing well with spoon. Cover and chill in refrigerator at least 3 hours.

Divide dough into fourths. Roll out each fourth on floured surface to ¼" thickness. Cut with floured 2" round cookie cutter. Place rounds, about 2" apart, on greased baking sheets.

Bake in 400° oven 8 to 10 minutes, or until a slight imprint remains when touched lightly with finger. Remove from baking sheets; cool on racks. Makes 12 dozen.

Double Orange Cookies

For a change of pace, fill the family cookie jar with these delicately flavored morsels thinly iced with a creamy orange glaze.

2¼ c. sifted flour	2 eggs
½ tsp. baking soda	1 tblsp. grated orange rind
½ tsp. salt	½ c. orange juice
⅔ c. shortening	½ c. chopped walnuts
1 c. sugar	Orange Icing (recipe follows)

Sift together flour, baking soda and salt; set aside.

Cream together shortening and sugar in bowl until light and fluffy, using electric mixer at medium speed. Add eggs, one at a time, beating well after each addition. Stir in orange rind.

Add dry ingredients alternately with orange juice to creamed mixture, beating well after each addition, using electric mixer at low speed. Stir in walnuts. Drop mixture by tablespoonfuls, about 2" apart, on greased baking sheets.

Bake in 375° oven 10 minutes, or until golden brown. Remove from baking sheets; cool on racks. Prepare Orange Icing. Frost cookies with Orange Icing. Makes 3 dozen.

Orange Icing: Combine 2½ tblsp. regular margarine and 1½ c. sifted confectioners' sugar in bowl. Add 1½ tblsp. orange juice and 2 tsp. grated orange rind. Stir until smooth, using a spoon.

Lemon Snowballs

Delicate lemon cookies look so attractive in their light dusting of confectioners' sugar. Pretty enough for a party.

1¾ c. sifted flour	1 egg
½ tsp. baking soda	3 tblsp. lemon juice
¼ tsp. cream of tartar	1 tblsp. water
½ c. shortening	½ c. chopped walnuts
⅔ c. sugar	Confectioners' sugar
2 tsp. grated lemon rind	

Sift together flour, baking soda and cream of tartar; set aside.

Cream together shortening, sugar and lemon rind in bowl until light and fluffy, using electric mixer at medium speed. Add egg; beat well.

Add dry ingredients alternately with lemon juice and water to creamed mixture, beating well after each addition, using a spoon. Stir in walnuts. Cover and chill in refrigerator at least 2 hours.

Shape dough into 1" balls, using floured hands. Place balls, about 1" apart, on ungreased baking sheets.

Bake in 350° oven 8 to 10 minutes, or until golden brown. Remove from baking sheets. Immediately roll in confectioners' sugar. Cool on racks. Makes 3½ dozen.

Lemon Meringue Bars

These meringue-topped lemon bars look fancy, but they aren't expensive or difficult to make. They're special enough for company.

1 c. sifted flour	2 eggs, separated
¼ tsp. salt	2 tsp. grated lemon rind
½ c. regular margarine	½ c. sugar
½ c. sifted confectioners' sugar	½ c. chopped walnuts

Sift together flour and salt; set aside.

Cream together margarine and confectioners' sugar in bowl until light and fluffy, using electric mixer at medium speed. Beat in egg yolks.

Stir dry ingredients into creamed mixture, mixing well with spoon. Stir in lemon rind. Spread mixture evenly in greased 8" square baking pan.

Bake in 350° oven 10 minutes, or until lightly browned. Remove from oven and place on cooling rack. Increase oven temperature to 400°.

Beat egg whites in bowl until stiff, moist peaks form, using electric mixer at high speed. Gradually beat in sugar, beating well after each addition. Fold in chopped walnuts. Spread meringue evenly over baked layer.

Bake in 400° oven 5 to 7 minutes, or until meringue is lightly browned. Cool slightly in pan on rack. Cut into 2" squares. Cool completely. Makes 16.

Potato Chip Cookies

Potato chips give these brown sugar-flavored cookies extra crunch. Children will be delighted with them.

1 c. shortening	1 tsp. vanilla
1 c. sugar	2 c. sifted flour
1 c. brown sugar, packed	1 c. crushed potato chips
2 eggs	

Cream together shortening, sugar and brown sugar in bowl until light and fluffy, using electric mixer at medium speed. Add eggs, one at a time, beating well after each addition. Beat in vanilla.

Gradually stir flour into creamed mixture, mixing well with spoon. Stir in potato chips. Drop mixture by rounded teaspoonfuls, about 2" apart, on greased baking sheets. Flatten each in one direction with floured tines of fork.

Bake in 350° oven 12 to 15 minutes, or until golden brown. Remove from baking sheets; cool on racks. Makes about 5 dozen.

Best-Ever Butterscotch Cookies

This recipe has been a favorite with Farm Journal readers for 25 years—you'll know why once you taste these butterscotch treats.

2½ c. sifted flour	1½ c. brown sugar, packed
1 tsp. baking soda	2 eggs
½ tsp. baking powder	1 tsp. vanilla
½ tsp. salt	⅔ c. chopped walnuts
1 tblsp. vinegar	Browned Frosting
Evaporated milk	(recipe follows)
½ c. regular margarine	Walnut halves

Sift together flour, baking soda, baking powder and salt; set aside.

Place vinegar in glass measuring cup. Add enough evaporated milk to make 1 c.; set aside.

Cream together margarine and brown sugar in bowl until light and fluffy, using electric mixer at medium speed. Add eggs, one at a time, beating well after each addition. Blend in vanilla.

Add dry ingredients alternately with evaporated milk mixture to creamed mixture, mixing well after each addition, using electric mixer at low speed. Stir in walnuts. Drop mixture by rounded tablespoonfuls, about 2½" apart, on greased baking sheets.

Bake in 350° oven 10 to 12 minutes, or until lightly browned. Remove from baking sheets; cool on racks. Prepare Browned Frosting. Frost cookies with Browned Frosting and top each with a walnut half. Makes about 5 dozen.

Browned Frosting: Melt ½ c. regular margarine in saucepan over medium heat. Continue heating, stirring constantly, until margarine stops bubbling and is nut-brown in color (do not scorch). Combine margarine with 2 c. sifted confectioners' sugar and 2 tblsp. boiling water in bowl. Beat until smooth and of spreading consistency, using a spoon. (Add more boiling water if necessary.)

Overnight Macaroons

An easily prepared cookie batter that's left to mellow overnight before baking. The next morning, bake like any drop cookie.

4 c. quick-cooking oats	2 eggs, beaten
2 c. brown sugar, packed	1 tsp. salt
1 c. cooking oil	1 tsp. almond extract

Combine oats, brown sugar and oil in bowl; mix well with spoon. Cover and let stand overnight at room temperature.

The next morning, add eggs, salt and almond extract to oat mixture. Stir well and let stand 5 minutes.

Drop mixture by teaspoonfuls, about 2" apart, on greased baking sheets.

Bake in 325° oven 15 minutes, or until lightly browned. Remove from baking sheets; cool on racks. Makes 4 dozen.

Spicy Raisin Drops

These spicy lemon-glazed mounds should be called "secret cookies." The secret of their interesting flavor and color is ketchup.

2¾ c. sifted flour	2 eggs
½ tsp. baking soda	1 tsp. vanilla
⅛ tsp. salt	¼ c. ketchup
1 c. regular margarine	¾ c. raisins
½ c. sugar	½ c. chopped walnuts
½ c. brown sugar, packed	Lemon Glaze (recipe follows)

Sift together flour, baking soda and salt; set aside.

Cream together margarine, sugar and brown sugar in bowl until light and fluffy, using electric mixer at medium speed. Add eggs, one at a time, beating well after each addition. Beat in vanilla.

Gradually add dry ingredients alternately with ketchup, stirring well after each addition. Stir in raisins and walnuts. Drop mixture by heaping teaspoonfuls, about 2" apart, on greased baking sheets.

Bake in 375° oven 10 to 12 minutes, or until edges are browned and no imprint remains when touched lightly with finger. Remove from baking sheets; cool slightly on racks. Prepare Lemon Glaze. While cookies are still warm, brush with Lemon Glaze, using pastry brush. Makes about 4 dozen.

Lemon Glaze: Combine 1½ c. sifted confectioners' sugar and 2 tblsp. lemon juice in bowl. Stir until smooth.

Nut-Raisin Cookies

You can add a pretty sparkle to these raisin-walnut treats by sprinkling with sugar crystals before popping them into the oven.

1½ c. sifted flour	1 egg
½ tsp. baking soda	½ tsp. vanilla
½ tsp. salt	3 tblsp. water
½ c. shortening	½ c. chopped walnuts
½ c. brown sugar, packed	½ c. raisins
¼ c. sugar	

Sift together flour, baking soda and salt; set aside.

Cream together shortening, brown sugar and sugar in bowl until light and fluffy, using electric mixer at medium speed. Add egg and vanilla; beat well.

Add dry ingredients alternately with water to creamed mixture, stirring well after each addition. Stir in walnuts and raisins. Drop mixture by teaspoonfuls, about 2" apart, on ungreased baking sheets.

Bake in 375° oven 10 minutes, or until golden brown. Remove from baking sheets; cool on racks. Makes about 3 dozen.

Frosted Carrot Bars

Shredded carrots add color, flavor and moistness to these cinnamon-spiced bars. The creamy frosting makes them hard to resist.

2 c. sifted flour	3 c. finely shredded, pared
2 tsp. baking soda	carrots (9 medium)
2 tsp. ground cinnamon	1½ c. flaked coconut
1 tsp. salt	1½ c. chopped walnuts
4 eggs	Cream Cheese Frosting
2 c. sugar	(recipe follows)
1½ c. cooking oil	

Sift together flour, baking soda, cinnamon and salt; set aside.

Beat eggs in bowl until light and lemon-colored, using electric mixer at high speed. Gradually beat in sugar.

Add dry ingredients alternately with oil to egg mixture, beating well after each addition, using electric mixer at low speed. Stir in carrots, coconut and walnuts. Spread in 2 greased 13x9x2" baking pans.

Bake in 350° oven 25 to 30 minutes, or until no imprint remains when touched lightly with finger. Cool in pans on racks. Prepare Cream Cheese Frosting. Spread cooled bars with Cream Cheese Frosting. Cut into 3x1" bars. Makes 78.

Cream Cheese Frosting: Combine 1 (3-oz.) pkg. cream cheese (softened) with 1 tblsp. milk in bowl. Stir until smooth. Add 2½ c. sifted confectioners' sugar, 3 tblsp. milk, 1 tsp. vanilla and ⅛ tsp. salt. Beat until smooth and creamy, using a spoon.

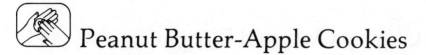

Peanut Butter-Apple Cookies

Although these resemble the traditional peanut butter cookies, they're spiced with cinnamon and flavored with grated apple.

1½ c. sifted flour	½ c. brown sugar, packed
1 tsp. baking soda	½ c. sugar
½ tsp. ground cinnamon	1 egg
½ tsp. salt	½ tsp. vanilla
½ c. shortening	1 medium apple, pared,
½ c. peanut butter	cored and grated

Sift together flour, baking soda, cinnamon and salt; set aside.

Cream together shortening, peanut butter, brown sugar and sugar in bowl until light and fluffy, using electric mixer at medium speed. Add egg and vanilla, beating well.

Gradually stir dry ingredients into creamed mixture, blending well with spoon. Stir in apple. Shape dough into 1" balls. Place balls, about 3" apart, on greased baking sheets. Flatten each with fork dipped in water, making a crisscross pattern.

Bake in 375° oven 10 minutes, or until golden brown. Remove from baking sheets; cool on racks. Makes 3½ dozen.

Coconut-Cornflake Crisps

Flaked coconut and cornflakes give cookies interesting flavor and texture. They're crunchy and chewy at the same time.

1 c. sifted flour	1 egg
1 tsp. baking powder	1 tsp. vanilla
½ c. shortening	1 c. flaked coconut
½ c. sugar	1 c. cornflakes
½ c. brown sugar, packed	Sugar

Sift together flour and baking powder; set aside.

Cream together shortening, ½ c. sugar and brown sugar in bowl until light and fluffy, using electric mixer at medium speed. Blend in egg and vanilla.

Gradually stir dry ingredients into creamed mixture, blending well. Stir in coconut and cornflakes. Cover and chill dough in refrigerator 30 minutes.

Shape dough into 1" balls. Place balls, about 3" apart, on greased baking sheets. Flatten each with greased bottom of drinking glass dipped in sugar.

Bake in 350° oven 10 minutes, or until golden brown. Remove from baking sheets; cool on racks. Makes 3½ dozen.

Chewy Oatmeal Drops

One farm woman substitutes bacon fat for half of the shortening in these cookies. Saves money and adds extra flavor.

2 c. sifted flour	1 tsp. vanilla
1 tsp. salt	1 tsp. baking soda
1 c. shortening	¼ c. boiling water
2 c. brown sugar, packed	2 c. quick-cooking oats
2 eggs	

Sift together flour and salt; set aside.

Cream together shortening and brown sugar in bowl until light and fluffy, using electric mixer at medium speed. Add eggs, one at a time, beating well after each addition. Blend in vanilla.

Combine baking soda and boiling water. Add dry ingredients alternately with soda mixture to creamed mixture, beating well after each addition, using electric mixer at low speed. Stir in oats. Drop mixture by teaspoonfuls, about 2" apart, on greased baking sheets.

Bake in 350° oven 12 minutes, or until golden brown. Cool slightly on baking sheets. Remove from baking sheets; cool on racks. Makes about 5 dozen.

Chocolate Nut Cookies

These easy-to-make refrigerator chocolate cookies recently won first prize at a county fair in Arizona. Mild chocolate flavor.

1½ c. sifted flour	1 c. sugar
½ c. baking cocoa	1 egg
½ tsp. baking soda	1 tsp. vanilla
½ tsp. salt	2 tblsp. milk
⅔ c. regular margarine	1 c. chopped walnuts

Sift together flour, cocoa, baking soda and salt; set aside.

Cream together margarine and sugar in bowl until light and fluffy, using electric mixer at medium speed. Add egg and vanilla; beat well.

Add dry ingredients alternately with milk to creamed mixture, beating well after each addition, using electric mixer at low speed. Stir in walnuts. Cover and chill dough in refrigerator at least 2 hours.

Divide dough in half. Shape each half into a 7" roll. Wrap rolls tightly in waxed paper or plastic wrap. Chill in refrigerator overnight.

Cut rolls into ¼" slices. Place rounds, about 2" apart, on greased baking sheets.

Bake in 375° oven 8 minutes, or until golden brown. Remove from baking sheets; cool on racks. Makes 6 dozen.

Homemade Cookie Mix

If your family likes chocolate cookies, keep this mix on hand. You'll be able to stir up a batch of fudgy cookies in a jiffy.

9 c. sifted flour	1 tblsp. salt
1/3 c. baking powder	1 tsp. cream of tartar
1/4 c. sugar	2 c. shortening

Sift together flour, baking powder, sugar, salt and cream of tartar 3 times. Place in large bowl. Cut in shortening until mixture resembles corn meal, using pastry blender or two knives. Store in covered container at room temperature. Use mix to make Chocolate Drop Cookies (recipe follows). Makes about 15 cups.

Chocolate Drop Cookies

You'll find these soft chocolate cookies perfect accompaniments to a dish of ice cream or sherbet.

3 c. Homemade Cookie Mix	1 egg
1 c. sugar	1 tsp. vanilla
1/3 c. baking cocoa	1/2 c. chopped walnuts
1/2 c. milk	

Combine Homemade Cookie Mix, sugar and cocoa in bowl; mix well.

Combine milk, egg and vanilla in another bowl; beat well with rotary beater. Stir milk mixture into dry ingredients; mix until well blended, using a spoon. Stir in walnuts. Drop mixture by teaspoonfuls, about 2" apart, on greased baking sheets.

Bake in 350° oven 12 to 15 minutes, or until no imprint remains when touched lightly with finger. Remove from baking sheets; cool on racks. Makes 4 dozen.

Frosted Chocolate Drops

Soft, cake-like chocolate drops swirled with a mocha frosting flavored with baking cocoa and coffee. A great after-school treat.

3⅓ c. sifted flour	2 eggs
¼ c. baking cocoa	2 tsp. vanilla
1 tsp. baking soda	1 c. milk
1 tsp. salt	Mocha Frosting
1 c. shortening	(recipe follows)
2 c. brown sugar, packed	

Sift together flour, cocoa, baking soda and salt; set aside.

Cream together shortening and brown sugar in bowl until light and fluffy, using electric mixer at medium speed. Add eggs, one at a time, beating well after each addition. Blend in vanilla.

Add dry ingredients alternately with milk to creamed mixture, beating well after each addition, using electric mixer at low speed. Drop mixture by teaspoonfuls, about 2" apart, on greased baking sheets.

Bake in 350° oven 10 minutes, or until no imprint remains when touched lightly with finger. Remove from baking sheets; cool on racks. Prepare Mocha Frosting. Frost cookies with Mocha Frosting. Makes about 7 dozen.

Mocha Frosting: Combine ¼ c. baking cocoa, ½ c. soft regular margarine, 1 tsp. vanilla and 3 c. sifted confectioners' sugar in bowl. Gradually stir in ¼ c. hot coffee. Beat until smooth and of spreading consistency, using a spoon.

Friendship Brownies

"I often make these for my family and friends," an Iowa farm woman wrote to us, "and everyone looks forward to them."

1½ c. sifted flour	2 c. sugar
½ c. baking cocoa	4 eggs
1 tsp. baking powder	2 tsp. vanilla
1 tsp. salt	1 c. chopped walnuts
⅔ c. regular margarine	Confectioners' sugar

Sift together flour, cocoa, baking powder and salt; set aside.

Cream together margarine and sugar in bowl until light and fluffy, using electric mixer at medium speed. Add eggs, one at a time, beating well after each addition. Blend in vanilla.

Gradually stir in dry ingredients, mixing well after each addition. Stir in walnuts. Spread mixture in greased 13x9x2" baking pan.

Bake in 350° oven 30 minutes, or until no imprint remains when touched lightly with finger. Cool in pan on rack. Dust with confectioners' sugar. Cut into 2¼" squares. Makes 24.

Marshmallow-Fudge Squares

Mildly flavored chocolate brownies with marshmallow topping. You'll find them easier to cut if you use a knife dipped in water.

¾ c. sifted flour	2 eggs
2 tblsp. baking cocoa	1 tsp. vanilla
¼ tsp. baking powder	½ c. chopped walnuts
¼ tsp. salt	1 (7-oz.) jar marshmallow
½ c. shortening	creme
¾ c. sugar	

Sift together flour, cocoa, baking powder and salt; set aside.

Cream together shortening and sugar in bowl until light and fluffy, using electric mixer at medium speed. Add eggs, one at a time, beating well after each addition. Blend in vanilla.

Gradually stir dry ingredients into creamed mixture, mixing well. Stir in walnuts. Spread mixture in greased and floured 12x8x2" (2-qt.) glass baking dish.

Bake in 350° oven 30 minutes, or until no imprint remains when touched lightly with finger. Immediately spread marshmallow creme evenly over top. Cool in pan on rack. Cut into 2" squares. Makes 24.

Chocolate-Coconut Brownies

A Delaware homemaker sent us the recipe for these moist milk chocolate brownies filled with lots of chewy coconut.

1½ c. sifted flour	2 c. sugar
½ c. baking cocoa	4 eggs
¼ tsp. salt	2 tsp. vanilla
½ c. regular margarine, melted	1 c. flaked coconut

Sift together flour, cocoa and salt; set aside.

Blend together melted margarine and sugar in bowl, using electric mixer at medium speed. Add eggs and vanilla; beat 2 more minutes.

Gradually add dry ingredients to creamed mixture, beating well after each addition, using electric mixer at low speed. Stir in coconut. Spread mixture in greased 13x9x2" baking pan.

Bake in 350° oven 25 minutes, or until no imprint remains when touched lightly with finger. Cool in pan on rack. Cut into 2¼" squares. Makes 24.

9 | To Give as a Gift

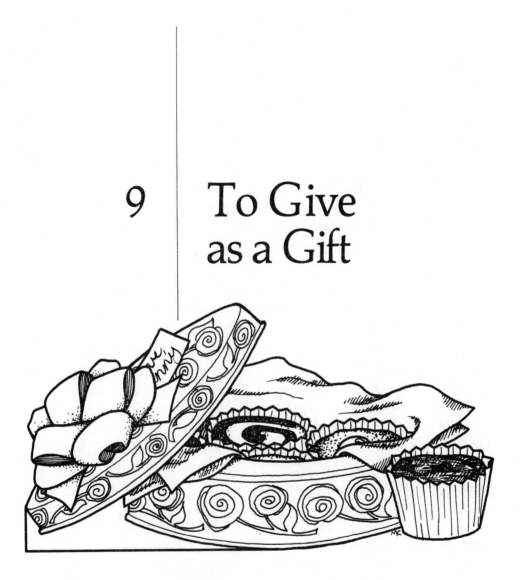

Whether it's for a birthday or a homecoming, or just because you're feeling thoughtful, a gift of cookies to a friend or relative will brighten the day for both of you.

The men on your gift list will appreciate farm-size Amish Oatmeal Cookies, generously filled with raisins and salted peanuts, or our Honest-to-Goodness Chocolate Chip Cookies, rich with morsels of chocolate and walnuts. Present a baker's dozen together with a handsome coffee mug and tie them up with a big red bow.

For Mother's Day, there's a recipe for elegant Chocolate-Filled Orange Crisps, delicately flavored press cookies sandwiched around a thin layer of melted chocolate. If she likes old-fashioned cookies, give her Crisp Gingersnaps—this version is both crunchy and chewy at the same time. Old-fashioned Fruit Bars, made with a colorful mix of candied fruit and walnuts, will appeal to every fruitcake lover. Arrange bars on a crystal cookie plate or a shiny new baking sheet, wrap in cellophane and top with a carnation or long-stemmed rose.

Children and adults alike will love our extra-rich Rocky Road Bars, a devilishly delicious concoction featuring a cake-like brownie bottom layered with a cream cheese filling, walnuts, chocolate morsels, miniature marshmallows and a creamy chocolate frosting. For peanut butter fans, there's a double treat in store: Peanut Butter Sandwich Cookies with a peanut butter cream filling. Pack them in a cookie tin with an assortment of toy cars, pens, inexpensive jewelry or balloons to surprise a child on his special day.

If your cookie gift needs to be mailed to someone who's far from home, choose soft cookies that won't crumble easily—bar cookies, brownies and drop cookies—and avoid cookies with moist fillings and sticky frostings. (For directions on packing cookies for mailing, see page 10.) Send favorites such as Soft Coconut-Oatmeal Drops, filled with chewy coconut, Soft Molasses Drops with plump raisins throughout or Apple-Pecan Drop Cookies sprinkled with confectioners' sugar.

Other good travelers are Walnut-Cinnamon Squares, unique bar cookies that can be flavored eight different ways, and Old-Fashioned Hermits, spicy drop cookies much like the ones sailors enjoyed during long ocean voyages. Chocolate-lovers will appreciate Chewy Coconut-Cherry Brownies and Chocolate Brownie Sticks—two recipes sent to us by Midwest farm women who have mailed these favorites to college students and out-of-town families.

Don't wait for a special occasion to surprise someone with a gift of homemade cookies: Cookies are a pleasure to give and a treat to receive any day of the year.

Pecan Drop Cookies

A Texas woman packs these soft drop cookies into decorated coffee cans and takes them to nursing homes several times a year.

½ c. butter or regular
  margarine
½ c. shortening
1 c. sifted confectioners'
  sugar

2 tsp. vanilla
2½ c. sifted cake flour
1 c. coarsely chopped pecans
Confectioners' sugar

Cream together butter, shortening and 1 c. confectioners' sugar in bowl until light and fluffy, using electric mixer at medium speed.

Add vanilla and cake flour, mixing well with spoon. Stir in pecans. Drop mixture by teaspoonfuls, about 2" apart, on greased baking sheets.

Bake in 325° oven 25 minutes, or until delicately browned. Remove from baking sheets; cool on racks. Roll in confectioners' sugar. Makes about 4 dozen.

Apple-Pecan Drop Cookies

This cookie is a good choice for mailing because it's not brittle. Pack tightly in a coffee can or cookie tin to keep fresh for weeks.

3 c. sifted flour
2 tsp. baking powder
1 tsp. baking soda
¼ c. shortening
1 c. brown sugar, packed
1 c. sugar
3 eggs

2 tsp. vanilla
½ c. dairy sour cream
2 c. finely chopped, pared
  apples
½ c. chopped pecans
Confectioners' sugar

Sift together flour, baking powder and baking soda; set aside.

Cream together shortening, brown sugar and sugar in bowl until light and fluffy, using electric mixer at medium speed. Add eggs, one at a time, beating well after each addition. Blend in vanilla and sour cream.

Gradually stir dry ingredients into creamed mixture, blending well. Stir in apples and pecans. Drop mixture by rounded teaspoonfuls, about 2" apart, on greased baking sheets.

Bake in 350° oven 12 minutes, or until lightly browned. Remove from baking sheets; cool on racks. Sprinkle each with confectioners' sugar. Makes 6 dozen.

Old-Fashioned Raisin Drop Cookies

"My son is in the service overseas and I often send these cookies to him because they stay fresh for weeks," wrote a Wisconsin woman.

2 c. raisins	¼ tsp. ground nutmeg
1 c. water	¼ tsp. ground allspice
1 tsp. baking soda	1 c. shortening
4 c. sifted flour	2 c. sugar
1 tsp. baking powder	3 eggs
2 tsp. salt	1 tsp. vanilla
1½ tsp. ground cinnamon	1 c. chopped walnuts

Combine raisins and water in 2-qt. saucepan. Cook over medium heat until mixture comes to a boil. Cover and simmer 5 minutes. Remove from heat. Drain cooking liquid, reserving ½ c. Combine raisins with ½ c. reserved liquid. Cool to lukewarm and stir in baking soda; set aside.

Sift together flour, baking powder, salt, cinnamon, nutmeg and allspice; set aside.

Cream together shortening and sugar in bowl until light and fluffy, using electric mixer at medium speed. Add eggs, one at a time, beating well after each addition. Blend in vanilla and raisin mixture.

Gradually stir dry ingredients into creamed mixture, mixing well. Stir in walnuts. Drop mixture by rounded teaspoonfuls, about 3" apart, on greased baking sheets.

Bake in 400° oven 8 to 10 minutes, or until golden brown. Remove from baking sheets; cool on racks. Makes 6½ dozen.

Sesame Cookie Crisps

Here's the perfect cookie for someone without a sweet tooth. These crunchy cookies are rolled in sesame seeds and cornflakes.

2 c. sifted flour	1 c. sugar
½ tsp. baking soda	1 egg
¼ tsp. salt	1 tsp. vanilla
1 c. butter or regular	¾ c. cornflake crumbs
margarine	¼ c. sesame seeds

Sift together flour, baking soda and salt; set aside.

Cream together butter and sugar in bowl until light and fluffy, using electric mixer at medium speed. Add egg and vanilla; beat well.

Gradually stir dry ingredients into creamed mixture, blending well. Stir in ½ c. of the cornflake crumbs. Shape dough into 1" balls.

Combine remaining ¼ c. cornflake crumbs and sesame seeds. Roll balls in sesame seed mixture. Place balls, about 2" apart, on ungreased baking sheets.

Bake in 375° oven 12 to 14 minutes, or until lightly browned. Remove from baking sheets; cool on racks. Makes 4 dozen.

Toffee Cookie Squares

Both chewy and crunchy, these brown sugar bar cookies are spread with melted chocolate and sprinkled with walnuts. Extra yummy!

2 c. sifted flour	1 egg yolk
½ tsp. salt	1 tsp. vanilla
½ c. butter or regular	1 (6-oz.) pkg. semisweet
margarine	chocolate pieces
½ c. shortening	½ c. chopped walnuts
1 c. brown sugar, packed	

Sift together flour and salt; set aside.

Cream together butter, shortening and brown sugar in bowl until light and fluffy, using electric mixer at medium speed. Add egg yolk and vanilla, beating well.

Gradually stir dry ingredients into creamed mixture, mixing well. Pat mixture into lightly greased 15½x10½x1″ jelly roll pan.

Bake in 325° oven 15 to 20 minutes, or until golden brown. Cool slightly in pan on rack.

Melt chocolate pieces over hot water, stirring until smooth. Spread chocolate evenly over warm bars. Sprinkle with walnuts. Cut into 2″ squares. Cool completely. Makes 35.

Southern Praline Bars

The flavor of these candy-like cookies resembles the traditional Southern praline. Very rich and downright delicious!

1½ c. sifted flour	2 eggs
1 tsp. baking powder	2 tsp. vanilla
1 tsp. salt	¾ c. chopped pecans
½ c. lard	Praline Frosting (recipe
1½ c. brown sugar, packed	follows)

Sift together flour, baking powder and salt; set aside.

Melt lard in 2-qt. saucepan over medium heat. Remove from heat. Add brown sugar, eggs and vanilla. Beat well, using a spoon. Stir in dry ingredients, mixing well. Stir in pecans. Spread mixture in greased 13x9x2″ baking pan.

Bake in 350° oven 25 to 30 minutes, or until golden brown. Cool slightly in pan on rack. Prepare Praline Frosting. Spread warm bars with Praline Frosting. Cool completely. Cut into 3x1″ bars. Makes 39.

Praline Frosting: Combine 2 tblsp. butter or regular margarine, ¼ c. brown sugar (packed) and 2 tblsp. light cream in saucepan. Cook over medium heat until butter is melted. Stir until smooth. Stir in 1 c. sifted confectioners' sugar. Beat until smooth, adding more confectioners' sugar, if necessary, to make frosting of spreading consistency.

American Sand Tarts

Each thin buttery round is decorated with a nut and a sprinkle of cinnamon. They look especially attractive in a doily-lined box.

1 c. butter or regular margarine	4 c. sifted flour
2¼ c. sugar	1 egg white, slightly beaten
2 eggs	Almonds or peanuts
	Ground cinnamon

Cream together butter and sugar in bowl until light and fluffy, using electric mixer at medium speed. Beat in eggs, one at a time, beating well after each addition.

Gradually stir flour into creamed mixture, mixing well. Cover and chill dough in refrigerator several hours.

Divide dough into fourths. Roll out each fourth on floured surface to ⅛" thickness. Cut with floured 2½" round cookie cutter. Place rounds, about 2" apart, on greased baking sheets. Brush centers of rounds with egg white and place one half of an almond or peanut in center of each. Brush again with egg white and sprinkle each cookie with a little cinnamon.

Bake in 400° oven 5 minutes, or until golden brown. Remove from baking sheets; cool on racks. Makes about 12 dozen.

Black Walnut Bars

Two-layer bar cookie featuring a crisp caramel-flavored bottom layer and brown sugary top with chopped black walnuts throughout.

2 c. sifted flour	2 tsp. vanilla
1 c. brown sugar, packed	2 tblsp. flour
1 c. butter or regular margarine	½ tsp. baking powder
4 eggs	½ tsp. salt
2 c. brown sugar, packed	2 c. chopped black walnuts

Mix together 2 c. flour and 1 c. brown sugar in bowl. Cut in butter until crumbs form, using pastry blender or two knives. Press mixture into well-greased 15½x10½x1" jelly roll pan.

Bake in 350° oven 10 minutes. Remove from oven and cool slightly on rack, about 10 minutes. Turn oven temperature to 375°.

Beat eggs in bowl until light and lemon-colored, using electric mixer at high speed. Gradually beat in 2 c. brown sugar and vanilla.

Stir together 2 tblsp. flour, baking powder and salt. Add to egg mixture along with walnuts. Spread mixture over baked crust in pan.

Bake in 375° oven about 20 minutes, or until lightly browned. Cool in pan on rack. Cut into 2½x1½" bars. Makes 48.

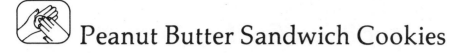

Peanut Butter Sandwich Cookies

Who could resist double-good peanut butter cookies like these? Surprise a young friend with them soon.

3 c. sifted flour	1 c. brown sugar, packed
2 tsp. baking soda	2 eggs
¼ tsp. salt	1 c. peanut butter
1 c. butter or regular	1 tsp. vanilla
margarine	Peanut Butter Filling (recipe
1 c. sugar	follows)

Sift together flour, baking soda and salt; set aside.

Cream together butter, sugar and brown sugar in bowl until light and fluffy, using electric mixer at medium speed. Add eggs, one at a time, beating well after each addition. Beat in peanut butter and vanilla.

Gradually stir dry ingredients into creamed mixture, mixing well. Form mixture into 1" balls. Place balls, about 2" apart, on greased baking sheets. Press each with floured tines of fork, making crisscross pattern.

Bake in 375° oven 8 minutes, or until golden brown. Remove from baking sheets; cool on racks. Prepare Peanut Butter Filling. When cookies are completely cooled, spread the bottom of one cookie with Peanut Butter Filling. Place another cookie on top, forming sandwich cookie. Makes 3½ dozen sandwich cookies.

Peanut Butter Filling: Combine ½ c. peanut butter, 3 c. sifted confectioners' sugar, 4 tblsp. milk and 1 tsp. vanilla in bowl. Beat until smooth and creamy, using electric mixer at medium speed.

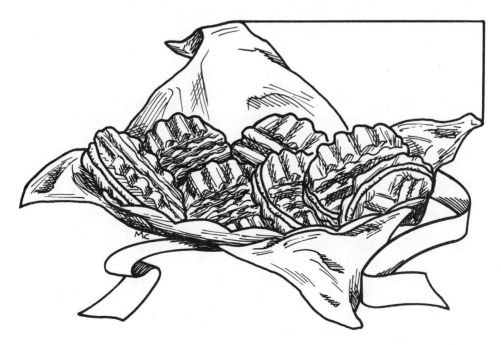

Basic Sugar Cookies

Next time you need a hostess gift, arrange two dozen of these sugar-topped cookies in a decorated coffee can tied with ribbon.

2½ c. sifted flour	1 c. sugar
3 tsp. baking powder	2 eggs
½ tsp. salt	1 tsp. vanilla
½ c. butter or regular margarine	Sugar

Sift together flour, baking powder and salt; set aside.

Cream together butter and 1 c. sugar in bowl until light and fluffy, using electric mixer at medium speed. Add eggs, one at a time, beating well after each addition. Add vanilla.

Gradually stir dry ingredients into creamed mixture, mixing well. Cover and chill dough in refrigerator 1 hour.

Divide dough in half. Roll out each half on lightly floured surface to ¼" thickness. Cut with floured 2" cookie cutter. Place rounds, about 2" apart, on ungreased baking sheets. Sprinkle tops with sugar.

Bake in 400° oven 8 to 10 minutes, or until golden brown. Remove from baking sheets; cool on racks. Makes 4½ dozen.

Buttery-Rich Shortbread

A superb cookie: This is one of the finest shortbreads ever tested in our Farm Journal Test Kitchens.

2 c. sifted flour	1 c. butter
¼ tsp. baking powder	½ c. sifted confectioners' sugar
¼ tsp. salt	

Sift together flour, baking powder and salt; set aside.

Cream together butter and confectioners' sugar in bowl until light and fluffy, using electric mixer at medium speed.

Gradually stir dry ingredients into creamed mixture, mixing well. Cover and chill in refrigerator 1 hour.

Roll out dough on floured surface to 9" square, about ¼" thick. Cut into 24 (2¼x1½") rectangles. Place rectangles, about 1" apart, on ungreased baking sheets. Prick each 3 times with tines of fork.

Bake in 300° oven 20 minutes, or until edges are lightly browned. Remove from baking sheets; cool on racks. Makes 24.

 # Raisin Shortbread Bars

Here's another version of shortbread. The topping is amply studded with raisins and walnuts on a rich buttery crust.

1 c. sifted flour	1 tsp. baking powder
¼ c. brown sugar, packed	1 tsp. vanilla
½ c. butter or regular	1 tsp. grated orange rind
margarine	½ tsp. salt
2 eggs	1½ c. chopped raisins
1 c. brown sugar, packed	1 c. chopped walnuts
2 tblsp. flour	Confectioners' sugar

Combine 1 c. flour and ¼ c. brown sugar in bowl. Cut in butter until mixture is crumbly, using pastry blender. Press crumb mixture into bottom of ungreased 13x9x2″ baking pan.

Bake in 375° oven 8 to 10 minutes, or until golden brown. Cool in pan on rack.

Beat eggs until foamy, using electric mixer at high speed. Add 1 c. brown sugar, 2 tblsp. flour, baking powder, vanilla, orange rind and salt; beat until thick and lemon-colored. Stir in raisins and walnuts. Spread mixture over cooled baked crust.

Bake in 375° oven 20 minutes, or until cake tester or wooden pick inserted in center comes out clean. Cool slightly in pan on rack. While still slightly warm, cut into 3¼x1⅛″ bars. Sprinkle with confectioners' sugar. Makes 32.

Raisin Meringue Kisses

Unique meringues, loaded with crispy cornflakes, raisins and coconut, keep best when stored in airtight container.

4 egg whites	2 c. cornflakes
¼ tsp. salt	1 c. chopped raisins
1 c. sugar	½ c. flaked coconut
1 tsp. vanilla	

Beat egg whites with salt in mixing bowl until soft peaks form, using electric mixer at high speed. Gradually add sugar, beating until very stiff peaks form. Beat in vanilla.

Stir in cornflakes, raisins and coconut. Drop mixture by heaping teaspoonfuls, about 2" apart, on greased baking sheets.

Bake in 350° oven 20 minutes, or until golden brown. Immediately remove from baking sheets; cool on racks. Makes 3½ dozen.

Six-in-One Refrigerator Cookies

This big-batch recipe turns out 18 dozen cookies in six different flavors, enough to celebrate several special occasions.

4 c. unsifted flour	½ c. shredded coconut
1 tsp. baking soda	½ c. finely chopped pecans
½ tsp. salt	1 tsp. ground cinnamon
2 c. butter or regular margarine	½ tsp. ground nutmeg
1 c. sugar	1 (1-oz.) square unsweetened chocolate, melted and cooled
1 c. brown sugar, packed	
2 eggs	¼ c. finely chopped red candied cherries
1 tsp. vanilla	

Mix together flour, baking soda and salt; set aside.

Cream together butter, sugar and brown sugar in bowl until light and fluffy, using electric mixer at medium speed. Add eggs, one at a time, beating well after each addition. Blend in vanilla.

Gradually stir dry ingredients into creamed mixture, mixing well.

Divide dough into 6 (1-c.) portions. Add coconut to one part, pecans to second, cinnamon and nutmeg to third, melted chocolate to fourth, and candied cherries to fifth. Leave the last portion plain. Cover and chill in refrigerator 30 minutes or longer.

Shape dough into 6 rolls, about 1¾" in diameter. Wrap tightly in plastic wrap or waxed paper and chill in refrigerator overnight.

Cut rolls into ⅛" slices. Place rounds, about 2" apart, on greased baking sheets.

Bake in 375° oven 10 to 12 minutes, or until golden brown. Remove from baking sheets; cool on racks. Makes 18 dozen.

Walnut-Cinnamon Squares

These simply delightful bars look fancy, but aren't difficult to make. You have a choice of eight different flavors.

2 c. sifted flour	1 c. sugar
1 tsp. ground cinnamon	1 egg, separated
1 c. butter or regular margarine	1 c. finely chopped walnuts

Sift together flour and cinnamon; set aside.

Cream together butter and sugar in bowl until light and fluffy, using electric mixer at medium speed. Add egg yolk; beat well.

Stir dry ingredients into creamed mixture, mixing well. Spread dough evenly in greased 15½x10½x1" jelly roll pan.

Beat egg white slightly with fork. Brush egg white over top of dough. Smooth surface with fingertips. Sprinkle walnuts over dough and press in gently with fingers.

Bake in 275° oven 1 hour, or until golden brown. While still warm, cut into 1½" squares. Cool in pan on rack. Makes 60.

Variations:

Austrian Almond Squares: Prepare dough as directed, but substitute 1 tsp. ground nutmeg for cinnamon and 1 c. chopped or sliced almonds for walnuts. Bake as directed.

Orange-Pecan Flats: Prepare dough as directed, but substitute 1 tblsp. grated orange rind for cinnamon and 1 c. chopped pecans for walnuts. Bake as directed.

Turkish Cardamoms: Prepare dough as directed, but substitute 1 tsp. ground cardamom for cinnamon and 1 c. chopped filberts or hazelnuts for walnuts. Bake as directed.

Macadamia Nut Gingers: Prepare dough as directed, but substitute 1 tsp. ground ginger for cinnamon and 1 c. finely chopped roasted macadamia nuts for walnuts. Bake as directed.

Peanut Salts: Prepare dough as directed, but substitute 1 c. brown sugar (packed) for white sugar. Omit cinnamon and substitute 1 c. chopped roasted peanuts for walnuts. Bake as directed.

Brown Sugar Spice Crisps: Prepare dough as directed, but substitute 1 c. brown sugar (packed) for white sugar. Increase ground cinnamon to 1½ tsp. and add ¾ tsp. ground nutmeg, ¾ tsp. ground ginger and ¼ tsp. ground cloves. Omit walnuts, topping dough only with egg white. Bake as directed.

Lemon or Lime Sugar Crisps: Prepare dough as directed, but substitute 2 tblsp. grated lemon or lime rind for cinnamon. Omit walnuts, topping dough only with egg white. Bake as directed.

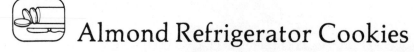

Almond Refrigerator Cookies

If you have a little extra time, make up several batches of this buttery cookie dough. The dough can be refrigerated up to three days.

2 c. sifted flour	½ tsp. almond extract
¾ c. sugar	1 egg yolk
¾ tsp. salt	1 tblsp. water
1 c. butter or regular	½ c. blanched whole
margarine	almonds, split into halves
½ tsp. vanilla	

Sift together flour, sugar and salt into bowl. Cut in butter until mixture is crumbly, using a pastry blender. Add vanilla and almond extract; mix with hands.

Divide dough in half. Shape each half into a long roll, 1½" in diameter. Wrap rolls tightly in plastic wrap or waxed paper. Chill in refrigerator 1 hour or until firm.

Cut rolls into ¼" slices. Place rounds, about 1" apart, on lightly greased baking sheets. Combine egg yolk and water; mix well. Brush top of each cookie lightly with egg yolk mixture. Press an almond half in center of each.

Bake in 400° oven 8 to 10 minutes, or until lightly browned. Cool slightly on baking sheets. Remove to cooling racks. Cool completely. Makes about 6½ dozen.

Lemon-Almond Riches

Each of these crunchy, lemony rounds is brightly decorated with almonds and a candied cherry.

2 c. sifted flour	1 tsp. water
¼ tsp. salt	Sugar
1 c. butter or regular	2 c. whole blanched almonds
margarine	(about ¾ lb.)
1 c. sugar	1 (4-oz.) pkg. red candied
1 egg, separated	cherries, cut into halves
1 tblsp. grated lemon rind	(about 1 c.)
½ c. finely chopped	
blanched almonds	

Sift together flour and salt; set aside.

Cream together butter and sugar in bowl until light and fluffy, using electric mixer at medium speed. Add egg yolk and lemon rind; beat well.

Stir dry ingredients into creamed mixture, mixing well. Stir in chopped almonds.

Divide dough in half. Roll out each half on floured surface to ¼" thickness. Cut with floured 2" round cookie cutter. Place rounds, about 2" apart, on greased baking sheets.

Slightly beat egg white and combine with water. Brush cookies with egg white mixture. Sprinkle each lightly with sugar. Press whole almonds on top of each round to resemble daisy petals, 5 almonds to a round. Place a cherry half in center of each.

Bake in 325° oven 15 minutes, or until browned around the edges. Remove from baking sheets; cool on racks. Makes 3½ dozen.

Tangy Lemon Squares

What hostess wouldn't be pleased with these buttery-rich bars topped with a tangy lemon filling and sprinkled with confectioners' sugar?

1 c. sifted flour	1 c. sugar
¼ c. sifted confectioners' sugar	3 tblsp. lemon juice
	2 tblsp. flour
½ c. butter or regular margarine	½ tsp. baking powder
	¼ tsp. grated lemon rind
2 eggs	Confectioners' sugar

Combine 1 c. flour and ¼ c. confectioners' sugar in bowl. Cut in butter until mixture forms fine crumbs, using pastry blender. Pat mixture into bottom of well-greased 9" square baking pan.

Bake in 350° oven 15 to 18 minutes, or until golden brown.

Meanwhile, combine eggs, sugar, lemon juice, 2 tblsp. flour, baking powder and lemon rind in bowl. Beat until smooth, using electric mixer at high speed. Pour mixture over warm baked crust.

Bake in 350° oven 25 minutes, or until no imprint remains when touched lightly with finger. Cool in pan on rack. When completely cooled, sprinkle with confectioners' sugar. Cut into 2¼" squares. Makes 16.

Chocolate-Filled Orange Crisps

Dozens of these extra-special tea cookies can be easily prepared by forcing the orange-flavored dough through a cookie press.

1 c. butter or regular margarine	2⅓ c. sifted flour
¾ c. sugar	3 drops red food coloring
1 egg	9 drops yellow food coloring
1½ tsp. grated orange rind	4 (1-oz.) squares
½ tsp. vanilla	semisweet chocolate,
½ tsp. salt	melted and cooled

Cream together butter and sugar in bowl until light and fluffy, using electric mixer at medium speed. Add egg, orange rind, vanilla and salt, beating until smooth.

Gradually stir flour into creamed mixture, mixing well. Blend in red and yellow food coloring.

Fit bar cookie design into cookie press. Placing one half of the dough in cookie press at a time, force dough through press in long strips, about 1" apart, on ungreased baking sheets. Cut long strips into small pieces at 1½" intervals.

Bake in 375° oven 6 to 7 minutes, or until lightly browned around the edges. Cut through strips at 1½" intervals again. Remove from baking sheets; cool on racks.

Spread the bottom of one half of the cookies with melted chocolate. Top with another cookie, forming a sandwich. Makes 4½ dozen.

Soft Molasses Drops

If you plan to send a homemade gift overseas, these soft cake-like drops are good mailers. They keep well, too.

¾ c. butter or regular margarine	2 tblsp. molasses
1½ c. brown sugar, packed	1 tsp. baking soda
3 eggs	3 c. sifted flour
1 tsp. vanilla	1 c. raisins

Cream together butter and brown sugar in bowl until light and fluffy, using electric mixer at medium speed. Add eggs, one at a time, beating well after each addition. Beat in vanilla.

Combine molasses and baking soda. Add molasses mixture to creamed mixture, mixing well. Gradually stir in flour. Stir in raisins. Drop mixture by teaspoonfuls, about 2" apart, on greased baking sheets.

Bake in 350° oven 8 minutes, or until lightly browned. Remove from baking sheets; cool on racks. Makes about 6 dozen.

Amish Oatmeal Cookies

Make these old-fashioned, man-sized cookies for Dad or Grandfather on his birthday or on Father's Day. What a great treat!

1½ c. raisins	1½ c. lard or shortening
1 c. salted peanuts	3 c. sugar
6 c. sifted flour	2 c. quick-cooking oats
3 tsp. baking powder	3 tsp. baking soda
1 tsp. salt	1 c. buttermilk
1 tsp. ground cinnamon	½ c. molasses
1 tsp. ground nutmeg	4 eggs

Grind raisins and peanuts in food grinder, using medium blade; set aside.

Sift together flour, baking powder, salt, cinnamon and nutmeg into very large bowl or dishpan. Cut in lard until mixture forms fine crumbs, using pastry blender. Add ground raisin mixture, sugar and oats. Mix well, using hands if necessary.

Dissolve baking soda in buttermilk in small bowl. Add molasses and 3 of the eggs to buttermilk mixture. Beat with rotary beater until blended.

Add buttermilk mixture to flour mixture; mix well with spoon. Drop mixture by heaping tablespoonfuls or a small ice cream scoop, about 3" apart, on greased baking sheets. Flatten each with bottom of drinking glass dipped in flour to 2½" round.

Beat remaining egg in small bowl until blended. Brush top of each round with egg.

Bake in 375° oven 8 to 10 minutes, or until golden brown. Remove from baking sheets; cool on racks. Makes 4½ dozen.

Chewy Oatmeal Cookies

Extra-chewy oatmeal cookies are hard to resist—especially when they're chock-full of coconut as these are.

2 c. sifted flour	1 c. sugar
1 tsp. baking powder	2 eggs
1 tsp. baking soda	1 tsp. vanilla
1 tsp. salt	1½ c. quick-cooking oats
1 c. shortening	1 c. flaked coconut
1 c. brown sugar, packed	

Sift together flour, baking powder, baking soda and salt; set aside.

Cream together shortening, brown sugar and sugar in bowl until light and fluffy, using electric mixer at medium speed. Add eggs, one at a time, beating well after each addition. Blend in vanilla.

Gradually add dry ingredients to creamed mixture, mixing well with spoon. Stir in oats and coconut. Shape dough into 1" balls. Place balls, about 2" apart, on greased baking sheets.

Bake in 350° oven 10 to 12 minutes, or until golden brown. Remove from baking sheets; cool on racks. Makes about 5 dozen.

Pecan-Oatmeal Cookies

Why not wrap up a dozen of these crackle-topped oatmeals as a surprise package for your letter carrier?

1½ c. sifted flour	1 c. sugar
1 tsp. baking powder	2 eggs
1 tsp. baking soda	1 tsp. vanilla
¼ tsp. salt	3 c. quick-cooking oats
1 c. butter or regular	Confectioners' sugar
margarine	48 small pecan halves
1 c. brown sugar, packed	

Sift together flour, baking powder, baking soda and salt; set aside.

Cream together butter, brown sugar and sugar in bowl until light and fluffy, using electric mixer at medium speed. Add eggs, one at a time, beating well after each addition. Blend in vanilla.

Gradually stir dry ingredients into creamed mixture, blending well. Stir in oats. Cover and chill in refrigerator 1 hour.

Shape dough into 1" balls. Place balls, about 3" apart, on greased baking sheets. Flatten each with greased bottom of drinking glass dipped in confectioners' sugar. Place a pecan half on top of each.

Bake in 375° oven 12 minutes, or until golden brown. Remove from baking sheets; cool on racks. Makes 4 dozen.

Soft Coconut Oatmeal Drops

Here's a favorite in our Farm Journal Test Kitchens. Why not surprise a friend with a dozen of these soft, cake-like oatmeals?

1¼ c. sifted flour	½ c. sugar
1 tsp. baking powder	2 eggs
1 tsp. baking soda	1 tsp. vanilla
½ tsp. salt	1 tblsp. milk
½ c. shortening	1 c. flaked coconut
½ c. brown sugar, packed	1 c. quick-cooking oats

Sift together flour, baking powder, baking soda and salt; set aside.

Cream together shortening, brown sugar and sugar in bowl until light and fluffy, using electric mixer at medium speed. Add eggs, one at a time, beating well after each addition. Blend in vanilla and milk.

Gradually stir dry ingredients into creamed mixture, blending well. Stir in coconut and oats. Drop mixture by rounded teaspoonfuls, about 3" apart, on greased baking sheets.

Bake in 350° oven 10 to 12 minutes, or until golden brown. Remove from baking sheets; cool on racks. Makes about 3½ dozen.

Refrigerator Oatmeal Cookies

Since oatmeal cookies are such favorites, we've included this refrigerator recipe. So simple: Just slice and bake at the last minute.

1½ c. sifted flour	1 c. sugar
1 tsp. baking soda	2 eggs
½ tsp. salt	1 tsp. vanilla
½ c. butter or regular	3 c. quick-cooking oats
margarine	½ c. chopped walnuts
½ c. shortening	½ c. flaked coconut
1 c. brown sugar, packed	

Sift together flour, baking soda and salt; set aside.

Cream together butter, shortening, brown sugar and sugar in bowl until light and fluffy, using electric mixer at medium speed. Add eggs, one at a time, beating well after each addition. Blend in vanilla.

Gradually stir dry ingredients into creamed mixture, blending well. Stir in oats. Divide dough in half. Stir walnuts into one half. Shape into 8" roll, about 1½" in diameter. Wrap in waxed paper.

Stir coconut into other half. Shape into 8" roll, about 1½" in diameter. Wrap in waxed paper. Chill wrapped rolls in refrigerator overnight.

Cut each roll into 24 slices, about ⅓" thick. Place slices, about 2" apart, on greased baking sheets.

Bake in 375° oven 10 minutes, or until golden brown. Remove from baking sheets; cool on racks. Makes 4 dozen.

Glazed Pineapple Bars

These vanilla-glazed bars have a tropical flavor. They're a perfect choice for those friends who have a real sweet tooth.

2¼ c. sifted flour	2 eggs
1½ c. sugar	1 tsp. vanilla
1½ tsp. baking soda	1⅓ c. flaked coconut
½ tsp. salt	½ c. chopped walnuts
1 (20-oz.) can crushed pineapple in juice	Vanilla Glaze (recipe follows)

Sift together flour, sugar, baking soda and salt into bowl. Add undrained pineapple, eggs and vanilla. Beat until smooth, using electric mixer at medium speed. Pour batter into greased 15½x10½x1" jelly roll pan. Sprinkle with coconut and walnuts.

Bake in 350° oven 20 minutes, or until no imprint remains when touched lightly with finger. Cool slightly in pan on rack. Prepare Vanilla Glaze. While bars are still warm, pour Vanilla Glaze over all. Cool completely. Cut into 4x1" bars. Makes 40.

Vanilla Glaze: Combine ¾ c. sugar, ½ c. butter or regular margarine and ¼ c. evaporated milk in 2-qt. saucepan; mix well. Cook over medium heat until mixture comes to a boil. Remove from heat.

Rich Anise Cookies

Unusual anise-flavored cookies, made with butter and cream cheese, sent to us by a Midwest dairy farmer's wife.

2½ c. sifted flour	1 c. sugar
½ tsp. salt	1 egg yolk
1 c. butter or regular margarine	½ tsp. vanilla
1 (3-oz.) pkg. cream cheese, softened	2 tsp. anise seeds, crushed

Sift together flour and salt; set aside.

Cream together butter, cream cheese and sugar in bowl until light and fluffy, using electric mixer at medium speed. Add egg yolk and vanilla; beat well.

Gradually stir dry ingredients into creamed mixture, mixing well. Stir in anise seeds.

Divide dough in half. Shape each half into a roll, 2" in diameter. Wrap rolls tightly in waxed paper. Chill in refrigerator at least 2 hours or overnight.

Cut rolls into ⅛" slices. Place rounds, about 2" apart, on ungreased baking sheets.

Bake in 350° oven 10 to 12 minutes, or until edges start to brown. Remove from baking sheets; cool on racks. Makes about 6 dozen.

Crisp Gingersnaps

Old-fashioned and sharply spiced, these gingersnaps are crisp and chewy at the same time. Pack in a gingham napkin.

2 c. sifted flour	¾ c. shortening
2 tsp. baking soda	1 c. sugar
¼ tsp. salt	¼ c. molasses
1 tsp. ground cinnamon	1 egg
1 tsp. ground ginger	Sugar
¼ tsp. ground cloves	

Sift together flour, baking soda, salt, cinnamon, ginger and cloves; set aside.

Cream together shortening and 1 c. sugar in bowl until light and fluffy, using electric mixer at medium speed. Blend in molasses and egg.

Gradually stir dry ingredeints into creamed mixture, blending well. Shape dough into 1¼" balls. Roll in sugar. Place balls, about 2" apart, on greased baking sheets.

Bake in 375° oven 12 minutes, or until a slight imprint remains when touched lightly with finger. Remove from baking sheets; cool on racks. Makes 3½ dozen.

Honest-to-Goodness Chocolate Chip Cookies

This all-time favorite, filled with lots of chocolate chips and walnuts, is still the most popular cookie in America.

2½ c. sifted flour	1 c. brown sugar, packed
1 tsp. baking soda	2 eggs
1 tsp. salt	1 tsp. vanilla
1 c. butter or regular	1 (12-oz.) pkg. semisweet
margarine	chocolate pieces
½ c. sugar	½ c. chopped walnuts

Sift together flour, baking soda and salt; set aside.

Cream together butter, sugar and brown sugar in bowl until light and fluffy, using electric mixer at medium speed. Add eggs, one at a time, beating well after each addition. Beat in vanilla.

Gradually stir dry ingredients into creamed mixture, mixing well. Stir in chocolate pieces and walnuts. Drop mixture by rounded teaspoonfuls, about 2" apart, on greased baking sheets.

Bake in 375° oven 8 to 10 minutes, or until golden brown. Remove from baking sheets; cool on racks. Makes 4 dozen.

Chocolate Sandwich Cookies

"My kids love the soft marshmallowy filling in these cake-like choco-late sandwich cookies," a Georgia farm woman recently wrote to us.

2 c. sifted flour
½ c. baking cocoa
1½ tsp. baking soda
½ tsp. baking powder
½ tsp. salt
½ c. butter or regular
    margarine

1 c. sugar
1 egg
1 tsp. vanilla
1 c. milk
Marshmallow Filling (recipe
    follows)

Sift together flour, cocoa, baking soda, baking powder and salt; set aside.

Cream together butter and sugar in bowl until light and fluffy, using electric mixer at medium speed. Add egg and vanilla; beat until well blended.

Add dry ingredients alternately with milk to creamed mixture, beating well after each addition, using electric mixer at low speed. Drop mixture by rounded tablespoonfuls, about 3" apart, on greased baking sheets. Make an indentation in center of each with back of spoon. (This helps cookies to flatten during baking.)

Bake in 400° oven 7 minutes, or until a slight imprint remains when touched lightly with finger. Remove from baking sheets; cool on racks. Prepare Marshmallow Filling. Spread the bottom of one cookie with Marshmallow Filling. Top with another cookie to form a sandwich. Makes 2½ dozen sandwich cookies.

Marshmallow Filling: Cream together ½ c. shortening and 2 c. sifted confectioners' sugar in bowl, using electric mixer at medium speed. Beat in 1 (7-oz.) jar marshmallow creme, 1 tsp. vanilla and 1 tblsp. milk. Beat until smooth and creamy.

Chocolate Cookies

These chocolate cookies are winners whether you serve them plain or frosted with butter cream icing and topped with a cherry.

¾ c. sifted flour	1 tsp. vanilla
¾ tsp. salt	3 (1-oz.) squares
½ c. shortening	unsweetened chocolate,
1 c. sugar	melted and cooled
2 eggs	

Sift together flour and salt; set aside.

Cream together shortening and sugar in bowl until light and fluffy, using electric mixer at medium speed. Add eggs, one at a time, beating well after each addition. Beat in vanilla.

Gradually add dry ingredients to creamed mixture, beating well after each addition, using electric mixer at low speed. Blend in chocolate. Drop mixture by teaspoonfuls, about 2″ apart, on greased baking sheets.

Bake in 325° oven 15 minutes, or until a slight imprint remains when touched lightly with finger. Remove from baking sheets; cool on racks. If you wish, frost with butter cream frosting (see Index for recipe) and decorate each with a maraschino cherry half. Makes about 2½ dozen.

Chocolate Linder Cookies

An Iowa farm woman freezes several batches of these delicate chocolate puffs to give to friends and neighbors at Christmas time.

2 c. unsifted flour	½ c. shortening
2 tsp. baking powder	2 c. sugar
¼ tsp. salt	4 eggs
4 (1-oz.) squares	2 tsp. vanilla
unsweetened chocolate	Sugar

Stir together flour, baking powder and salt; set aside.

Combine chocolate and shortening in medium saucepan. Cook over low heat until melted. Remove from heat.

Add 2 c. sugar to chocolate mixture; mix well with spoon. Add eggs, one at a time, beating well after each addition. Blend in vanilla. Stir in dry ingredients, mixing well. Cover and chill mixture in refrigerator 2 to 3 hours.

Shape mixture into 1″ balls. Roll in sugar. Place balls, about 2″ apart, on greased baking sheets.

Bake in 375° oven 9 to 10 minutes, or until no imprint remains when touched lightly with finger. Remove from baking sheets; cool on racks. Makes 6 dozen.

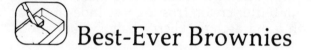

Chocolate Chip Blonde Brownies

For an unusual wedding shower gift, pack a dozen of these flavorful bar cookies inside a colorful coffeepot or teakettle.

¾ c. sifted flour
½ tsp. baking powder
½ tsp. salt
¼ tsp. baking soda
⅓ c. melted butter or regular margarine

¾ c. brown sugar, packed
1 egg
1 tsp. vanilla
½ c. semisweet chocolate pieces

Sift together flour, baking powder, salt and baking soda; set aside.

Combine butter, brown sugar, egg and vanilla in bowl; mix well with spoon.

Stir dry ingredients into brown sugar mixture; blend well. Stir in chocolate pieces. Spread mixture in greased 8" square baking pan.

Bake in 350° oven 20 minutes, or until no imprint remains when touched lightly with finger. Cool in pan on rack. Cut into 2x1" bars. Makes 32.

Best-Ever Brownies

If you have avid chocolate fans on your gift list, they'll appreciate a box of these chewy fudge brownies.

¾ c. sifted flour
½ tsp. baking powder
¼ tsp. salt
½ c. butter or regular margarine
1 c. sugar
2 eggs

1 tsp. vanilla
2 (1-oz.) squares unsweetened chocolate, melted and cooled
1 c. chopped walnuts
¼ c. sifted confectioners' sugar

Sift together flour, baking powder and salt; set aside.

Cream together butter and sugar in bowl until light and fluffy, using electric mixer at medium speed. Add eggs, one at a time, beating well after each addition. Blend in vanilla and chocolate.

Add dry ingredients to creamed mixture, blending well with spoon. Stir in walnuts. Spread mixture in greased 9" square baking pan. Dust confectioners' sugar evenly over top.

Bake in 350° oven 35 minutes, or until no imprint remains when touched lightly with finger. Cool in pan on rack. Cut into 2¼" squares. Makes 16.

Rocky Road Bars

A Wisconsin farm wife told us that her family prefers these super-rich layered brownies to a box of chocolate candy.

½ c. butter or regular
  margarine
1 (1-oz.) square
  unsweetened chocolate
1 c. sifted flour
1 tsp. baking powder
2 eggs
1 c. sugar
1 tsp. vanilla
½ c. chopped walnuts
1 (8-oz.) pkg. cream cheese,
  softened

¼ c. butter or regular
  margarine
½ c. sugar
1 egg
½ tsp. vanilla
2 tblsp. flour
¼ c. chopped walnuts
1 (6-oz.) pkg. semisweet
  chocolate pieces
2 c. miniature marshmallows
Chocolate Cream Cheese
  Frosting (recipe follows)

Combine ½ c. butter and 1-oz. chocolate in small saucepan. Melt over low heat. Remove from heat; cool to room temperature.

Sift together 1 c. flour and baking powder; set aside.

Beat together 2 eggs, 1 c. sugar and 1 tsp. vanilla in bowl. Beat until smooth, using electric mixer at medium speed. Blend in chocolate mixture, beating well.

Stir in dry ingredients; mix well. Stir in ½ c. walnuts. Spread mixture in greased 13x9x2" baking pan.

Reserve 2 oz. cream cheese for frosting. Place remaining cream cheese in bowl. Cream together cream cheese, ¼ c. butter and ½ c. sugar until light and fluffy, using electric mixer at medium speed. Add 1 egg, ½ tsp. vanilla and 2 tblsp. flour; blend well. Stir in ¼ c. walnuts. Spread over chocolate batter. Sprinkle with chocolate pieces.

Bake in 325° oven 35 minutes, or until a cake tester or wooden pick inserted in center comes out clean. Remove from oven. Sprinkle with marshmallows and return to oven for 2 minutes, or until marshmallows are softened. Cool slightly in pan on rack. Meanwhile, prepare Chocolate Cream Cheese Frosting. While brownies are still warm, frost with Chocolate Cream Cheese Frosting. Cool completely. Cut into 3x 1" bars. Makes 39.

Chocolate Cream Cheese Frosting: Combine 1 (1-oz.) square unsweetened chocolate and ¼ c. butter or regular margarine in saucepan. Cook over low heat until melted. Cool well. Combine reserved 2 oz. cream cheese (softened), ¼ c. milk, 1 tsp. vanilla, 3 c. sifted confectioners' sugar and cooled chocolate mixture in bowl. Beat until frosting is smooth and creamy, using electric mixer at medium speed.

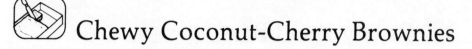

Chewy Coconut-Cherry Brownies

"This is an ideal brownie to mail to college students," an Illinois farm wife told us. It's loaded with cherries and coconut.

3 (1-oz.) squares unsweetened chocolate	1 tsp. vanilla
½ c. butter or regular margarine	1 c. sifted flour
3 eggs	1⅓ c. flaked coconut
¼ tsp. salt	⅓ c. chopped red maraschino cherries, well drained
2 c. sugar	

Combine chocolate and butter in small saucepan. Cook over low heat until chocolate and butter are melted. Remove from heat; cool to room temperature.

Combine eggs and salt in mixing bowl. Beat until foamy, using electric mixer at high speed. Gradually add sugar, beating until thick and lemon-colored. Blend in cooled chocolate mixture and vanilla. Add flour; stir well to mix. Stir in coconut and maraschino cherries. Pour mixture into greased 13x9x2" baking pan.

Bake in 375° oven 25 minutes, or until no imprint remains when touched lightly with finger. Cool in pan on rack. Cut into 2¼x1" bars. Makes 52.

Chocolate Brownie Sticks

Every year a Wisconsin homemaker sends her son a big box filled with chocolate sticks for his birthday—it's always his favorite present.

¾ c. butter or regular margarine	2 eggs
2 (1-oz.) squares unsweetened chocolate	1 tsp. vanilla
	1 c. unsifted flour
1 c. sugar	½ c. chopped pecans
	Confectioners' sugar

Combine butter and chocolate in saucepan. Cook over low heat until melted. Remove from heat; cool to room temperature.

Beat together sugar, eggs and vanilla in bowl until light and lemon-colored, using electric mixer at high speed. Blend in cooled chocolate mixture. Stir in flour; mix well. Stir in pecans. Pour mixture into greased 13x9x2" baking pan.

Bake in 350° oven 15 minutes, or until no imprint remains when touched lightly with finger. Cool slightly in pan on rack. While still warm, cut into 3x1" bars. Cool completely. Dust with confectioners' sugar. Makes 39.

Frosted Chocolate Squares

Cocoa-flavored brownies with a creamy chocolate frosting are just right for those who don't care for extra-rich fudge brownies.

1 c. butter or regular margarine	½ c. dairy sour cream
½ c. baking cocoa	2 c. sugar
1 c. water	2 eggs
2 c. sifted flour	Chocolate Frosting (recipe follows)
1 tsp. baking soda	¾ c. chopped pecans
¾ tsp. salt	

Combine butter, baking cocoa and water in 2-qt. saucepan. Cook over medium heat, stirring constantly, until mixture comes to a boil. Remove from heat; cool slightly.

Sift together flour, baking soda and salt; set aside.

Beat together sour cream, sugar and eggs in bowl until well blended, using electric mixer at medium speed.

Add dry ingredients alternately with cocoa mixture to sour cream mixture, beating well after each addition, using electric mixer at low speed. Pour batter into 2 greased 13x9x2" baking pans.

Bake in 350° oven 15 to 20 minutes, or until no imprint remains when touched lightly with finger. Cool in pans on racks. Prepare Chocolate Frosting. Frost bars with Chocolate Frosting. Sprinkle with pecans. Cut each pan into 2¼" squares. Makes 48.

Chocolate Frosting: Combine 2¼ c. sifted confectioners' sugar, ¼ c. soft butter or regular margarine, 2 tblsp. baking cocoa and 3 tblsp. milk in bowl. Beat until smooth, using a spoon.

Golden Fruit Cookies

Lightly spiced fruit cookies made with mixed dried fruit that's stewed before adding to the dough.

1 c. mixed dried fruit	½ c. sugar
Water	3 eggs
3½ c. sifted flour	2 tblsp. molasses
1 tsp. baking soda	1 tsp. vanilla
1 tsp. ground cloves	1 c. raisins
1 tsp. ground cinnamon	1½ c. chopped walnuts
½ tsp. salt	2 tsp. grated lemon rind
1 c. shortening	

Cook dried fruit in water in saucepan according to package directions. Remove from heat. Drain fruit, reserving ¼ c. liquid. Cut up fruit and set aside.

Sift together flour, baking soda, cloves, cinnamon and salt; set aside.

Cream together shortening and sugar in bowl until light and fluffy, using electric mixer at medium speed. Add eggs, one at a time, beating well after each addition. Beat in molasses and vanilla.

Add dry ingredients alternately with reserved liquid to creamed mixture, beating well after each addition, using electric mixer at low speed. Stir in stewed fruit, raisins, walnuts and lemon rind. Drop mixture by teaspoonfuls, about 2" apart, on greased baking sheets.

Bake in 350° oven 10 to 12 minutes, or until golden brown. Remove from baking sheets; cool on racks. Makes about 6 dozen.

Fruit Blossom Cookies

A bright fruit filling peeks through the centers of these delicious, old-fashioned sugar cookies.

2 c. sifted flour	½ tsp. vanilla
1½ tsp. baking powder	2 tblsp. milk
¼ tsp. salt	Apricot, Pineapple and
⅔ c. shortening	Cherry Fillings (recipes
¾ c. sugar	follow)
1 egg	

Sift together flour, baking powder and salt; set aside.

Cream together shortening and sugar in bowl until light and fluffy, using electric mixer at medium speed. Add egg and vanilla; beat well.

Add dry ingredients alternately with milk to creamed mixture, mixing well with spoon. Cover and chill in refrigerator 1 hour. Prepare desired filling (recipes follow).

Divide dough in half. Roll out each half on floured surface to ⅛" thickness. Cut out 24 rounds, using floured 3" scalloped cookie cutter. Place rounds, about 1½" apart, on greased baking sheets. Place ½ tsp. of desired filling in center of rounds.

Cut out 24 more rounds. Cut out centers of each with floured 1" round cookie cutter. Place these rounds on top of filled ones and press edges together with tines of fork to seal.

Bake in 350° oven 10 to 12 minutes, or until golden brown. Remove from baking sheets; cool on racks. Makes 2 dozen.

Apricot Filling: Combine ¼ c. chopped dried apricots, 1½ tsp. orange juice, ¼ tsp. lemon juice, 3 tblsp. water and 1 tsp. flour in saucepan. Cook over medium heat, stirring constantly, until it comes to a boil. Simmer 5 minutes. Remove from heat and cool completely.

Pineapple Filling: Combine ¼ c. crushed pineapple (undrained) and ¾ tsp. cornstarch in saucepan. Cook over medium heat, stirring, until clear and thickened. Remove from heat and cool completely.

Cherry Filling: Mash ¼ c. prepared cherry pie filling. Add a few drops almond extract, if desired.

Fruit Bars

If you want to make these fruited bars even more appealing, top with vanilla glaze and decorate with candied cherries.

2 c. raisins	2 tsp. ground cinnamon
1½ c. mixed candied fruit	1 tsp. baking soda
1 c. chopped walnuts	1 c. butter or regular
½ c. orange or pineapple	margarine
juice	1 c. sugar
2 tsp. vanilla	1 c. brown sugar, packed
4½ c. sifted flour	2 eggs
2 tsp. baking powder	

Place raisins in bowl. Add enough hot water to cover and let stand 5 minutes. Drain raisins and blot dry with paper towels. Combine raisins, mixed candied fruit, walnuts, orange juice and vanilla in bowl. Set aside.

Sift together flour, baking powder, cinnamon and baking soda; set aside.

Cream together butter, sugar and brown sugar in bowl until light and fluffy, using electric mixer at medium speed. Add eggs, one at a time, beating well after each addition.

Gradually stir dry ingredients into creamed mixture, mixing well. Stir in fruit-nut mixture. Cover and chill in refrigerator 1½ hours or overnight.

Spread dough in greased 15½x10½x1" jelly roll pan.

Bake in 400° oven 15 to 20 minutes, or until lightly browned. Cool in pan on rack. Cut into 2½x1½" bars. Makes 48.

Holiday Fruitcake Cookies

Especially for fruitcake lovers—a festive recipe for drop cookies filled with pecans, cherries, dates and mixed candied fruits.

4 c. sifted flour	2 c. cut-up pitted dates
1 tsp. baking soda	1 c. chopped pecans
1 tsp. salt	1 c. red candied cherries, cut
1 c. shortening	into quarters
2 c. brown sugar, packed	1 c. mixed candied fruit
2 eggs	Red or green candied
⅔ c. buttermilk	cherries, cut into halves

Sift together flour, baking soda and salt; set aside.

Cream together shortening and brown sugar in bowl until light and fluffy, using electric mixer at medium speed. Add eggs, one at a time, beating well after each addition.

Add dry ingredients alternately with buttermilk to creamed mixture, beating well after each addition, using electric mixer at low speed. Stir in dates, pecans, 1 c. candied cherries and candied fruit. Cover and chill dough in refrigerator at least 1 hour.

Drop dough by teaspoonfuls, about 2" apart, on greased baking sheets. Top each cookie with red or green cherry half.

Bake in 375° oven 8 to 10 minutes, or until golden brown. Remove from baking sheets; cool on racks. Makes 8 dozen.

Old-Fashioned Hermits

This spicy version of hermits will be appreciated by people who like old-fashioned cookies. Good rolled in confectioners' sugar.

3½ c. sifted flour	2 c. brown sugar, packed
1 tsp. baking soda	2 eggs
1 tsp. salt	½ c. cold coffee
1 tsp. ground cinnamon	2½ c. raisins or currants
1 tsp. ground nutmeg	1½ c. chopped walnuts
1 c. shortening	

Sift together flour, baking soda, salt, cinnamon and nutmeg; set aside.

Cream together shortening and brown sugar in bowl until light and fluffy, using electric mixer at medium speed. Add eggs, one at a time, beating well after each addition.

Add dry ingredients alternately with cold coffee to creamed mixture, beating well after each addition, using electric mixer at low speed. Stir in raisins and walnuts. Drop mixture by rounded teaspoonfuls, about 2" apart, on greased baking sheets.

Bake in 375° oven 8 to 10 minutes, or until a slight imprint remains when touched lightly with finger. Remove from baking sheets; cool on racks. Makes about 7½ dozen.

10 | For Very Special Occasions

Because they can be made in advance, cookies can't be surpassed as a festive dessert for a large group of people, whether you're entertaining a bride-to-be, celebrating a birth, welcoming new neighbors, or honoring old friends. A silver tray or a tiered plate stacked high with an assortment of crisp meringues, sparkling sugar cookies, wafer-thin lace cookies or creamy chocolate confections will tempt every one of your guests.

Many of these recipes tend to be expensive because they're extra-rich in ingredients such as butter, pecans, almonds and heavy cream. Our English Shortbread uses half a pound of butter, but it's well worth it—your guests will savor every buttery bite.

Some of these recipes require a little extra time and trouble, too, but your efforts will be rewarded. For example, Lemon Meringue Tarts feature a tangy lemon filling in miniature meringue shells that few will be able to resist.

Because butter cookies are universal favorites, we've included recipes for a baker's dozen—rolled, molded, drop and pressed. There are delicate Cinnamon Crescents, double-rich with butter and sour cream; Frosted Diamonds, swirled with White Mountain Frosting and sprinkled with pink sugar; crispy Brown-Rim Butter Cookies; and three delectable versions of pressed cookies, including Lindsborg Letter Spritz, cookies that can be shaped into the initials of the honoree. You can vary the decorations to suit the occasion by using pink or yellow decorating sugars, chocolate jimmies, multicolored confection sprinkles and silver or gold dragées.

If you're looking for a dainty, decorative cookie, try a brittle-crisp lace recipe—we offer a choice of four, including Lacy Pecan Cookies, crunchy little cylinders with a candy-like texture, and orange-flavored Florentines brushed with melted chocolate.

When you want to add a touch of romance to the buffet table, there's a recipe for Chocolate Mint Creams, crisp chocolate wafers bound together with a creamy mint filling, each one dipped in chocolate glaze and topped with a pastel rosebud.

Moist, rich bar cookies also are popular party selections because they're so easy to prepare. Some don't even require an electric mixer: Almond-Raspberry Bars have a rich double crust filled with red raspberry preserves and drizzled with an almond-scented icing, and tangy Apricot Snowdrifts, rolled in confectioners' sugar and topped with candied cherries, are pretty any time of year.

Each and every cookie in this chapter will look pretty and taste extra-special. Best of all, most of them can be made in advance and frozen until the big day arrives.

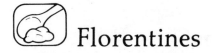 Florentines

These chocolate-coated lace cookies, a delightful combination of candied orange peel and chocolate, are as crunchy as candy.

¾ c. heavy cream	¾ c. very finely chopped
¼ c. sugar	candied orange peel (4 oz.)
¼ c. sifted flour	2 (4-oz.) bars German sweet
½ c. very finely chopped	chocolate
blanched almonds	

Combine heavy cream and sugar in bowl; stir to blend. Add flour, almonds and candied orange peel; mix well.

Drop mixture by scant teaspoonfuls, about 1¼" apart, on heavily greased and floured baking sheets. Flatten each with a spatula.

Bake in 350° oven 10 to 12 minutes, or until cookies begin to brown lightly around the edges. (Centers of cookies will be bubbling when you remove them from oven.) Let stand 2 to 3 minutes, or until they become firmer. Remove from baking sheets; cool on racks.

Meanwhile, melt chocolate over hot, not boiling, water. Stir until smooth. When cookies are cooled, turn upside down and brush with melted chocolate. Let dry several hours or overnight at room temperature to give chocolate time to set. Makes 4 dozen.

Lacy Pecan Cookies

Fancy cylindrical-shaped sweets like these are perfect party fare. With just a little practice, anyone can turn out these beauties.

⅔ c. finely ground pecans	1 tblsp. flour
½ c. sugar	2 tblsp. milk
½ c. butter or regular	½ tsp. vanilla
margarine	

Combine pecans, sugar, butter, flour, milk and vanilla in 10" skillet. Cook over medium heat, stirring constantly, until butter is melted and mixture is blended. Keep mixture warm over low heat.

Drop batter by teaspoonfuls, about 3" apart, on greased baking sheets. (Place 4 cookies on each baking sheet.)

Bake in 350° oven 5 minutes, or until golden brown. Cool on baking sheet 1 minute. Loosen cookies with pancake turner. Turn over and roll around the handle of a wooden spoon. Slide off and cool on rack. Work quickly. If cookies become too hard to shape, return to oven for 1 minute to soften. Makes 32.

Pecan Lace Roll-Ups

Another party-perfect lace cookie that will add interest to a cookie tray for either a shower or a small wedding celebration.

2 eggs	¼ c. sifted flour
⅔ c. brown sugar, packed	⅔ c. finely chopped pecans
1 tsp. vanilla	
¼ c. melted butter or regular margarine	

Beat eggs in bowl until thick and lemon-colored, using electric mixer at high speed. Add brown sugar, 1 tblsp. at a time, beating constantly. Beat in vanilla. Slowly add butter. Stir in flour and pecans.

Drop batter by tablespoonfuls, about 3" apart, on well-greased baking sheets. (Place no more than 4 on one baking sheet.) Spread each into 4" circle, using back of spoon.

Bake in 375° oven 5 to 6 minutes, or until browned around edges. Loosen cookies with a wide spatula. Turn cookies over. Place the handle of a wooden spoon on one end of cookie and quickly roll up loosely to make a cylinder. Place on rack to cool. Repeat with other baked cookies. If cookies become too hard to shape, return to oven for 1 minute to soften. Makes 15.

Swedish Lace Cookies

These saddle-shaped lace cookies are formed while they're still warm by wrapping them around a foil-covered broomstick.

½ c. butter or regular margarine, melted	⅔ c. sugar
1½ c. regular rolled oats	1 tsp. baking powder
1 egg	1 tblsp. flour
	Dash of salt

Pour melted butter over oats in bowl; set aside.

Beat egg in bowl until light and lemon-colored, using a rotary beater. Beat in sugar. Then add baking powder, flour and salt; mix well. Stir in oat mixture.

Drop batter by tablespoonfuls, about 3" apart, on greased and lightly floured baking sheets. (Place 4 cookies on each baking sheet.)

Bake in 375° oven 8 to 10 minutes, or until golden brown.

Place baking sheet on cooling rack and let stand 1 minute. Lift cookies off quickly with wide spatula and place over a broomstick wrapped in aluminum foil. Gently press cookies to make them the shape of a saddle. Work quickly; if cookies become too cold, they'll break in the shaping process. If cookies become too hard, return to oven 1 minute to soften. Makes 20.

English Shortbread

This plain butter cookie has long been popular in both Western Europe and the United States simply because it's so delicious.

3 c. sifted flour	½ c. sugar
1 tsp. baking powder	1 egg
1 c. butter or regular margarine	

Sift together flour and baking powder; set aside.

Cream together butter and sugar in bowl until light and fluffy, using electric mixer at medium speed. Beat in egg.

Add dry ingredients to creamed mixture, stirring well to blend. Knead dough lightly until it holds together.

Roll out dough on floured surface to 14" square. Cut into 49 (2") squares. Place squares, about 2" apart, on ungreased baking sheets. Prick each with fork.

Bake in 325° oven 12 minutes, or until lightly browned. Remove from baking sheets; cool on racks. Makes 49.

Brown-Rim Butter Cookies

For an extra-thin vanilla wafer to complement ice cream or sherbet, choose these crunchy, easily made brown-edged cookies.

2½ c. sifted flour	½ c. shortening
1 tsp. salt	⅔ c. sugar
½ c. butter or regular margarine	2 eggs
	1 tsp. vanilla

Sift together flour and salt; set aside.

Cream together butter, shortening and sugar in bowl until light and fluffy, using electric mixer at medium speed. Add eggs, one at a time, beating well after each addition. Blend in vanilla.

Gradually stir dry ingredients into creamed mixture, blending well. Drop mixture by teaspoonfuls, about 3" apart, on greased baking sheets. Flatten each to 2¾" rounds with bottom of drinking glass dipped in water.

Bake in 375° oven 8 minutes, or until lightly browned around the edges. Remove from baking sheets; cool on racks. Makes 4 dozen.

Winning Sugar Cookies

Rich and buttery, these sugar cookies seem to melt in your mouth. They're popular candidates for an assortment of party cookies.

4 c. sifted flour	1 c. sugar
1 tsp. baking soda	1 c. sifted confectioners' sugar
1 tsp. cream of tartar	
½ tsp. salt	2 eggs
1 c. butter or regular margarine	1 c. cooking oil
	1 tsp. vanilla

Sift together flour, baking soda, cream of tartar and salt; set aside.

Cream together butter, sugar and confectioners' sugar in bowl until light and fluffy, using electric mixer at medium speed. Add eggs, one at a time, beating well after each addition. Blend in oil and vanilla.

Gradually add dry ingredients to creamed mixture; mix well with spoon. Cover and chill dough in refrigerator 8 hours or overnight.

Shape dough in 1" balls. Place balls, about 2" apart, on ungreased baking sheets.

Bake in 350° oven 10 to 12 minutes, or until golden brown. Remove from baking sheets; cool on racks. Makes about 7 dozen.

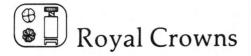

Spritz Pressed Cookies

Although almond-flavored spritz are often served at Christmas time, they're also perfect for year 'round entertaining.

1 c. butter or regular margarine	1 egg yolk
⅔ c. sifted confectioners' sugar	1 tsp. almond extract
1 egg	2¾ c. sifted flour
	Quartered red and green candied cherries

Cream together butter and confectioners' sugar in bowl until light and fluffy, using electric mixer at medium speed. Beat in egg, egg yolk and almond extract; blend well.

Gradually stir flour into creamed mixture, mixing well.

Fit flower or crown design into cookie press. Place one half of the dough in cookie press at a time, forcing dough through press, about 1" apart, on ungreased baking sheets. Place 1 quarter of red or green candied cherry in center of each.

Bake in 400° oven 7 to 10 minutes, or until set but not browned. Remove from baking sheets; cool on racks. Makes about 6 dozen.

Royal Crowns

Your cookie press will make short work of making dozens of these pretty cookies. Decorate with candied cherries or colored sugar.

4 hard-cooked egg yolks	½ tsp. almond extract
½ tsp. salt	2½ c. sifted flour
1 c. butter or regular margarine	Red or green candied cherries, cut into quarters
⅔ c. sugar	

Force egg yolks through a coarse sieve with the back of a spoon. Add salt; set aside.

Cream together butter and sugar in bowl until light and fluffy, using electric mixer at medium speed. Beat in almond extract and egg yolks.

Gradually stir flour into creamed mixture, mixing well.

Fit crown design into cookie press. Place one half of the dough in cookie press at a time, forcing dough through press, about 1" apart, on ungreased baking sheets. Press 1 quarter of red or green candied cherry in the center of each.

Bake in 375° oven 7 to 10 minutes, or until set but not browned. Remove from baking sheets; cool on racks. Makes 6 dozen.

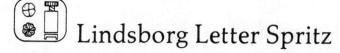

Lindsborg Letter Spritz

You can personalize refreshments for a small wedding reception by shaping these cookies into the initials of the bridal couple.

2 c. sifted flour	¾ c. sugar
1 tsp. baking powder	1 egg yolk
⅛ tsp. salt	¾ tsp. vanilla
1 c. butter or regular margarine	

Sift together flour, baking powder and salt; set aside.

Cream together butter and sugar in bowl until light and fluffy, using electric mixer at medium speed. Beat in egg yolk and vanilla.

Gradually stir dry ingredients into creamed mixture, mixing well. Shape dough into a ball. Wrap tightly in plastic wrap or waxed paper. Chill in refrigerator several hours or overnight.

Let dough warm slightly before placing in cookie press. Fit star design into cookie press. Place one half of the dough in cookie press at a time, forcing dough through press in long straight strips on ungreased baking sheets. Cut each strip into 4" pieces and shape into letter desired. (You will need to add pieces of dough to form some letters.) Place letters, about 1" apart, on ungreased baking sheets.

Bake in 350° oven 8 to 10 minutes, or until edges of cookies are golden brown. Remove from baking sheets; cool on racks. Makes about 6 dozen.

Pecan Fingers

Watch the cookies disappear when you feature these delicious pecan-studded logs rolled in confectioners' sugar.

2 c. sifted flour	½ c. sugar
¼ tsp. salt	2 tsp. vanilla
1 c. butter or regular margarine	1 c. pecan halves
	Confectioners' sugar

Sift together flour and salt; set aside.

Cream together butter and sugar in bowl until light and fluffy, using electric mixer at medium speed. Beat in vanilla.

Gradually stir dry ingredients into creamed mixture, mixing well. Using rounded teaspoonfuls of dough, shape dough around each pecan half, using floured hands. Place, about 1" apart, on lightly greased baking sheets.

Bake in 350° oven 15 to 18 minutes, or until lightly browned. Remove from baking sheets; cool slightly on racks. While cookies are still warm, roll in confectioners' sugar. Cool completely. Makes about 4½ dozen.

 Swedish Butter Nut Cookies

Interesting bar-shaped cookies that are molded by hand before rolling in ground walnuts. They're perfect for a bridal shower.

2 c. butter or regular
  margarine
1½ c. sugar
6 egg yolks

1 tsp. almond extract
4½ c. sifted flour
1 egg white, slightly beaten
1 c. ground walnuts

Cream together butter and sugar in bowl until light and fluffy, using electric mixer at medium speed. Blend in egg yolks and almond extract.

Gradually add flour to creamed mixture; mix well with spoon.

Shape dough into 2" strips about ½" thick. Dip in egg white, then in walnuts. Place, about 2" apart, on ungreased baking sheets.

Bake in 425° oven 8 to 10 minutes, or until golden brown. Remove from baking sheets; cool on racks. Makes 12 dozen.

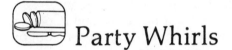 Party Whirls

A basic refrigerator dough makes lovely cookies whirled with circles of pink, white and brown. Excellent served with punch.

3 c. sifted flour
½ tsp. salt
½ tsp. ground cinnamon
1 c. butter or regular
  margarine
1 c. sugar

2 eggs
½ tsp. vanilla
3 drops red food coloring
½ (1-oz.) square
  semisweet chocolate,
  melted and cooled

Sift together flour, salt and cinnamon; set aside.

Cream together butter and sugar in bowl until light and fluffy, using electric mixer at medium speed. Add eggs, one at a time, beating well after each addition. Blend in vanilla.

Gradually stir dry ingredients into creamed mixture, mixing well.

Divide dough into thirds. Tint one third pink with red food coloring; add chocolate to the second, and leave the last third untinted.

Roll each third of dough separately on lightly floured waxed paper into a 13x10" rectangle. Cover baking sheet with waxed paper. Invert untinted dough on baking sheet; remove paper. Repeat with pink and chocolate dough. Cut edges with knife to straighten if necessary. Cover and chill in refrigerator until firm.

Roll up dough tightly as for jelly roll, using waxed paper to help shape log. Wrap tightly in waxed paper and chill.

Cut roll into ¼" slices. Place rounds, about 1" apart, on ungreased baking sheets.

Bake in 400° oven 8 minutes, or until golden brown. Remove from baking sheets; cool on racks. Makes about 7 dozen.

Filled Vanilla Wafers

Flaky rounds filled with a pink butter cream. These cookies are ideal for tea parties, wedding receptions or women's luncheons.

1 c. soft butter or regular margarine	Sugar
2 c. sifted flour	Butter Cream Filling (recipe follows)
⅓ c. heavy cream	

Cream butter in bowl until soft and creamy, using electric mixer at medium speed.

Add flour alternately with heavy cream to butter, beating well after each addition, using electric mixer at low speed. Cover and chill dough in refrigerator 2 hours.

Divide dough into thirds. Use one third of the dough at a time, keeping remaining dough in refrigerator. Roll out each third on floured surface to ⅛" thickness. Cut with floured 1½" round cookie cutter with scalloped edge. Place rounds, about 1" apart, on ungreased baking sheets. Prick tops with fork; sprinkle with sugar.

Bake in 375° oven 7 minutes, or until set but not browned. Cool on baking sheets on racks 3 minutes. Remove from baking sheets; cool on racks. When completely cooled, spread one cookie with Butter Cream Filling. Top with another cookie to form sandwich cookie. Makes 4 dozen sandwich cookies.

Butter Cream Filling: Combine ¾ c. sifted confectioners' sugar, ¼ c. soft butter or regular margarine, 1 tsp. vanilla and 3 drops red food coloring in bowl. Beat until smooth, using electric mixer at low speed.

Frosted Diamonds

These frosted butter cookies are perfect for a wedding shower. Change color of sugar topping to match the bridesmaids' dresses.

3 c. sifted flour	1 tsp. vanilla
⅛ tsp. salt	1 tsp. caraway seeds
¼ c. butter or regular margarine	White Mountain Frosting (recipe follows)
¼ c. shortening	¼ c. coarse pink decorating sugar
½ c. sugar	
2 eggs	

Sift together flour and salt; set aside.

Cream together butter, shortening and sugar in bowl until light and fluffy, using electric mixer at medium speed. Add eggs, one at a time, beating well after each addition. Blend in vanilla.

Gradually add dry ingredients to creamed mixture, mixing well with spoon. Stir in caraway seeds.

Divide dough in half. Roll out each half on floured surface to ⅛" thickness. Cut into 2" diamonds with sharp knife or cookie cutter. Place diamonds, about 2" apart, on greased baking sheets.

Bake in 325° oven 10 to 12 minutes, or until golden brown. Remove from baking sheets; cool on racks. Prepare White Mountain Frosting. Frost cookies with White Mountain Frosting; sprinkle with pink sugar. Makes about 6½ dozen.

White Mountain Frosting: Combine 1 c. sugar, ⅛ tsp. cream of tartar and ¼ c. water in small saucepan. Place over medium heat and cook, stirring constantly, until sugar dissolves. Continue cooking to soft ball stage (236°) on candy thermometer. Meanwhile, add ⅛ tsp. salt to 1 egg white; beat until stiff, using electric mixer at high speed. Pour hot syrup in a fine stream into egg white, beating constantly, until frosting is of spreading consistency.

Extra-Special Tea Cookies

These buttery, bite-size wafers are topped with a pale pink cream cheese mixture and drizzled with a thin chocolate icing.

½ c. butter or regular
   margarine
½ c. sifted confectioners'
   sugar
¼ tsp. salt
1 tsp. vanilla

1¼ c. sifted flour
Creamy Nut Topping
   (recipe follows)
Chocolate Icing
   (recipe follows)

Cream together butter, confectioners' sugar, salt and vanilla in bowl until light and fluffy, using electric mixer at medium speed. Gradually stir in flour, mixing well.

Roll out dough on lightly floured surface to ¼" thickness. Cut in 1" rounds, using cookie cutter or doughnut hole cutter. Place rounds, about 1" apart, on ungreased baking sheets.

Bake in 350° oven 12 minutes, or until lightly browned. Remove from baking sheets; cool on racks.

Prepare Creamy Nut Topping and Chocolate Icing. Top each cookie with ½ tsp. of Creamy Nut Topping. Then drizzle tops with Chocolate Icing. Makes 6½ dozen.

Creamy Nut Topping: Place 1 (3-oz.) pkg. cream cheese in bowl. Beat until creamy, using electric mixer at high speed. Add 1 c. sifted confectioners' sugar, 2 tblsp. flour, 1 tsp. vanilla and 2 drops red food coloring; mix well. Stir in ½ c. chopped walnuts and ½ c. flaked coconut.

Chocolate Icing: Combine ½ c. semisweet chocolate pieces, 2 tblsp. butter or regular margarine and 2 tblsp. water in saucepan. Cook over low heat, stirring constantly, until chocolate melts. Stir in ½ c. sifted confectioners' sugar, beating until smooth.

Jelly-Filled Butter Cookies

When it's your turn to serve refreshments, bake these colorful cookies. Vary the jelly filling, using three or more flavors.

2 c. sifted flour	2 egg yolks
¼ tsp. salt	½ tsp. vanilla
1 c. butter or regular margarine	1 c. finely chopped pecans
½ c. brown sugar, packed	½ c. red currant jelly

Sift together flour and salt; set aside.

Cream together butter and brown sugar in bowl until light and fluffy, using electric mixer at medium speed. Add egg yolks and vanilla, beating well.

Gradually stir dry ingredients into creamed mixture, blending well. Shape dough into 1" balls. Roll in chopped pecans. Place balls, about 2" apart, on ungreased baking sheets.

Bake in 350° oven 5 minutes. Remove from oven and make depression in center of each cookie, using a thimble or your finger. Return to oven and bake 8 minutes longer, or until golden brown. Remove from baking sheets; cool on racks. When cookies are completely cooled, fill each with approximately ½ tsp. currant jelly. Makes 3½ dozen.

Cinnamon Crescents

These buttery-rich cookies are perfect for a midmorning coffee break. They're also special enough to serve with a party punch.

1 c. butter or regular margarine	¾ c. sugar
2 c. sifted flour	¾ c. finely chopped walnuts
1 egg yolk	1 tsp. ground cinnamon
¾ c. dairy sour cream	1 egg white, slightly beaten
	1 tblsp. water

Cut butter into flour in bowl until mixture resembles coarse crumbs, using pastry blender. Stir in egg yolk and sour cream. Mix with fork until dough forms a ball. Wrap in plastic wrap. Chill in refrigerator 2 hours.

Combine sugar, walnuts and cinnamon.

Divide dough into fourths. Roll each fourth into 11" circle on floured surface. Sprinkle with one quarter walnut-sugar mixture. Cut into 16 wedges. Roll up wedges, starting at widest end. Place rolls, about 2" apart, on ungreased baking sheets. Brush with combined egg white and water.

Bake in 350° oven 20 minutes, or until golden brown. Remove from baking sheets; cool on racks. Makes 64.

Snow-Capped Coconut Cookies

A Nebraska family has been enjoying these sugar-topped cookies for more than 25 years. Chopped pecans add crunch.

2 c. sifted flour	½ c. brown sugar, packed
1 tsp. baking soda	2 eggs
1 tsp. cream of tartar	1 tsp. vanilla
¼ tsp. salt	1 c. flaked coconut
¾ c. butter or regular margarine	½ c. chopped pecans
1 c. sugar	Sugar

Sift together flour, baking soda, cream of tartar and salt; set aside.

Cream together butter, 1 c. sugar and brown sugar in bowl until light and fluffy, using electric mixer at medium speed. Add eggs, one at a time, beating well after each addition. Blend in vanilla.

Gradually stir dry ingredients into creamed mixture, blending well. Stir in coconut and pecans. Cover and chill in refrigerator 3 hours, or until firm enough to shape.

Shape dough into 1¼" balls. Dip tops into cold water and then in sugar. Place balls, sugared side up, about 3" apart, on greased baking sheets.

Bake in 350° oven 12 minutes, or until golden brown. Remove from baking sheets; cool on racks. Makes 4 dozen.

Butter Pecan Chocolate Bars

Chocolate and caramel are swirled together over the crunchy crumb crust of these rich bars. The recipe is from a Nebraska farm wife.

2 c. sifted flour	⅔ c. butter or regular margarine
1 c. brown sugar, packed	½ c. brown sugar, packed
½ c. butter or regular margarine	1 (6-oz.) pkg. milk chocolate pieces
1 c. pecan halves	

Combine flour and 1 c. brown sugar in bowl. Cut in ½ c. butter until crumbly, using pastry blender. Press mixture into ungreased 13x9x2" baking pan. Sprinkle pecan halves over crust.

Combine ⅔ c. butter and ½ c. brown sugar in small saucepan. Cook over medium heat, stirring constantly, until mixture boils. Boil 1 minute. Pour over pecan halves.

Bake in 350° oven 20 minutes, or until bubbly and crust is light brown. Remove from oven. Sprinkle chocolate pieces over all. Let stand 5 minutes so chocolate melts slightly. Swirl chocolate through caramel layer for marbled effect. Cool in pan on rack. Cut into 3x1" bars. Makes 39.

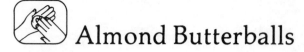 Almond Butterballs

You can use either blanched or unblanched almonds for this recipe. It's up to you—either one adds crunchiness.

1 c. butter or regular margarine	⅛ tsp. almond extract
¼ c. sifted confectioners' sugar	2 c. sifted flour
1 tsp. vanilla	1 c. chopped almonds
	Confectioners' sugar

Cream together butter and ¼ c. confectioners' sugar in bowl until light and fluffy, using electric mixer at medium speed. Beat in vanilla and almond extract.

Gradually stir flour into creamed mixture, mixing well. Stir in almonds; mix well. Shape dough into 1" balls. Place balls, about 1½" apart, on greased baking sheets.

Bake in 350° oven 20 minutes, or until delicately browned. Remove from baking sheets; cool slightly on racks. While cookies are still warm, roll in confectioners' sugar. Cool completely. Makes 6 dozen.

Almond Refrigerator Squares

These square-shaped refrigerator cookies won a Grand Champion ribbon for a Kansas farm wife. Attractive and yet so easy to make.

2 c. sifted flour	1 tsp. almond extract
½ tsp. baking powder	½ tsp. vanilla
1 c. butter or regular margarine	½ c. chopped toasted almonds
½ c. sugar	Sugar
2 tblsp. water	

Sift together flour and baking powder; set aside.

Cream together butter, ½ c. sugar, water, almond extract and vanilla in bowl until light and fluffy, using electric mixer at medium speed.

Gradually stir dry ingredients into creamed mixture, mixing well. Stir in almonds; mix well. Cover and chill in refrigerator 1 hour.

Use an empty 12" long plastic wrap, waxed paper or aluminum foil carton. Grease a 10" long sheet of waxed paper and place in carton. Press dough into carton. Wrap waxed paper securely over dough. Chill in refrigerator 8 hours or overnight.

Cut dough into ¼" thick slices. Place, about 2" apart, on ungreased baking sheets.

Bake in 350° oven 12 to 15 minutes, or until golden brown. Remove from baking sheets and roll in sugar. Cool on racks. Makes 4 dozen.

Chinese Almond Cookies

Crunchy with almonds and rich with butter, these flavorful treats adapt well to many occasions, from birthdays to special holidays.

3 c. sifted flour	1 egg
1 tsp. baking powder	1 tsp. almond extract
¼ tsp. salt	½ tsp. vanilla
1 c. butter or regular margarine	½ c. chopped toasted almonds
1½ c. sugar	

Sift together flour, baking powder and salt; set aside.

Cream together butter and sugar in bowl until light and fluffy, using electric mixer at medium speed. Add egg, almond extract and vanilla; blend well.

Gradually stir dry ingredients into creamed mixture; mix well.

Divide dough in half. Roll out each half on floured surface to ¼" thickness. Cut with floured 2" round cookie cutter. Place rounds, about 2" apart, on greased baking sheets. Sprinkle each with almonds. Press almonds down lightly into each.

Bake in 325° oven 15 minutes, or until golden brown. Remove from baking sheets; cool on racks. Makes 4 dozen.

Almond-Raspberry Bars

These blue-ribbon bars feature a raspberry jam filling, a rich pastry crust and an almond-scented icing.

1½ c. sifted flour	½ c. ground blanched almonds
½ c. sugar	1 egg
½ tsp. baking powder	½ tsp. almond extract
½ tsp. ground cinnamon	¾ c. raspberry jam
½ c. butter or regular margarine	Vanilla Icing (recipe follows)

Sift together flour, sugar, baking powder and cinnamon into a bowl. Cut in butter until mixture is crumbly, using a pastry blender. Add almonds, egg and almond extract; mix well. Spread one half of the dough in an 8" square on waxed paper. Cover and chill in refrigerator.

Meanwhile, press remaining dough into ungreased 8" square baking pan. Spread with raspberry jam. Top with chilled dough.

Bake in 350° oven 35 to 40 minutes, or until golden brown. Cool in pan on rack. Prepare Vanilla Icing. Drizzle with Vanilla Icing. Cut into 2x1" bars. Makes 32.

Vanilla Icing: Combine ½ c. sifted confectioners' sugar, 2 tsp. milk and ¼ tsp. almond extract in bowl. Beat until smooth, using a spoon.

Lemon Meringue Tarts

A light and lemony custard filling in crisp miniature meringue shells. These delicate morsels are perfect for a reception.

2 eggs, separated	½ c. water
⅛ tsp. cream of tartar	2 tsp. butter or regular
¼ tsp. vanilla	margarine
1 c. sugar	½ tsp. grated lemon rind
2 tblsp. cornstarch	2 tblsp. lemon juice
⅛ tsp. salt	½ c. heavy cream, whipped

Combine egg whites, cream of tartar and vanilla in bowl. Beat until foamy, using electric mixer at high speed. Gradually beat in ½ c. of the sugar. Continue beating until stiff peaks form. Drop mixture by heaping teaspoonfuls, about 1½" apart, on baking sheets covered with brown paper. Make an indentation in the center of each with back of a spoon.

Bake in 275° oven 45 minutes, or until set. Turn off oven and let stand in warm oven 30 minutes more. Remove from baking sheets; cool on racks.

To make filling, combine remaining ½ c. sugar, cornstarch and salt in 2-qt. saucepan; mix well. Stir in water. Cook over medium heat, stirring constantly, until mixture thickens. Beat egg yolks slightly. Stir a little hot mixture into egg yolks; mix well. Then stir egg yolk mixture into hot mixture, mixing well. Cook over low heat 2 minutes more, stirring constantly. Remove from heat. Stir in butter, lemon rind and lemon juice. Cool to room temperature.

Fold whipped cream into cooled lemon mixture. Fill meringue shells. Refrigerate until serving time. Makes 30.

Lemon-Cheese Cookies

Unusual cookies with a butter and cream cheese base. Each one is rolled in crumbled cornflakes before baking.

1 c. sifted flour	½ c. sugar
2 tsp. baking powder	1 tsp. grated lemon rind
¼ tsp. salt	¼ tsp. lemon extract
½ c. butter or regular	1¼ c. coarsely crumbled
margarine	cornflakes
1 (3-oz.) pkg. cream cheese, softened	

Stir together flour, baking powder and salt; set aside.

Cream together butter, cream cheese and sugar in bowl until light and fluffy, using electric mixer at medium speed. Blend in lemon rind and lemon extract.

Gradually add dry ingredients to creamed mixture; mix well with spoon. Cover and chill dough in refrigerator about 1 hour.

Shape dough into 1″ balls. Roll each in cornflake crumbs. Place balls, about 2″ apart, on ungreased baking sheets.

Bake in 350° oven 12 to 15 minutes, or until golden brown. Remove from baking sheets; cool on racks. Makes about 3 dozen.

Tart Lemon Squares

If you like a tangy lemon-flavored bar cookie, here's the one for you. It was the Grand Champion winner at a Wisconsin county fair.

1 c. sifted flour	2 tblsp. flour
¼ c. sifted confectioners' sugar	½ tsp. baking powder
⅛ tsp. salt	⅛ tsp. salt
½ c. butter or regular	2 eggs, slightly beaten
margarine	2 tblsp. lemon juice
1 c. sugar	1 tsp. grated lemon rind
	Lemon Glaze (recipe follows)

Combine 1 c. flour, ¼ c. confectioners' sugar and ⅛ tsp. salt in bowl. Cut in butter until mixture is crumbly, using pastry blender. Press crumb mixture into greased 12x8x2″ (2-qt.) glass baking dish.

Bake in 325° oven 15 minutes.

Combine sugar, 2 tblsp. flour, baking powder, ⅛ tsp. salt, eggs, lemon juice and lemon rind in bowl. Mix thoroughly. Spread evenly over baked crust.

Bake in 325° oven 25 minutes, or until golden brown. Cool in pan on rack. Prepare Lemon Glaze. Spread bars with Lemon Glaze. Cut into 2″ squares. Makes 24.

Lemon Glaze: Combine ½ c. sifted confectioners' sugar, 1 tblsp. lemon juice, 1 tblsp. melted butter or regular margarine and 1 drop yellow food coloring in bowl. Blend until smooth, using a spoon.

Apricot Snowdrifts

These colorful bar cookies feature a golden crumb crust and tangy apricot filling. Each one is decorated with a cherry half.

⅔ c. dried apricots	2 eggs
⅓ c. sifted flour	1 c. brown sugar, packed
½ tsp. baking powder	½ c. chopped walnuts
¼ tsp. salt	½ tsp. vanilla
1 c. sifted flour	Confectioners' sugar
¼ c. sugar	Candied red cherries
½ c. butter or regular margarine	

Cook apricots in boiling water in saucepan over medium heat for 10 minutes. Remove from heat. Drain. Cool and cut up apricots; set aside.

Sift together ⅓ c. flour, baking powder and salt; set aside.

Combine 1 c. flour, sugar and butter in bowl. Mix until crumbly, using a pastry blender. Press crumb mixture into greased 9" square baking pan. Bake in 350° oven 18 minutes.

Beat eggs in bowl until light and lemon-colored, using electric mixer at high speed. Slowly beat in brown sugar, blending well. Add dry ingredients; stir well. Add apricots, walnuts and vanilla. Spread mixture over baked layer.

Bake in 350° oven 25 minutes, or until golden brown. Cool in pan on rack. Cut into 2¼x1" bars, using a wet knife. Roll bars in confectioners' sugar. Decorate each bar with candied cherry half. Makes 36.

 # Strawberry Meringue Bars

A Virginia farm woman told us that her family loves strawberries. She uses her own homemade strawberry preserves in this recipe.

⅔ c. shortening	½ c. sugar
⅓ c. sugar	1 c. finely chopped walnuts
2 eggs, separated	1 (10-oz.) jar strawberry
1½ c. sifted flour	preserves (1 c.)

Cream together shortening and ⅓ c. sugar in bowl until light and fluffy, using electric mixer at medium speed. Beat in egg yolks. Stir in flour, mixing well. Press mixture into bottom of ungreased 13x9x2" baking pan.

Bake in 350° oven 15 minutes, or until golden brown.

Meanwhile, beat egg whites in another bowl until frothy, using electric mixer at high speed. Gradually add ½ c. sugar, beating until stiff, glossy peaks form. Fold in walnuts.

Spread strawberry preserves over baked crust. Carefully spread walnut-meringue mixture on top.

Bake in 350° oven 25 minutes, or until meringue is golden brown. Cool in pan on rack. Cut into 3¼x1⅛" bars. Makes 32.

Mint Chip Meringues

If you don't care for mint with chocolate, substitute regular semisweet chocolate morsels for the mint-flavored ones.

2 egg whites	1 (6-oz.) pkg. semisweet mint
¾ tsp. cream of tartar	chocolate pieces
¼ tsp. salt	4 drops green food coloring
¾ c. sugar	

Beat egg whites, cream of tartar and salt in bowl until soft peaks form, using electric mixer at high speed. Gradually add sugar, beating until stiff peaks form.

Fold in mint chocolate pieces and food coloring. Drop mixture by teaspoonfuls, about 2" apart, on waxed paper-lined baking sheets.

Place in 350° oven and turn off heat. Leave meringues in oven at least 12 hours. Remove from baking sheets. Makes 2½ dozen.

Grated Chocolate Meringues

These meringues have a subtle chocolate flavor. Just the right addition to a special-occasion assortment of cookies.

2½ c. sifted flour
2 tsp. baking powder
¼ tsp. salt
½ c. shortening
2 c. sugar
3 eggs

2 tsp. vanilla
2 (1-oz.) squares semisweet
    chocolate, grated
Sugar
Whole blanched almonds

Sift together flour, baking powder and salt; set aside.

Cream together shortening and 2 c. sugar in bowl until light and fluffy, using electric mixer at medium speed. Add eggs, one at a time, beating well after each addition. Beat in vanilla.

Stir dry ingredients into creamed mixture, mixing well. Stir in chocolate. Drop mixture by teaspoonfuls, about 2" apart, on greased baking sheets. Flatten each with the bottom of a drinking glass dipped in sugar. Place almond in the center of each.

Bake in 350° oven 12 minutes, or until lightly browned. Remove from baking sheets; cool on racks. Makes about 4½ dozen.

German Chocolate-Cheese Brownies

Once we tested this recipe in Farm Journal's Test Kitchens, we knew why an Iowa farm wife chose it as her favorite for any occasion.

2 (4-oz.) pkg. German sweet
    chocolate
6 tblsp. butter or regular
    margarine
2 (3-oz.) pkg. cream cheese
4 tblsp. butter or regular
    margarine
½ c. sugar
2 eggs
2 tblsp. flour

1 tsp. vanilla
4 eggs
1½ c. sugar
1 c. sifted flour
1 tsp. baking powder
½ tsp. salt
½ tsp. almond extract
2 tsp. vanilla
1 c. chopped toasted
    almonds

Combine sweet chocolate and 6 tblsp. butter in 2-qt. saucepan. Place over low heat, stirring occasionally, until melted. Remove from heat; cool to room temperature.

Cream together cream cheese and 4 tblsp. butter in bowl, using electric mixer at medium speed. Add ½ c. sugar, beating until light and fluffy. Blend in 2 eggs, 2 tblsp. flour and 1 tsp. vanilla.

Beat 4 eggs in another bowl until foamy, using electric mixer at high speed. Gradually add 1½ c. sugar, beating until mixture is thick and lemon-colored.

Sift together 1 c. flour, baking powder and salt. Add to egg mixture, mixing well. Blend in cooled chocolate mixture, almond extract and 2 tsp. vanilla. Stir in almonds. Reserve 2 c. of chocolate batter. Spread remaining chocolate batter in greased 13x9x2" baking pan. Spread cream cheese mixture over first layer. Spoon reserved 2 c. chocolate batter over all. Use a metal spatula to swirl layers to give a marbled effect.

Bake in 350° oven 50 minutes, or until no imprint remains when touched lightly with finger. Cool in pan on rack. Cut into 2¼" squares. Makes 24.

Orange and Fudge Brownies

An orange-flavored filling is sandwiched in the middle of this unusual brownie shared by a Rhode Island farm woman.

1½ c. sifted flour	1 c. sugar
6 tblsp. baking cocoa	¾ c. sifted flour
¼ tsp. salt	1 tsp. grated orange rind
1 c. butter or regular	½ tsp. almond extract
margarine	1 egg
2 c. sugar	2 tblsp. orange juice
4 eggs	Fudge Frosting
2 tsp. vanilla	(recipe follows)

Sift together 1½ c. flour, cocoa and salt; set aside.

Cream together butter and 2 c. sugar in bowl until light and fluffy, using electric mixer at medium speed. Add 4 eggs, one at a time, beating well after each addition. Add vanilla.

Gradually stir dry ingredients into creamed mixture, mixing well. Set aside.

Combine 1 c. sugar and ¾ c. flour in a bowl. Add orange rind, almond extract, 1 egg and orange juice; blend well. Spread one half of fudge batter in greased 13x9x2" pan. Top with orange batter. Spread remaining fudge batter over all.

Bake in 350° oven 30 minutes, or until no imprint remains when touched lightly with finger. Cool in pan on rack. Prepare Fudge Frosting. Frost cooled bars with Fudge Frosting. Cut into 3x1" bars. Makes 39.

Fudge Frosting: Combine 1½ c. sifted confectioners' sugar, 3 tblsp. soft butter or regular margarine, 3 tblsp. baking cocoa, 3 tblsp. milk and ½ tsp. vanilla in bowl. Beat until smooth, using a spoon.

 # Tri-Level Brownies

A South Carolina farm woman told us that she makes these triple-rich brownies when her family craves something extra-chocolaty.

½ c. sifted flour	⅔ c. sifted flour
¼ tsp. baking soda	¼ tsp. baking powder
¼ tsp. salt	¼ tsp. salt
1 c. quick-cooking oats	¾ c. sugar
½ c. brown sugar, packed	1 egg
⅔ c. melted butter or regular margarine	½ tsp. vanilla
	¼ c. milk
1 (1-oz.) square unsweetened chocolate	½ c. chopped walnuts
	Chocolate Icing
¼ c. butter or regular margarine	(recipe follows)

Sift together ½ c. flour, baking soda and ¼ tsp. salt into bowl. Add quick-cooking oats, brown sugar and ⅔ c. melted butter. Mix until crumbly, using fork. Press crumb mixture into greased 12x8x2″ (2-qt.) glass baking dish.

Bake in 350° oven 10 minutes. Cool slightly on rack.

Melt chocolate and ¼ c. butter in saucepan over very low heat, stirring constantly. Remove from heat and cool slightly.

Sift together ⅔ c. flour, baking powder and ¼ tsp. salt; set aside.

Combine chocolate mixture, sugar, egg and vanilla in bowl. Beat 1 minute or until well blended, using electric mixer at medium speed.

Add dry ingredients alternately with milk to chocolate mixture, beating well after each addition, using electric mixer at low speed. Stir in walnuts. Spread mixture over baked crust.

Bake in 350° oven 25 minutes, or until no imprint remains when touched lightly with finger. Cool in baking dish on rack. Prepare Chocolate Icing. Frost brownies with Chocolate Icing. Cut into 2″ squares. Makes 24.

Chocolate Icing: Melt 2 tblsp. butter or regular margarine and 1 (1-oz.) square unsweetened chocolate over very low heat, stirring constantly. Remove from heat; cool slightly. Combine 1½ c. sifted confectioners' sugar, 2 tblsp. hot water and 1 tsp. vanilla in bowl. Stir in chocolate mixture, beating until smooth and creamy.

Chocolate-Cream Cheese Cookies

Cream cheese gives these chocolate drop cookies an irresistibly rich flavor. Just the dessert for true chocolate lovers.

2¼ c. sifted flour	1 egg
1½ tsp. baking soda	1 tsp. vanilla
½ tsp. salt	2 tblsp. milk
1 c. butter or regular	2 (1-oz.) squares
margarine	unsweetened chocolate,
1 (3-oz.) pkg. cream cheese	melted and cooled
1½ c. sugar	½ c. chopped walnuts

Sift together flour, baking soda and salt; set aside.

Cream together butter, cream cheese and sugar in bowl until light and fluffy, using electric mixer at medium speed. Add egg, vanilla, milk and chocolate; beat well.

Gradually stir dry ingredients into creamed mixture, mixing well. Stir in walnuts. Drop mixture by teaspoonfuls, about 2" apart, on greased baking sheets.

Bake in 350° oven 10 minutes, or until top springs back when touched lightly with finger. Remove from baking sheets; cool on racks. Makes 6 dozen.

Caramel-Chocolate Bars

These marvelous brownies are favorites in our Farm Journal Test Kitchens. They're rich with melted caramels and crunchy with nuts.

1 (14-oz.) bag caramels	¾ c. melted butter or regular
⅓ c. evaporated milk	margarine
1 (18½-oz.) box Swiss	1 (6-oz.) pkg. semisweet
chocolate cake mix	chocolate pieces
⅓ c. evaporated milk	1 c. chopped walnuts

Combine caramels and ⅓ c. evaporated milk in top of double boiler. Cover and place over boiling water until melted, stirring occasionally. Keep warm.

Combine cake mix, ⅓ c. evaporated milk and butter in bowl. Beat until smooth, using electric mixer at medium speed. (Mixture will be thick.) Spread one half of mixture in greased 13x9x2" baking pan.

Bake in 350° oven 6 minutes. Remove from oven and cool on rack 2 minutes. Spread hot caramel mixture carefully over baked layer. Sprinkle with chocolate pieces.

Stir ½ c. of the walnuts into remaining cake batter. Drop batter by spoonfuls over all. Sprinkle with remaining ½ c. walnuts.

Bake in 350° oven 18 minutes, or until top springs back when touched lightly with finger. Cool in pan on rack. Cut into 3¼x1⅛" bars. Makes 32.

Chocolate Peppermint Bars

Peppermint and chocolate are a nice combination for the Christmas holidays, but these cookies are good any time. So pretty, too!

2 (1-oz.) squares unsweetened chocolate	3 tblsp. butter or regular margarine
½ c. butter or regular margarine	5 tsp. milk
2 eggs	1 tsp. peppermint extract
1 c. sugar	1½ (1-oz.) squares unsweetened chocolate
½ c. sifted flour	1½ tblsp. butter or regular margarine
½ c. chopped toasted almonds	1 tblsp. crushed peppermint candy
1½ c. sifted confectioners' sugar	

Combine 2 oz. chocolate and ½ c. butter in saucepan. Cook over low heat until melted. Remove from heat; cool well.

Beat together eggs and sugar in bowl until thick and lemon-colored, using electric mixer at high speed. Blend in chocolate mixture and flour. Beat until smooth. Stir in almonds. Spread in greased 8" square baking pan.

Bake in 350° oven 25 minutes, or until a cake tester or wooden pick inserted in center comes out clean. Cool in pan on rack.

Combine confectioners' sugar, 3 tblsp. butter, milk and peppermint extract in bowl. Beat until smooth, using electric mixer at medium speed. Spread mixture on cooled brownies. Cover and chill in refrigerator until cream layer is firm.

Melt 1½ oz. chocolate with 1½ tblsp. butter over hot water. Cool slightly and spread over cream layer. Sprinkle with peppermint candy. Let stand until chocolate is set. Cut into 2x1" bars. Makes 32.

Brownies with Browned Butter Frosting

Chocolate drizzled over a beige butter-cream frosting forms a contrasting topping for this moist pecan-filled brownie.

1 c. butter or regular margarine	1¼ c. sifted flour
4 (1-oz.) squares unsweetened chocolate	1 c. chopped pecans
2 c. sugar	Browned Butter Frosting (recipe follows)
4 eggs	½ (1-oz.) square unsweetened chocolate
1 tsp. vanilla	

Combine butter and 4 oz. chocolate in small saucepan. Cook over low heat until butter and chocolate are melted. Remove from heat; cool to room temperature.

Beat together sugar and eggs in bowl 2 minutes, using electric mixer at high speed. Blend in cooled chocolate mixture and vanilla. Stir in flour; mix well. Stir in pecans. Spread mixture in greased 13x9x2" baking pan.

Bake in 350° oven 35 minutes, or until no imprint remains when touched lightly with finger. Cool in pan on rack. Prepare Browned Butter Frosting. Frost brownies with Browned Butter Frosting.

Melt ½ oz. chocolate in custard cup in hot, but not boiling water. Drizzle over frosting. Let stand until chocolate sets. Cut into 2¼" squares. Makes 24.

Browned Butter Frosting: Melt ¼ c. butter in small saucepan over low heat. Continue heating, stirring constantly, until delicately browned. Remove from heat. Combine 2 c. sifted confectioners' sugar, 2 tblsp. light cream and 1 tsp. vanilla in bowl. Add browned butter. Beat until smooth and creamy, using electric mixer at medium speed.

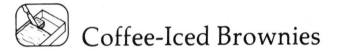 # Coffee-Iced Brownies

Here's another fudgy brownie, this one a very dark chocolate. It's studded with pecans and has a coffee-flavored frosting.

⅔ c. sifted flour
¼ c. baking cocoa
2 eggs
1 c. sugar
⅓ c. butter or regular
  margarine

1 tsp. vanilla
½ c. chopped pecans
Coffee Icing (recipe follows)

Sift together flour and baking cocoa; set aside.

Beat together eggs and sugar in bowl until thick and lemon-colored, using electric mixer at high speed for 2 minutes. Add butter and vanilla; beat well.

Blend in dry ingredients, using electric mixer at low speed. Stir in pecans. Spread batter in greased 8" square baking pan.

Bake in 350° oven 25 minutes, or until no imprint remains when touched lightly with finger. Cool in pan on rack. Prepare Coffee Icing. Frost brownies with Coffee Icing. Cut into 2" squares. Makes 16.

Coffee Icing: Combine 1¾ c. sifted confectioners' sugar, 1 tblsp. baking cocoa, 1 tblsp. butter or regular margarine, 2 tblsp. strong hot coffee and 1 tsp. vanilla in bowl. Beat until smooth, using a spoon.

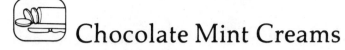 Chocolate Mint Creams

Rosebud-decorated cookies filled with mint cream and dipped into a glossy chocolate glaze. Beautiful!

2½ c. sifted flour
1 tsp. baking soda
1 tsp. cream of tartar
⅛ tsp. salt
1 c. butter or regular
   margarine
1½ c. sifted confectioners'
   sugar
1 egg
1 tsp. vanilla

2 (1-oz.) squares
   unsweetened chocolate,
   melted and cooled
Mint Cream Filling
   (recipe follows)
Shiny Chocolate Glaze
   (recipe follows)
Easy Decorating Icing
   (recipe follows)

Sift together flour, baking soda, cream of tartar and salt; set aside.

Cream together butter and confectioners' sugar in bowl until light and fluffy, using electric mixer at medium speed. Add egg, vanilla and cooled chocolate, mixing well.

Gradually stir in dry ingredients, mixing well. Divide dough in half. Shape each half into a 10" roll. Wrap in waxed paper or plastic wrap. Chill in refrigerator several hours.

Cut rolls into slices, about ⅙" thick. Place rounds, about 1" apart, on greased baking sheets.

Bake in 350° oven 10 minutes, or until no imprint remains when touched lightly with finger. Remove from baking sheets; cool on racks.

Prepare Mint Cream Filling and Shiny Chocolate Glaze. Spread one cookie with Mint Cream Filling. Top with another cookie, forming a sandwich cookie. Dip each sandwich cookie in Shiny Chocolate Glaze, so glaze covers half of cookie. Leave other half unglazed. Place cookies on racks over waxed paper until glaze dries.

Prepare Easy Decorating Icing. Decorate each cookie with a rosebud and leaf made with Easy Decorating Icing. Makes 2½ dozen.

Mint Cream Filling: Cream together ¼ c. butter or regular margarine and 2 c. sifted confectioners' sugar in bowl, using electric mixer at medium speed. Add ⅛ tsp. mint flavoring and 5 tsp. milk; blend well. Add 1 more tsp. milk, if necessary, to make a creamy filling.

Shiny Chocolate Glaze: Melt together 2 (1-oz.) squares unsweetened chocolate and 2 tblsp. butter or regular margarine in saucepan over heat. Remove from heat. Stir in 2 c. sifted confectioners' sugar and 5 tblsp. milk, blending well. Add 1 more tblsp. milk, if necessary, to make a glaze that coats the cookies.

Easy Decorating Icing: Cream together 3 tblsp. butter or regular margarine in bowl, using electric mixer at medium speed. Blend in ½ tsp. vanilla. Add 3 tsp. milk, 1 tsp. at a time, beating until icing is stiff enough to hold its shape. Tint icing as desired, using paste food coloring. Makes about 1 cup.

Triple Chocolate Cookies

Crunchy drop cookies filled with chocolate morsels and topped with chocolate icing—a favorite of one New York family.

2 c. sifted flour	2 eggs
1 tsp. baking powder	1 tsp. vanilla
½ tsp. baking soda	½ c. dairy sour cream
¼ tsp. salt	½ c. semisweet chocolate
½ c. butter or regular	pieces
margarine	½ c. chopped walnuts
2½ (1-oz.) squares	Chocolate Frosting
unsweetened chocolate	(recipe follows)
1 c. sugar	

Sift together flour, baking powder, baking soda and salt; set aside.

Combine butter and unsweetened chocolate in saucepan. Cook over low heat until melted. Remove from heat. Cool to room temperature.

Combine sugar, eggs, vanilla and cooled chocolate mixture in bowl. Beat until blended, using electric mixer at medium speed.

Add dry ingredients alternately with sour cream to chocolate mixture, beating well after each addition, using electric mixer at low speed. Stir in chocolate pieces and walnuts. Cover and chill in refrigerator at least 2 hours.

Drop mixture by teaspoonfuls, about 2" apart, on greased baking sheets.

Bake in 375° oven 10 to 12 minutes, or until no imprint remains when touched lightly with finger. Remove from baking sheets; cool on racks. Prepare Chocolate Frosting. Frost cookies with Chocolate Frosting. Makes 4 dozen.

Chocolate Frosting: Melt 2 (1-oz.) squares unsweetened chocolate and 2 tblsp. butter or regular margarine in saucepan over low heat. Remove from heat. Add 2 c. sifted confectioners' sugar and 4 tblsp. milk. Beat until smooth and creamy, using a spoon.

Chewy Coconut Macaroons

To keep these pretty beige macaroons fresh for your party, store in airtight containers until time to serve.

⅓ c. sifted flour	¾ c. sugar
¼ tsp. baking powder	1 tblsp. butter or regular
⅛ tsp. salt	margarine, melted
2 eggs	2⅔ c. flaked coconut
1 tsp. vanilla	

Sift together flour, baking powder and salt; set aside.

Beat together eggs and vanilla in bowl until foamy, using electric mixer at high speed. Gradually beat in sugar. Continue beating at high speed until thick and lemon-colored. Blend in butter.

Gradually add dry ingredients to egg mixture, using electric mixer at low speed. Fold in coconut. Drop mixture by rounded teaspoonfuls, about 2" apart, on greased baking sheets.

Bake in 325° oven 15 minutes, or until golden brown around the edges. Remove from baking sheets; cool on racks. Makes 2½ dozen.

Orange-Chocolate Cookies

These orange cookies are flavored with bits of chocolate and a whisper of nutmeg—an interesting combination.

2 c. sifted flour	1 c. sugar
½ tsp. baking powder	1 egg
½ tsp. baking soda	1 tblsp. grated orange rind
½ tsp. salt	1 tsp. orange juice
¼ tsp. ground nutmeg	½ c. sour milk*
½ c. butter or regular	1 (6-oz.) pkg. semisweet
margarine	chocolate pieces

Sift together flour, baking powder, baking soda, salt and nutmeg; set aside.

Cream together butter and sugar in bowl until light and fluffy, using electric mixer at medium speed. Add egg, orange rind and orange juice; blend well.

Add dry ingredients alternately with sour milk to creamed mixture, beating well after each addition, using electric mixer at low speed. Stir in chocolate pieces. Drop mixture by rounded teaspoonfuls, about 3" apart, on greased baking sheets.

Bake in 350° oven 15 minutes, or until golden brown. Remove from baking sheets; cool on racks. Makes 4 dozen.

*Note: To sour milk, place 1½ tsp. vinegar in measuring cup. Add enough milk to make ½ c.

Prize-Winning Cream Cheese Bars

It's hard to believe these fabulous bar cookies are so easy to prepare. They won a blue ribbon at a county fair in Wisconsin.

¾ c. butter or regular margarine
½ c. sugar
2 c. sifted flour
¼ tsp. salt
½ tsp. vanilla

¼ c. butter or regular margarine
1 (3-oz.) pkg. cream cheese, softened
¾ c. brown sugar, packed
1 c. chopped walnuts

Combine ¾ c. butter, sugar, flour, salt and vanilla in bowl. Beat until fine crumbs form, using electric mixer at low speed. Set aside 1 c. crumb mixture for topping. Press remaining crumb mixture into ungreased 13x9x2" baking pan.

Cream together ¼ c. butter, cream cheese and brown sugar in another bowl until light and fluffy, using electric mixer at medium speed. Stir in walnuts. Drop mixture in large spoonfuls over top of crumb crust.

Bake in 375° oven 5 minutes. Remove from oven. Spread cheese mixture evenly over crumb crust. Sprinkle with reserved crumbs. Return to oven. Bake 25 to 30 minutes, or until golden brown. Cool in pan on rack. Cut into 3x1½" bars. Makes 24.

Tutti-Frutti Squares

Fruit-and-nut bars like these are perfect for long-distance mailing at holiday time because they mellow with age.

¾ c. sifted flour
1½ tsp. baking powder
½ tsp. salt
2 eggs
1 c. sifted confectioners' sugar
3 tblsp. melted shortening
1 c. chopped pitted dates

1 c. chopped walnuts
¼ c. chopped candied orange peel
¼ c. chopped candied lemon peel
¼ c. chopped candied pineapple
Confectioners' sugar

Sift together flour, baking powder and salt; set aside.

Beat eggs in bowl until light and lemon-colored, using electric mixer at high speed. Slowly beat in 1 c. confectioners' sugar and shortening.

Gradually stir dry ingredients into creamed mixture, mixing well. Stir in dates, walnuts, orange peel, lemon peel and pineapple. Spread mixture in greased 8" square baking pan.

Bake in 350° oven 35 to 40 minutes, or until no imprint remains when touched lightly with finger. Cool in pan on rack 10 minutes. Cut into 2" squares. Cool completely. Roll cookies in confectioners' sugar. Makes 16.

Cherry-Topped Oatmeal Cookies

This popular oatmeal cookie is pretty enough for the holiday cookie plate. A cherry half is pressed into each one before baking.

1 c. sifted flour	1 egg
½ tsp. baking soda	⅓ c. water
1 tsp. salt	1 tsp. vanilla
¾ c. shortening	3 c. quick-cooking oats
1 c. brown sugar, packed	30 red candied cherries, cut
½ c. sugar	into halves

Sift together flour, baking soda and salt; set aside.

Cream together shortening, brown sugar and sugar in bowl until light and fluffy, using electric mixer at medium speed. Add egg, water and vanilla, beating well.

Gradually stir dry ingredients into creamed mixture, blending well. Stir in oats. Drop mixture by rounded teaspoonfuls, about 3" apart, on greased baking sheets. Press a candied cherry half in center of each cookie.

Bake in 350° oven 15 minutes, or until golden brown. Remove from baking sheets; cool on racks. Makes 5 dozen.

Crispy Thin Gingersnaps

This recipe is very popular in one North Dakota farm home. White sugar is used instead of brown in this thin, chewy ginger cookie.

2 c. sifted flour	1 c. sugar
2 tsp. baking soda	1 egg
1 tsp. ground cloves	¼ c. molasses
1 tsp. ground ginger	Sugar
1 tsp. ground cinnamon	
¾ c. butter or regular margarine	

Sift together flour, baking soda, cloves, ginger and cinnamon; set aside.

Cream together butter and 1 c. sugar in bowl until light and fluffy, using electric mixer at medium speed. Add egg and molasses, beating well.

Gradually stir dry ingredients into creamed mixture, blending well. Cover and chill in refrigerator at least 4 hours, or until dough is firm enough to shape.

Shape dough into 1" balls. Roll in sugar. Place balls, about 2" apart, on greased baking sheets.

Bake in 350° oven 8 minutes, or until no imprint remains when touched lightly with finger. Remove from baking sheets; cool on racks. Makes 3 dozen.

 # French Bars

Cinnamon-spiced bars, loaded with walnuts, dates and coconut, are swirled with a creamy orange-flavored frosting.

2¼ c. unsifted flour
1½ tsp. baking soda
1 tsp. ground cinnamon
½ tsp. salt
4 eggs
2¼ c. brown sugar, packed

1½ c. sour evaporated milk*
1½ c. chopped walnuts
1½ c. cut-up pitted dates
1 c. toasted flaked coconut
Orange Butter Frosting
  (recipe follows)

Mix together flour, baking soda, cinnamon and salt; set aside.

Beat eggs and brown sugar in bowl until thick, using electric mixer at high speed. Stir in soured evaporated milk.

Gradually stir dry ingredients into egg mixture, mixing well. Stir in walnuts, dates and coconut. Do not overmix batter. Spread batter evenly in 2 lightly greased 15½x10½x1" jelly roll pans.

Bake in 350° oven about 20 minutes, or until top springs back when touched lightly with finger. Cool in pans on racks. Prepare Orange Butter Frosting. Frost bars with Orange Butter Frosting. Cut into 2½x1½" bars. Makes 96.

*Note: To sour evaporated milk, pour 1½ tblsp. vinegar into 2-c. measure. Add enough evaporated milk to make 1½ c.

Orange Butter Frosting: Combine 1 (1-lb.) box confectioners' sugar (sifted), ¼ c. butter or regular margarine, ¼ c. orange juice, ½ tsp. salt and 1 tsp. grated orange rind in bowl. Beat until creamy, using electric mixer at low speed.

11 | Country Christmas Favorites

Christmas is a time of celebration and joy—a time for sharing. Farm and ranch families have always opened up their hearts and their homes to friends and relatives during this festive time. In most homes, cookie baking is as much a part of this joyous season as decorating the family tree, giving gifts and sharing a holiday dinner.

Every farm family splurges on special holiday foods, and country kitchens burst with extra bags of walnuts, boxes of brown sugar, lots of creamy butter and pounds and pounds of flour. Right after Thanksgiving, farm women across the country begin turning out a parade of jaunty gingerbread figures, iced sugar cookies and fruit-studded bars. We'd like to share 58 of these top Christmas cookie recipes we've collected over the years.

To create a really special Christmas tree, decorate it with homemade cookies. Two of our meringue cookies make lovely decorations—the pale pink Meringue Candy Canes, and the Meringue Christmas Wreaths sprinkled with green decorating sugar; just tie each one with ribbon and hang it from the boughs of the tree. Our recipe for Hand-Painted Butter Cookies was sent to us from a New York woman whose family joins in the decorating fun, hand-painting the cookies in fanciful designs with food coloring. Gaily decorated gingerbread people or animals also make great ornaments—just wrap each in plastic wrap and tie with a bow. When your holiday guests leave, give each one a gingerbread cookie—a nice personal gift.

You'll find some once-a-year specials for the buffet table, too. Christmas Cherry Bells are rich in chopped pecans and spiced with ginger and cinnamon; they're shaped by hand from rounds of dough, so no bell-shaped cookie cutter is needed. The Date-Filled Poinsettias, sparkling with crystals of red sugar, are as flavorful as they are pretty.

Many farm families serve heirloom cookies from other countries during the holidays. Farmers of German descent enjoy anise-flavored Springerle, small picture cookies made with a special rolling pin, and extra-spicy Chocolate Lebkuchen, chewy bars laden with morsels of chocolate, fruit and nuts. Norwegian-American families in the Midwest make lots of crisp pastry twists called Fattigman, deep-fried and dusted with confectioners' sugar, or the soft, cake-like Kringla, ring-shaped cookies with a delicate flavor and a light vanilla glaze.

Fruitcake lovers have a choice of six candied fruit-studded treats in this chapter, including Iced Ambrosia Drops, Holiday Fruit Bars and Extra-Easy Fruitcake Squares. The last confection doesn't even require any mixing—it's just layered into the pan. If chocolate is your favorite flavor no matter what the season, there's a sumptuous selection of ways to combine chocolate with peppermint, mincemeat, coconut, marshmallows, walnuts and pecans.

Since everyone has a favorite version of the classic sugar cookie, it was almost impossible to limit the selection to just 10 for this chapter. The first recipe, Rolled Sugar Cookies, is one of our best. These buttery-rich cookies will be a hit whether they're offered as part of a holiday cookie assortment or served as a late-evening snack to drop-in guests. If you prefer a cookie with a hint of nutmeg and cinnamon, try the extra-thin and crisp White Christmas Cookies. For all novice bakers, we've included No-Stick Rolled Butter Cookies—an extra-easy rolled cookie recipe that assures you success every time. And if you like sugar cookies but don't like rolling them out, bake these hand-shaped ones: Heirloom Sugar Cookies, dusted with confectioners' sugar, or crackle-topped Crisp Sugar Cookies.

Each one of these cookies is part of a happy tradition for some farm family; we hope some of them will become annual traditions in your home, too.

Rolled Sugar Cookies

One of our best sugar cookies—ideal for Christmas entertaining. For a touch of color, just sprinkle with decorating sugar before baking.

2 eggs	2 tsp. cream of tartar
1 c. sugar	1 tsp. baking soda
1 tsp. vanilla	1 c. butter or regular
3 c. sifted flour	margarine

Beat eggs in bowl thoroughly, using electric mixer at high speed. Add sugar and vanilla; beat well.

Sift together flour, cream of tartar and baking soda into another bowl. Cut in butter until mixture is crumbly, using pastry blender. Add egg mixture, stirring until dough is moist enough to hold together. Cover and chill in refrigerator 20 minutes.

Divide dough into fourths. Roll out each fourth on lightly floured surface to ¼" thickness. Cut with floured 2" cookie cutter. Place, about 2" apart, on greased baking sheets.

Bake in 400° oven 8 to 10 minutes, or until golden brown. Remove from baking sheets; cool on racks. Makes about 5½ dozen.

White Christmas Cookies

A big-batch recipe that turns out thin fragile cookies with a hint of nutmeg and cinnamon. For a smaller batch, cut recipe in half.

4 c. sifted flour	½ c. shortening
⅛ tsp. ground nutmeg	2 c. sugar
⅛ tsp. ground cinnamon	4 eggs
½ c. butter or regular margarine	

Sift together flour, nutmeg and cinnamon; set aside.

Cream together butter, shortening and sugar in bowl until light and fluffy, using electric mixer at medium speed. Beat in eggs, one at a time, beating well after each addition.

Gradually stir dry ingredients into creamed mixture, mixing well. (Dough will be stiff.) Store in covered bowl in refrigerator overnight.

Divide dough into fourths. Roll out each fourth on lightly floured surface to ⅛" thickness. Cut into star shapes. Place, 2" apart, on greased baking sheets.

Bake in 350° oven 10 to 12 minutes, or until crisp and straw-colored. Remove from baking sheets; cool on racks. Makes 16 dozen.

No-Stick Rolled Butter Cookies

Here's a no-fail recipe that has won several blue ribbons. The dough won't stick to the rolling pin, so it's easy to handle.

3 c. sifted flour	2 eggs
1 tsp. baking soda	1 c. sugar
2 tsp. cream of tartar	1 tsp. vanilla
1 c. butter or regular margarine	Sugar

Sift together flour, baking soda and cream of tartar into bowl. Cut in butter until mixture is crumbly, using pastry blender.

Beat eggs, 1 c. sugar and vanilla in another bowl until well blended, using rotary beater. Stir egg mixture into crumb mixture, mixing until blended. Cover and chill in refrigerator 15 minutes.

Divide dough into fourths. Roll out each fourth of dough on floured surface to ⅛" thickness. Cut with floured 2" round cookie cutter. Place rounds, about 2" apart, on greased baking sheets. Sprinkle each with sugar.

Bake in 350° oven 10 minutes, or until golden brown. Remove from baking sheets; cool on racks. Makes 4 dozen.

Hand-Painted Butter Cookies

These colorful cookies are pretty enough to hang on the tree. Since they're painted with food coloring, they're edible, too.

4½ c. sifted flour	1 c. sugar
¼ tsp. salt	2 eggs
1½ c. butter or regular margarine	1 tsp. grated lemon rind
	Food coloring

Sift together flour and salt; set aside.

Cream together butter and sugar in bowl until light and fluffy, using electric mixer at medium speed. Add eggs and lemon rind; beat well.

Gradually add dry ingredients to creamed mixture, mixing well with spoon. Cover and chill dough in refrigerator 3 to 4 hours.

Divide dough into fourths. Roll out one fourth at a time on lightly floured surface to ⅛" thickness. Cut into desired shapes with floured cookie cutters. Place, about 2" apart, on greased baking sheets.

Bake in 400° oven 6 to 8 minutes, or until golden brown. If cookies will be used as tree decorations, twist a small hole in the top of each cookie with a toothpick. Cool slightly. Remove from baking sheets; cool completely on racks. Makes 6 dozen.

To decorate cookies: Pour food coloring in small saucers. Add a few drops of water. You can make many beautiful colors by mixing the basic colors. Use narrow brushes for fine lines and wider brushes for large areas. Rinse brush out in water when you change colors so that your colors will be clear and not murky. With colors of your choice, paint your own original designs on the cookies.

To hang cookies on the tree, draw narrow colored cord through the hole in each cookie.

Danish Christmas Cookies

*For a festive touch, frost each buttery round with your favorite con-
fectioners' sugar icing and top with a bright red cherry half.*

1 c. butter or regular	½ tsp. almond extract
margarine	½ tsp. vanilla
½ c. sugar	2½ c. sifted flour
½ tsp. lemon extract	

Cream together butter and sugar in bowl until light and fluffy, using electric mixer at medium speed. Beat in lemon extract, almond extract and vanilla. Gradually stir in flour, mixing well. Cover with plastic wrap. Chill in refrigerator 30 minutes.

Shape dough into 13" roll. Wrap in plastic wrap and chill in refrigerator 8 hours or overnight. (Can be stored 2 days.)

Cut into ¼" slices. Place rounds, about 2" apart, on greased baking sheets.

Bake in 350° oven 8 minutes, or until golden brown. Remove from baking sheets; cool on racks. Frost with confectioners' sugar icing, if you wish (see Index for recipe). Makes about 4 dozen.

Heirloom Sugar Cookies

*Another Danish sugar cookie—this one's shaped into balls. This treas-
ured heirloom recipe was sent to us by a Minnesota farm wife.*

2 c. sifted flour	¼ c. sugar
¼ tsp. salt	2 tsp. vanilla
1 c. butter or regular	1 c. chopped walnuts
margarine	Confectioners' sugar

Sift together flour and salt; set aside.

Cream together butter and sugar in bowl until light and fluffy, using electric mixer at medium speed. Beat in vanilla.

Gradually add dry ingredients to creamed mixture, mixing well with spoon. Stir in walnuts. Shape dough into 1" balls. Place balls, about 2" apart, on greased baking sheets.

Bake in 350° oven 12 minutes, or until golden brown. Remove from baking sheets; cool on racks. Roll cookies in confectioners' sugar. Makes about 3½ dozen.

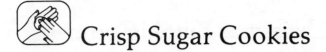

Crisp Sugar Cookies

Old-fashioned crackle-topped sugar cookies are perfect for the holidays when you don't have time to make rolled sugar cookies.

2½ c. sifted flour	½ c. shortening
1 tsp. baking soda	½ c. brown sugar, packed
1 tsp. cream of tartar	½ c. sugar
½ tsp. salt	1 egg
½ c. butter or regular margarine	1 tsp. vanilla
	Sugar

Sift together flour, baking soda, cream of tartar and salt; set aside.

Cream together butter, shortening, brown sugar and ½ c. sugar in bowl until light and fluffy, using electric mixer at medium speed. Beat in egg and vanilla.

Gradually stir dry ingredients into creamed mixture, blending well. Shape dough into 1¼" balls. Roll in sugar. Place balls, about 2" apart, on greased baking sheets. Flatten each with greased bottom of drinking glass.

Bake in 425° oven 6 minutes, or until lightly browned and crackled on top. Remove from baking sheets; cool on racks. Makes 4 dozen.

Christmas Jewel Cookies

To make these mouth-watering butter cookies look even more special, we suggest spreading them with your favorite vanilla glaze.

1 c. butter or regular margarine	1 tsp. vanilla
½ c. sugar	2 c. sifted flour
3 hard-cooked egg yolks	Strawberry or currant jelly

Cream together butter and sugar in bowl until light and fluffy, using electric mixer at medium speed. Break up egg yolks and beat into creamed mixture; blend well. Add vanilla.

Gradually stir flour into creamed mixture, mixing well. Cover and chill in refrigerator 1 hour.

Shape dough into 1" balls. Place balls, about 2" apart, on ungreased baking sheets. Make a small dent in top of each cookie with finger.

Bake in 375° oven 10 minutes, or until golden brown. Remove from oven and fill dents with jelly. Return to oven and bake 1 to 2 more minutes to set jelly. If you wish, top with your favorite vanilla glaze while cookies are still warm (see Index for recipe). Remove from baking sheets; cool on racks. Makes 5 dozen.

Frosted Christmas Butter Cookies

Sour cream, brown sugar and butter make these cookies absolutely divine. They're easily made, too, because they're drop cookies.

3 c. sifted flour	1 c. brown sugar, packed
1 tsp. baking soda	3 eggs
1 tsp. cream of tartar	1 c. dairy sour cream
1 c. butter or regular margarine	Vanilla Frosting (recipe follows)
1 c. sugar	

Sift together flour, baking soda and cream of tartar; set aside.

Cream together butter, sugar and brown sugar in bowl until light and fluffy, using electric mixer at medium speed. Add eggs, one at a time, beating well after each addition.

Add dry ingredients alternately with sour cream to creamed mixture, beating well after each addition, using electric mixer at low speed. Drop mixture by rounded teaspoonfuls, about 3" apart, on greased baking sheets.

Bake in 350° oven 8 to 10 minutes, or until edges are browned. Remove from baking sheets; cool on racks. Prepare Vanilla Frosting. Frost cookies with Vanilla Frosting. Makes 7 dozen.

Vanilla Frosting: Combine 4 c. sifted confectioners' sugar, 1 tsp. vanilla and 4 tblsp. milk in bowl. Beat until smooth, using a spoon. Add 1 more tblsp. milk, if necessary, to make frosting of spreading consistency.

Cinnamon Sugar Puffs

The recipe for these puffy drop cookies, sprinkled with sugar and cinnamon, was sent to us by a Pennsylvania homemaker.

4 c. sifted flour	3 eggs
2 tsp. baking powder	1 c. dairy sour cream
1 tsp. baking soda	1 tsp. vanilla
1 tsp. salt	3 tblsp. sugar
1 c. lard	½ tsp. ground cinnamon
2 c. sugar	

Sift together flour, baking powder, baking soda and salt; set aside.

Cream together lard and 2 c. sugar in bowl until light and fluffy, using electric mixer at medium speed. Add eggs, one at a time, beating well after each addition. Blend in sour cream and vanilla.

Gradually stir dry ingredients into creamed mixture, blending well. Drop mixture by rounded teaspoonfuls, about 3" apart, on greased baking sheets. Combine 3 tblsp. sugar and cinnamon. Sprinkle sugar-cinnamon mixture over each cookie.

Bake in 375° oven 10 minutes, or until golden brown. Remove from baking sheets; cool on racks. Makes 5 dozen.

Spiced Christmas Cookies

This extra-spicy gingerbread dough is rolled out very thin. A single batch makes 19 dozen, but the recipe may be halved.

5 c. sifted flour
1 tblsp. ground cinnamon
1½ tsp. ground ginger
½ tsp. ground cloves
½ c. butter or regular
  margarine

½ c. shortening
1½ c. brown sugar, packed
2 c. molasses
2 tblsp. light cream or dairy
  half-and-half

Sift together flour, cinnamon, ginger and cloves; set aside.

Cream together butter, shortening and brown sugar in bowl until light and fluffy, using electric mixer at medium speed. Beat in molasses and cream.

Gradually stir dry ingredients into creamed mixture, mixing well. Cover and chill in refrigerator overnight.

Divide dough into fourths. Roll out each fourth on lightly floured surface to ⅛" thickness. Cut with floured cookie cutters. Place, about 1½" apart, on greased baking sheets.

Bake in 350° oven 10 to 12 minutes, or until no imprint remains when touched lightly with finger. Remove from baking sheets; cool on racks. Makes 19 dozen.

Molasses-Ginger Cookies

This is a milder version of a gingerbread cookie and this recipe makes only 2½ dozen—perfect size for smaller families.

½ c. shortening
½ c. sugar
½ c. light molasses
½ tblsp. vinegar
3 c. sifted flour

½ tsp. baking soda
½ tsp. ground cinnamon
½ tsp. ground ginger
¼ tsp. salt
1 egg, beaten

Combine shortening, sugar, molasses and vinegar in small saucepan. Cook over medium heat until it comes to a boil. Remove from heat. Cool completely.

Sift together flour, baking soda, cinnamon, ginger and salt; set aside.

Stir egg into molasses mixture. Gradually stir dry ingredients into molasses mixture, mixing well. Cover and chill in refrigerator 1 hour.

Divide dough in half. Use one half of dough at a time, keeping remaining dough in refrigerator. Roll out each half of dough on floured surface to ⅛" thickness. Cut into desired shapes with floured cookie cutters. Place, about 1" apart, on greased baking sheets.

Bake in 375° oven 10 minutes, or until a slight imprint remains when touched lightly with finger. Remove from baking sheets; cool on racks. Makes about 2½ dozen.

Gingerbread Men

Spicy gingerbread figures are fun to decorate. Using your favorite confectioners' sugar icing, add faces, jackets, buttons and shoes.

5 c. sifted flour	1 c. shortening
2 tsp. ground ginger	1 c. sugar
1½ tsp. baking soda	1 egg
1 tsp. ground cinnamon	1 c. molasses
1 tsp. ground cloves	2 tblsp. vinegar
½ tsp. salt	

Sift together flour, ginger, baking soda, cinnamon, cloves and salt; set aside.

Cream together shortening and sugar in bowl until light and fluffy, using electric mixer at medium speed. Add egg, molasses and vinegar; beat well.

Gradually stir dry ingredients into creamed mixture, mixing well. Cover and chill in refrigerator at least 3 hours.

Divide dough into fourths. Use one fourth of dough at a time, keeping remaining dough in refrigerator. Roll out each fourth of dough on floured surface to ⅛" thickness. Cut with floured gingerbread cookie cutter. Place cookies, about 1½" apart, on greased baking sheets.

Bake in 375° oven 5 to 6 minutes, or until no imprint remains when touched lightly with finger. Cool on baking sheets a few seconds. Remove from baking sheets; cool on racks. Decorate with confectioners' sugar icing (see Index for recipe). Makes 5 dozen 4" cookies.

Spicy Molasses Cookies

If you like gingerbread cookies but don't want to bother rolling out the dough, try these chewy, crackle-topped treats.

4 c. sifted flour	1½ c. melted shortening
4 tsp. baking soda	2 c. sugar
2 tsp. ground cinnamon	2 eggs
1 tsp. salt	½ c. molasses
1 tsp. ground cloves	Sugar
1 tsp. ground ginger	

Stir together flour, baking soda, cinnamon, salt, cloves and ginger; set aside.

Combine melted shortening and 2 c. sugar in bowl; beat until blended, using electric mixer at medium speed. Add eggs, one at a time, beating well after each addition. Gradually stir in molasses.

Gradually add dry ingredients to molasses mixture, mixing well with a spoon. Cover and chill dough in refrigerator 8 hours or overnight.

Shape dough into 1" balls. Roll each in sugar. Place balls, about 2" apart, on ungreased baking sheets.

Bake in 375° oven 8 to 10 minutes, or until golden brown. Let cool slightly on baking sheets. Remove from baking sheets; cool completely on racks. Makes about 7 dozen.

German Refrigerator Cookies

The Wisconsin woman who shared this recipe wrote, "I don't remember a Christmas when we didn't have dozens of these."

2 c. sifted flour	½ c. lard
1 tsp. baking soda	2 c. sugar
½ tsp. ground cardamom	1 egg
½ c. butter or regular margarine	

Sift together flour, baking soda and cardamom; set aside.

Cream together butter, lard and sugar in bowl until light and fluffy, using electric mixer at medium speed. Add egg; beat well.

Stir dry ingredients into creamed mixture, mixing well. Cover and chill in refrigerator overnight.

Shape dough into 1" balls. Place, about 1½" apart, on greased baking sheets.

Bake in 325° oven 10 minutes, or until golden brown. Remove from baking sheets; cool on racks. Makes 5 dozen.

German Spice Cookies

A sharply spiced ginger cookie that's shaped into balls before baking. This heirloom recipe was brought to this country from Germany.

6½ c. sifted flour	1 c. shortening
2 tsp. ground cinnamon	2 c. brown sugar, packed
1 tsp. baking soda	3 eggs
1 tsp. ground ginger	⅔ c. molasses
1 tsp. ground cloves	1 tsp. vanilla
½ tsp. salt	⅓ c. sour milk*

Sift together flour, cinnamon, baking soda, ginger, cloves and salt; set aside.

Cream together shortening and brown sugar in bowl until light and fluffy, using electric mixer at medium speed. Add eggs, one at a time, beating well after each addition. Beat in molasses and vanilla.

Add dry ingredients alternately with sour milk to creamed mixture, beating well after each addition, using electric mixer at low speed. Cover and chill dough in refrigerator 1 hour.

Shape dough into 1" balls. Place balls, about 2" apart, on greased baking sheets.

Bake in 350° oven 15 minutes, or until golden brown. Remove from baking sheets; cool on racks. Makes 8 dozen.

*Note: To sour milk, place 1 tsp. vinegar in glass measuring cup. Add enough milk to fill to ⅓ c.

Chocolate Lebkuchen

"I'd like to share my German Lebkuchen with you. It's filled with spices, honey and chocolate chips," wrote an Indiana woman.

2¾ c. sifted flour	2 tblsp. water
2 tsp. ground cinnamon	2 eggs
1½ tsp. ground cardamom	¼ c. orange juice
1 tsp. baking powder	1 (12-oz.) pkg. semisweet
1 tsp. baking soda	chocolate pieces
½ tsp. ground cloves	1 c. chopped walnuts
1¼ c. sugar	½ c. mixed candied fruit
¾ c. honey	Confectioners' sugar

Sift together flour, cinnamon, cardamom, baking powder, baking soda and cloves; set aside.

Combine sugar, honey and water in 2-qt. saucepan. Cook over medium heat, stirring constantly, until it comes to a boil. Remove from heat. Pour into large bowl. Cool to room temperature.

Add eggs and orange juice to cooled honey mixture. Beat 1 minute, using electric mixer at medium speed.

Add dry ingredients to egg mixture, beating 2 minutes at medium speed. Stir in chocolate pieces, walnuts and candied fruit. Spread batter in greased 15½x10½x1" jelly roll pan.

Bake in 325° oven 35 minutes, or until top springs back when touched lightly with finger. Cool in pan on rack. Cover with aluminum foil. Store 3 days at room temperature to develop flavor. Dust with confectioners' sugar. Cut into 2" squares. Makes 35.

 Lebkuchen

This German cookie was popular before the advent of freezers because it kept so well. It's still a tradition in many farm homes.

¾ c. honey	½ tsp. salt
¾ c. sugar	¼ tsp. ground cloves
1 egg	⅓ c. chopped citron
1 tsp. grated lemon rind	½ c. chopped blanched
1 tblsp. milk	almonds
2¾ c. sifted flour	1 c. sifted confectioners'
1 tsp. ground cinnamon	sugar
1 tsp. ground allspice	4 tsp. water

Heat honey in large saucepan over medium heat. Do not boil. Remove from heat. Stir in sugar. Add egg, beating well with spoon. Stir in lemon rind and milk; set aside.

Sift together flour, cinnamon, allspice, salt and cloves. Stir dry ingredients into honey mixture, mixing well. Stir in citron and almonds. Form dough into a ball. Wrap in waxed paper and chill in refrigerator several hours or overnight.

Divide dough in half and let stand 15 minutes at room temperature. Spread dough in 2 greased 13x9x2" baking pans.

Bake in 400° oven 15 minutes, or until lightly browned. Cool slightly in pans on racks. Combine confectioners' sugar and water in bowl; mix well. Brush top of warm bars with confectioners' sugar icing. While still warm, cut into 3x1" bars. Remove from baking pans; cool on racks. Store in airtight containers. Can be stored for several weeks. Makes 78.

Holland Spice Cookies

A Midwest farmer's wife sent us this heirloom recipe. These spicy cookies may be iced and decorated with candied fruit.

4½ c. sifted flour
3 tsp. ground cinnamon
1 tsp. salt
½ tsp. baking soda
½ tsp. ground nutmeg
¼ tsp. ground cloves

1 c. butter or regular
  margarine
1 c. lard
2 c. brown sugar, packed
½ c. dairy sour cream
½ c. chopped walnuts

Sift together flour, cinnamon, salt, baking soda, nutmeg and cloves; set aside.

Cream together butter, lard and brown sugar in bowl until light and fluffy, using electric mixer at medium speed. Beat in sour cream.

Gradually add dry ingredients to creamed mixture, mixing well with a spoon. Stir in walnuts. Cover and chill in refrigerator 1 hour.

Shape dough into 4 (6") rolls. Wrap each tightly in plastic wrap or waxed paper. Chill in refrigerator overnight.

Cut rolls into ¼" slices. Place rounds, about 2" apart, on greased baking sheets.

Bake in 350° oven 8 to 10 minutes, or until golden brown. Remove from baking sheets; cool on racks. If you wish, frost with confectioners' sugar frosting (see Index for recipe) and decorate with pieces of candied fruit. Makes 8 dozen.

Scandinavian Spritz

These dainty butter cookies can be decorated with bits of green or red candied cherries and silver or gold dragées.

2¼ c. sifted flour
½ tsp. baking powder
¼ tsp. salt
1 c. butter or regular
  margarine

¾ c. sugar
3 egg yolks
1 tsp. almond extract

Sift together flour, baking powder and salt; set aside.

Cream together butter and sugar in bowl until light and fluffy, using electric mixer at medium speed. Add egg yolks and almond extract.

Gradually stir dry ingredients into creamed mixture, using hands if dough becomes crumbly.

Fit desired design into cookie press. Place one half of the dough in cookie press at a time, forcing dough through press, about 1" apart, on ungreased baking sheets.

Bake in 400° oven 7 to 10 minutes, or until set but not browned. Remove from baking sheets; cool on racks. Makes about 6 dozen.

Fattigman

These crisp twists of pastry are traditional favorites among Norwegian-American communities in Wisconsin and Minnesota.

2¼ c. sifted flour	1 tblsp. melted butter or
¼ tsp. ground nutmeg	regular margarine
6 egg yolks	1 tblsp. grated lemon rind
½ tsp. salt	Cooking oil
⅓ c. light cream	Confectioners' sugar
⅓ c. sugar	

Sift together flour and nutmeg; set aside.

Beat together egg yolks and salt in bowl until thick and light, using electric mixer at high speed. Beat in light cream, sugar and butter.

Gradually add dry ingredients to egg yolk mixture with lemon rind, mixing well with a spoon. Cover and chill in refrigerator 1 hour.

Divide dough into fourths. Roll out one fourth of dough at a time, keeping remaining dough chilled. Roll to ¹/₁₆" thickness. Cut into strips about 1½" wide with sharp knife. Cut diagonally at 4" intervals. Make 1" slits lengthwise in center of each piece. Slip one end through slit to form a knot.

Fry a few at a time in deep, hot oil at 350° for 1 to 2 minutes or until golden. Remove from oil with slotted spoon. Drain on paper towels. Sprinkle with confectioners' sugar. Store in an airtight container. Makes 6 dozen.

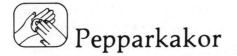

Pepparkakor

There are many versions of this Swedish gingersnap. This one contains a sprinkle of black pepper for added zing.

3½ c. sifted flour	1 c. lard
1 tblsp. ground ginger	1 c. sugar
1 tsp. baking soda	1 c. light molasses
1 tsp. salt	Sugar
½ tsp. pepper	

Sift together flour, ginger, baking soda, salt and pepper; set aside.

Cream together lard and 1 c. sugar in bowl until light and fluffy, using electric mixer at medium speed. Beat in molasses.

Add dry ingredients to creamed mixture, mixing well with a spoon. Cover and chill dough in refrigerator at least 2 hours.

Shape dough into 1" balls. Roll balls in sugar. Place balls, about 1½" apart, on greased baking sheets.

Bake in 350° oven 12 to 15 minutes, or until lightly browned. Cool on baking sheets 1 minute. Remove from baking sheets; cool on racks. Makes about 7 dozen.

Springerle

These unique sugar cookies get their classic look from a springerle rolling pin—each cookie looks like a tiny picture (see illustration).

4 c. sifted cake flour	2 c. sugar
1 tsp. baking powder	2 tblsp. butter or regular
¼ tsp. salt	margarine, melted
4 eggs	1 tblsp. anise seeds

Sift together cake flour, baking powder and salt; set aside.

Beat eggs in bowl until thoroughly mixed, using electric mixer at high speed. Gradually add sugar, beating well at high speed for 10 minutes.

Add dry ingredients to egg mixture alternately with melted butter, beating well after each addition. Cover and chill dough in refrigerator at least 1 hour.

Divide dough in half. Use one half of dough at a time, keeping remaining dough in refrigerator. Roll out each half of dough on floured surface to about ½" thickness. Lightly flour springerle rolling pin and roll over dough just once to press in designs.

Lightly grease baking sheets and sprinkle evenly with anise seeds. Lift dough carefully to baking sheets and cover loosely with waxed paper. Let stand at room temperature overnight.

The next morning, cut dough into square-shaped cookies following lines made by springerle rolling pin. Separate, about ½" apart, on baking sheets.

Bake in 350° oven 5 minutes. Then reduce heat to 300° and continue baking 10 minutes more, or until cookies turn a light straw color. Remove from baking sheets; cool on racks. Makes 3½ dozen.

 # Kringla

Slightly soft, ring-shaped cookies dressed in a delicate vanilla icing. They're certain to add interest to your cookie tray.

3¼ c. sifted flour	1 c. sugar
2½ tsp. baking powder	1 egg
1 tsp. baking soda	1 tsp. vanilla
½ tsp. salt	1 c. buttermilk
½ c. butter or regular margarine	Vanilla Glaze (recipe follows)

Sift together flour, baking powder, baking soda and salt; set aside.

Cream together butter and sugar in bowl until light and fluffy, using electric mixer at medium speed. Add egg and vanilla; beat well.

Add dry ingredients alternately with buttermilk to creamed mixture, beating well after each addition, using electric mixer at low speed. Cover and chill in refrigerator several hours or overnight.

Roll 1 tblsp. of dough on a floured surface, making a 5" stick. Place on greased baking sheet. Shape each stick into a ring and join ends. Repeat with remaining dough.

Bake in 350° oven 12 minutes, or until golden brown. Remove from baking sheets; cool on racks. Prepare Vanilla Glaze. Spread cookies with Vanilla Glaze. Makes about 5½ dozen.

Vanilla Glaze: Combine 1½ c. sifted confectioners' sugar, 1½ tblsp. water and 1 tsp. vanilla. Beat until smooth, using a spoon. If necessary, add more water to make a thin glaze.

French Lace Cookies

Taste-tempting lacy cookies, rich with finely chopped walnuts, add an elegant touch to any Yuletide cookie assortment.

½ c. dark corn syrup	⅔ c. brown sugar, packed
½ c. butter or regular margarine	1 c. sifted flour
	1 c. finely chopped walnuts

Combine corn syrup, butter and brown sugar in 2-qt. saucepan. Cook over medium heat, stirring constantly, until it comes to a boil. Remove from heat.

Gradually stir in flour and walnuts, mixing well. Drop mixture by level measuring teaspoonfuls, about 3" apart, on aluminum foil-covered baking sheets.

Bake in 375° oven 5 to 6 minutes, or until golden brown. Let cool on baking sheets 5 minutes. Remove from baking sheets by pulling foil away from cookies. Cool on racks. Makes 5 dozen.

Date-Filled Poinsettias

These plump, pinwheel-shaped cookies are filled with a mixture of dates and peanuts, then sprinkled with bright red sugar.

6 c. sifted flour
2 tsp. baking powder
1 tsp. baking soda
¼ tsp. salt
1 c. lard
2 c. sugar
2 eggs
1 tsp. vanilla

½ tsp. lemon extract
2 tblsp. grated orange rind
¼ c. orange juice
1 c. dairy sour cream
Date-Peanut Filling (recipe follows)
Red decorating sugar

Sift together flour, baking powder, baking soda and salt; set aside.

Cream together lard and sugar in bowl until light and fluffy, using electric mixer at medium speed. Add eggs, one at a time, beating well after each addition. Blend in vanilla, lemon extract, orange rind and orange juice.

Add dry ingredients alternately with sour cream to creamed mixture, beating well after each addition, using electric mixer at low speed. Cover and chill dough in refrigerator 3 hours. Meanwhile, prepare Date-Peanut Filling; set aside.

Divide dough into fourths. Use one fourth of the dough at a time, keeping remaining dough in refrigerator. Roll out on floured surface to 12" square. Cut into 16 (3") squares. To make poinsettias: Make diagonal cuts in each 3" square from corners to within ½" of center. Place about 1 tsp. Date-Peanut Filling in center of square. Fold right sides of each diagonal cut to center over filling, forming pinwheel. Place filled cookies, about 2" apart, on greased baking sheets. Sprinkle each with red decorating sugar.

Bake in 350° oven 8 to 10 minutes, or until golden brown. Remove from baking sheets; cool on racks. Makes 64.

Date-Peanut Filling: Combine 1 c. chopped pitted dates, ⅔ c. water and 2 tblsp. lemon juice in 2-qt. saucepan. Cook over medium heat, stirring constantly, until mixture thickens. Remove from heat. Stir in ½ c. chopped salted peanuts. Cool completely.

Christmas Cherry Bells

You can make these cheerful cookies just by folding circles of dough—no bell-shaped cookie cutter is needed.

3 c. sifted flour	1 egg
½ tsp. baking soda	1 tblsp. light cream
½ tsp. salt	1½ c. finely chopped pecans
½ tsp. ground ginger	⅓ c. brown sugar, packed
½ tsp. ground cinnamon	3 tblsp. maraschino cherry
1 c. butter or regular	juice
margarine	1 tblsp. butter or regular
1¼ c. brown sugar, packed	margarine
¼ c. dark corn syrup	Maraschino cherries

Sift together flour, baking soda, salt, ginger and cinnamon; set aside.

Cream together 1 c. butter and 1¼ c. brown sugar in bowl until light and fluffy, using electric mixer at medium speed. Add corn syrup, egg and light cream; beat well.

Gradually stir dry ingredients into creamed mixture, mixing well. Cover and chill in refrigerator 1 hour.

Divide dough into thirds. Roll out each third on floured surface to ⅛" thickness. Cut with floured 2½" round cookie cutter. Place rounds, about 2" apart, on ungreased baking sheets.

Combine pecans, ⅓ c. brown sugar, cherry juice and 1 tblsp. butter in bowl; mix well. Place ½ tsp. pecan filling in center of each round. Shape into bell by folding sides to center over filling, overlapping slightly. Fold edges so that top is narrower than bottom. Place a piece of maraschino cherry at bottom of bell for clapper.

Bake in 325° oven 12 to 15 minutes, or until golden brown. Remove from baking sheets; cool on racks. Makes about 6 dozen.

Pumpkin Pie Squares

A delicious variation of the traditional pumpkin pie—serves 24. Top each of these bar cookies with a puff of whipped cream.

1 c. sifted flour
½ c. quick-cooking oats
½ c. brown sugar, packed
½ c. butter or regular
  margarine
1 (16-oz.) can mashed
  pumpkin (2 c.)
1 (13½-oz.) can evaporated
  milk
2 eggs

¾ c. sugar
1 tsp. ground cinnamon
½ tsp. salt
½ tsp. ground ginger
¼ tsp. ground cloves
½ c. chopped pecans
½ c. brown sugar, packed
2 tblsp. butter or regular
  margarine

Combine flour, oats, ½ c. brown sugar and ½ c. butter in bowl. Mix until crumbly, using electric mixer at low speed. Press dough into bottom and ½" up sides of ungreased 13x9x2" baking pan. Bake in 350° oven 15 minutes.

Combine pumpkin, evaporated milk, eggs, sugar, cinnamon, salt, ginger and cloves in bowl. Beat well, using rotary beater. Pour into baked crust.

Bake in 350° oven 20 minutes.

Combine pecans, ½ c. brown sugar and 2 tblsp. butter; sprinkle over pumpkin filling. Return to oven and bake 15 minutes, or until filling is set. Cool in pan on rack. Cut into 2¼" squares. Makes 24.

Mincemeat Pie Bars

When topped with a scoop of vanilla ice cream, these mincemeat pastries make a great holiday dessert for a large group.

2½ c. sifted flour
1 tsp. salt
1 c. shortening

5 to 6 tblsp. water
2 c. prepared mincemeat
2 tblsp. sugar

Combine flour and salt in bowl. Cut in shortening until crumbly, using a pastry blender. Add enough water until dough holds together, mixing with fork.

Divide dough in half. Roll out one half on floured surface to make a 14x9" rectangle. Place on ungreased baking sheet. Spread mincemeat to within ½" of edges.

Roll out remaining one half of dough to 14x9" rectangle. Place over mincemeat; seal edges with fork. Prick top with fork. Sprinkle with sugar.

Bake in 400° oven 30 minutes, or until golden brown. Cool slightly in pan on rack. Cut into 2" squares. Serve warm or cold. Makes 28.

Candy Cane Cookies

Children will be delighted with these Christmasy red and white candy canes. They look especially festive with big green bows.

3½ c. sifted flour	1 egg
1 tsp. salt	1 tsp. vanilla
1¼ c. butter or regular margarine	¼ tsp. almond extract
	8 drops red food coloring
1 c. sifted confectioners' sugar	1 egg, beaten
	Red decorating sugar

Sift together flour and salt; set aside.

Cream together butter and confectioners' sugar in bowl until light and fluffy, using electric mixer at medium speed. Add 1 egg, vanilla and almond extract; beat well.

Stir dry ingredients into creamed mixture, mixing well.

Divide dough in half. Add red food coloring to one half. Using 1 measuring teaspoon of red dough, shape into 4″ long rope by rolling on floured surface. Using 1 measuring teaspoon of uncolored dough, shape into 4″ long rope by rolling on floured surface. Twist one plain rope and one red rope together and shape into a candy cane. Place, about 2″ apart, on ungreased baking sheets. Brush with beaten egg. Sprinkle each with red sugar.

Bake in 350° oven 10 to 12 minutes, or until lightly browned. Remove from baking sheets; cool on racks. Makes 4½ dozen.

Meringue Candy Canes

These pretty pink candy canes are decorated with red sugar. To keep them crisp, be sure to store in airtight containers.

4 egg whites	1 c. sugar
¼ tsp. cream of tartar	Red food coloring
½ tsp. vanilla	Red decorating sugar

Beat together egg whites, cream of tartar and vanilla in large bowl until foamy, using electric mixer at high speed. Gradually add sugar and continue beating until stiff peaks form. Tint pink with a few drops of red food coloring.

Fill a large pastry bag fitted with a medium star tip (#4) with meringue mixture. Pipe mixture into 3½″ long candy canes, about 1″ apart, on baking sheets covered with brown paper. Sprinkle each with red decorating sugar.

Bake in 275° oven 45 minutes, or until set but not browned. Turn off oven and leave meringues in oven 1 hour to dry out. Remove from oven. When meringues are completely cool, remove from paper. Store in an airtight container. If you wish, you can tie candy canes with red or green ribbons, and hang them on the tree. Makes 5 dozen.

Meringue Christmas Wreaths

If you wish to tint wreaths a pale green color, add a few drops of green food coloring to the egg whites after you add the sugar.

4 egg whites	1 c. sugar
¼ tsp. cream of tartar	Green decorating sugar
½ tsp. vanilla	

Beat together egg whites, cream of tartar and vanilla in large bowl until foamy, using electric mixer at high speed. Gradually add sugar and continue beating until stiff peaks form.

Fill a large pastry bag fitted with a large star tip (#6) with meringue mixture. Pipe mixture into 3" rings, about 1" apart, on baking sheets covered with brown paper. Sprinkle each with green decorating sugar.

Bake in 275° oven 1 hour, or until set but not browned. Turn off oven and leave meringues in oven 1 hour to dry out. Remove from oven. When meringues are completely cool, remove from paper. Store in an airtight container. If you wish, you can pull red or green ribbons through wreaths, and hang them on the tree. Makes 27.

Walnut Meringue Cookies

A quick and easy meringue cookie filled with crispy rice cereal and finely chopped walnuts. It has a delicate cinnamon flavor.

2 egg whites	1 tsp. ground cinnamon
Dash of salt	2 c. toasted rice cereal
½ c. sugar	1 c. finely chopped walnuts

Beat egg whites with salt in bowl until foamy, using electric mixer at high speed. Gradually add sugar and cinnamon, beating until mixture is stiff and glossy. Fold in rice cereal and walnuts. Drop mixture by teaspoonfuls, about 3" apart, on well-greased baking sheets.

Bake in 350° oven 10 minutes, or until very lightly browned. Remove from baking sheets; cool on racks. Store in an airtight container. Makes 3 dozen.

Chocolate-Walnut Kisses

These light, airy meringue cookies are filled with chocolate chips, cornflakes and coconut. They're both chewy and crunchy.

3 egg whites	1 c. flaked coconut
½ tsp. cream of tartar	½ c. semisweet chocolate
1 c. sugar	pieces
½ tsp. vanilla	½ c. chopped walnuts
3 c. cornflakes	

Beat egg whites with cream of tartar in bowl until foamy, using electric mixer at high speed. Gradually beat in sugar, beating until stiff peaks form. Add vanilla.

Combine cornflakes, coconut, chocolate pieces and walnuts in large bowl. Carefully fold in egg white mixture. Drop by heaping teaspoonfuls, about 2" apart, on lightly greased baking sheets.

Bake in 350° oven 15 minutes, or until lightly browned. Immediately remove from baking sheets; cool on racks. (If kisses become too hard to remove from baking sheets, return to oven a few minutes to soften.) Store in an airtight container. Makes 4 dozen.

Chocolate-Covered Turtle Cookies

These whimsical cookies are shaped like tiny turtles. Fun to make and a great addition to any get-together.

1½ c. sifted flour	2 eggs
¼ tsp. baking soda	1 tsp. vanilla
¼ tsp. baking powder	8 oz. large pecan halves (160
½ c. butter or regular	halves)
margarine	Chocolate Icing (recipe
½ c. brown sugar, packed	follows)

Sift together flour, baking soda and baking powder; set aside.

Cream together butter and brown sugar in bowl until light and fluffy, using electric mixer at medium speed. Add eggs, one at a time, beating well after each addition. Beat in vanilla.

Gradually stir dry ingredients into creamed mixture, mixing well. Arrange pecan halves in clusters of 4, about 2" apart, on ungreased baking sheets, placing halves in the form of a cross. Drop dough, by rounded teaspoonfuls, in center of each cluster.

Bake in 350° oven 10 minutes, or until golden brown. Remove from baking sheets; cool on racks. Prepare Chocolate Icing. Frost centers of each cookie with Chocolate Icing. Makes 40.

Chocolate Icing: Combine 1 c. sifted confectioners' sugar, 1 tblsp. butter or regular margarine, 1½ (1-oz.) squares unsweetened chocolate (melted and cooled) and 3 tblsp milk in bowl. Stir until smooth.

Chocolate-Mincemeat Jumbles

One South Dakota farm woman makes these mincemeat chocolate chips and packs them in gift boxes for shut-ins every Christmas.

2½ c. unsifted flour	1 c. sugar
2 tsp. baking soda	3 eggs
1 tsp. salt	1 (6-oz.) pkg. semisweet
½ c. butter or regular	chocolate pieces
margarine	1 c. prepared mincemeat

Stir together flour, baking soda and salt; set aside.

Cream together butter and sugar in bowl until light and fluffy, using electric mixer at medium speed. Add eggs, one at a time, beating well after each addition.

Gradually add dry ingredients to creamed mixture, mixing well with a spoon. Stir in chocolate pieces and mincemeat. Drop mixture by tablespoonfuls, about 3" apart, on lightly greased baking sheets.

Bake in 375° oven 9 minutes, or until lightly browned. Cool on baking sheets a few seconds. Remove from baking sheets; cool on racks. Makes about 4½ dozen.

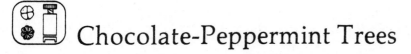 # Chocolate-Peppermint Trees

Tiny chocolate sandwich cookies are dipped in a melted peppermint-flavored confection coating for an interesting decorative touch.

3½ c. sifted flour	1 tsp. vanilla
¼ tsp. salt	4 (1-oz.) squares
1½ c. butter or regular	unsweetened chocolate,
margarine	melted and cooled
1 c. sugar	Peppermint Filling (recipe
3 egg yolks	follows)

Sift together flour and salt; set aside.

Cream together butter and sugar in bowl until light and fluffy, using electric mixer at medium speed. Add egg yolks and vanilla; beat well. Blend in chocolate.

Gradually stir dry ingredients into creamed mixture, mixing well.

Fit tree design into cookie press. Place one half of the dough in cookie press at a time, forcing dough through press, about 1" apart, on ungreased baking sheets.

Bake in 375° oven 8 to 10 minutes, or until set but not browned. Cool cookies on baking sheets 2 minutes. Remove from baking sheets; cool on racks.

Prepare Peppermint Filling. Spread the bottom of one cookie with Peppermint Filling. Top with another cookie to form a sandwich cookie. Fill all the cookies. Then dip each sandwich into remaining Peppermint Filling so that filling coats half of cookie. Leave other half uncoated. Place on waxed paper until coating sets. Makes 5½ dozen sandwich cookies.

Peppermint Filling: Melt 8 oz. cut-up white confection coating in top of double boiler over hot water. When melted, stir in 2 drops green food coloring and ¼ tsp. peppermint extract. Keep mixture warm over hot water. (White confection coating is also called white chocolate or summer coating. It is sold by the pound in candy stores.)

Rich Peppermint Brownies

Peppermint-flavored chocolate brownies frosted with pale green icing and feathered with melted chocolate.

1 c. butter or regular margarine	2 tsp. vanilla
5 (1-oz.) squares unsweetened chocolate	½ tsp. peppermint extract
1¾ c. sifted flour	1 c. chopped pecans
1 tsp. salt	Peppermint Frosting (recipe follows)
5 eggs	½ (1-oz.) square unsweetened chocolate
2¼ c. sugar	

Combine butter and 5 oz. chocolate in saucepan. Place over low heat until melted. Remove from heat; cool to room temperature.

Sift together flour and salt; set aside.

Combine eggs and sugar in bowl. Beat 2 minutes or until light and fluffy, using electric mixer at high speed. Add cooled chocolate mixture, vanilla and peppermint extract; blend well.

Add dry ingredients to chocolate mixture, mixing well with spoon. Stir in pecans. Pour mixture into greased 15½x10½x1" jelly roll pan.

Bake in 325° oven 25 minutes, or until no imprint remains when touched lightly with finger. Cool in pan on rack. Prepare Peppermint Frosting. Frost bars with Peppermint Frosting.

Melt ½ oz. chocolate in small custard cup in hot water. Drizzle in 5 parallel lines the length of the pan. Gently move a toothpick across the chocolate lines at even intervals. Let stand until chocolate sets. Cut into 2½x1½" bars. Makes 48.

Peppermint Frosting: Combine 3 c. sifted confectioners' sugar, 6 tblsp. cooking oil, 3 tblsp. milk, ½ tsp. peppermint extract and 1 to 2 drops green food coloring in bowl. Beat until smooth, using a spoon.

Mississippi Mud Bars

Three-layer brownies loaded with coconut and pecans, spread with marshmallow creme and topped with cocoa frosting.

1 c. butter or regular margarine	1⅓ c. flaked coconut
2 c. sugar	1½ c. chopped pecans
¼ c. baking cocoa	1 (7½-oz.) jar marshmallow creme
4 eggs	Cocoa Frosting (recipe follows)
1 tsp. vanilla	
1½ c. sifted flour	

Cream together butter, sugar and cocoa in bowl until light and fluffy, using electric mixer at medium speed. Add eggs and vanilla. Beat 2 more minutes at medium speed.

Gradually stir flour into creamed mixture, mixing well. Stir in coconut and pecans. Spread in greased 15½x10½x1" jelly roll pan.

Bake in 350° oven 30 minutes, or until top springs back when touched lightly with finger. Remove from oven; spoon marshmallow creme over all. Let stand 5 minutes. Spread carefully with metal spatula. Prepare Cocoa Frosting. While brownies are still warm, frost with Cocoa Frosting. Cool completely. Cut into 4x1" bars. Makes 40.

Cocoa Frosting: Combine ½ c. butter or regular margarine and ½ c. baking cocoa in saucepan. Place over low heat until butter melts. Cool slightly. Combine 4 c. sifted confectioners' sugar, ½ c. evaporated milk and 1 tsp. vanilla in bowl. Add cooled cocoa mixture. Beat until smooth, using electric mixer at low speed.

Fudge-Marshmallow Brownies

Chocolate fans will love a box of these sinfully rich brownies with a chewy marshmallow layer and a thin chocolate glaze.

1 c. butter or regular margarine	2 c. sugar
⅓ c. baking cocoa	1½ c. chopped pecans
1½ c. sifted flour	3 c. miniature marshmallows
Pinch of salt	Chocolate Glaze (recipe follows)
4 eggs	

Combine butter and cocoa in small saucepan. Cook over low heat, stirring constantly, until butter melts and mixture is smooth. Remove from heat and cool slightly.

Sift together flour and salt; set aside.

Combine eggs and sugar in bowl and beat until well blended, using electric mixer at medium speed.

Add dry ingredients alternately with cocoa mixture to egg mixture, beating well after each addition, using electric mixer at low speed. Stir in pecans. Spread mixture in greased 15½x10½x1" jelly roll pan.

Bake in 350° oven 20 minutes, or until no imprint remains when top is touched lightly with finger. Remove from oven; sprinkle with marshmallows. Return to oven 2 minutes more to soften marshmallows. Remove from oven. Press marshmallows to flatten. Cool slightly in pan on rack. Prepare Chocolate Glaze. While bars are still warm, pour Chocolate Glaze over bars. Cool completely. Cut into 2" squares. Makes 35.

Chocolate Glaze: Combine 2 (1-oz.) squares unsweetened chocolate and ¼ c. butter or regular margarine in saucepan. Cook over low heat, stirring constantly, until melted. Remove from heat; cool slightly. Combine 2¼ c. sifted confectioners' sugar, ¼ c. hot water, 1 tsp. vanilla and ⅛ tsp. salt in bowl. Stir in chocolate mixture. Beat until mixture becomes smooth and begins to thicken, using a spoon.

Brownie Walnut Drops

"I always make lots of these crackle-topped cookies at Christmas time for my cookie plate and for gifts, too," wrote a Kansas farm woman.

2 (4-oz.) pkg. German sweet chocolate	¼ tsp. ground cinnamon
1 tblsp. butter or regular margarine	⅛ tsp. salt
¼ c. unsifted flour	2 eggs
¼ tsp. baking powder	½ tsp. vanilla
	¾ c. sugar
	¾ c. chopped walnuts

Combine chocolate and butter in small saucepan. Cook over low heat until melted. Remove from heat; cool to room temperature.

Stir together flour, baking powder, cinnamon and salt; set aside.

Beat eggs and vanilla in bowl until foamy, using electric mixer at high speed. Gradually add sugar, beating until thick and lemon-colored, about 5 minutes. Blend in cooled chocolate mixture.

Add dry ingredients to chocolate mixture, mixing well with spoon. Stir in walnuts. Drop mixture by rounded teaspoonfuls, about 2" apart, on greased baking sheets.

Bake in 350° oven 10 minutes, or until no imprint remains when touched lightly with finger. Cool slightly on baking sheets. Remove from baking sheets; cool on racks. Makes 2½ dozen.

Refrigerator Chocolate Pinwheels

These pretty swirled cookies are easy to make—just roll up chocolate and vanilla dough like a jelly roll.

3 c. sifted flour	2 eggs
2 tsp. baking powder	2 tsp. vanilla
½ tsp. salt	2 (1-oz.) squares
1 c. butter or regular margarine	unsweetened chocolate, melted and cooled
1 c. sugar	

Sift together flour, baking powder and salt; set aside.

Cream together butter and sugar in bowl until light and fluffy, using electric mixer at medium speed. Add eggs, one at a time, beating well after each addition. Beat in vanilla.

Gradually stir dry ingredients into creamed mixture, blending well.

Divide dough in half. Blend chocolate into one half. Cover dough and refrigerate at least 1½ hours.

Divide chocolate dough and vanilla dough into halves. Return un-used portions to refrigerator.

Roll out chocolate dough on waxed paper to 12x10" rectangle. Roll out vanilla dough on waxed paper to 12x10" rectangle. Place chocolate dough on top of vanilla dough, waxed paper side up. Peel off waxed paper. Roll up dough like jelly roll, starting from wide edge and peeling off waxed paper from vanilla dough as you roll. Wrap roll in waxed paper and refrigerate until firm enough to slice, about 1½ hours. Repeat with remaining refrigerated chocolate and vanilla dough.

Cut each roll into 48 slices, about ¼" thick. Place slices, about 2" apart, on greased baking sheets.

Bake in 375° oven 7 minutes, or until lightly browned. Remove from baking sheets; cool on racks. Makes 8 dozen.

Fruitcake Squares

Orange-flavored fruitcake bars are especially good served with cups of steaming hot fruit punch.

1½ c. coarsely chopped pitted dates	1 c. sifted flour
1 c. golden raisins	1½ tsp. salt
1 c. dark raisins	4 eggs
1 c. coarsely chopped walnuts	1 c. brown sugar, packed
½ c. halved candied cherries	1 tblsp. grated orange rind
½ c. chopped candied pineapple	1 tsp. vanilla
	½ c. sugar
	¼ c. orange juice

Combine dates, golden raisins, dark raisins, walnuts, cherries and pineapple. Sift together flour and salt. Sprinkle fruit with ¼ c. of the flour mixture and stir to coat. Set aside.

Beat eggs in bowl until frothy, using electric mixer at medium speed. Beat in brown sugar, orange rind and vanilla. Stir in flour mix-ture and fruit mixture, mixing well. Spread in greased 15½x10½x1" jelly roll pan.

Bake in 325° oven 30 to 35 minutes, or until lightly browned. Cool slightly in pan on rack. Combine sugar and orange juice in small saucepan. Cook over medium heat, stirring constantly, until mixture comes to a boil and sugar is dissolved. Brush sugar syrup over warm bars. Cool completely. Cut into 2½x1½" bars. Makes 48.

Holiday Fruit Bars

These two-layer bars begin with a candy-like crust; the topping is gently spiced with cinnamon and allspice.

1⅓ c. sifted flour	¼ c. melted butter or regular
¾ tsp. baking powder	margarine
¼ tsp. salt	½ c. dark raisins
½ c. brown sugar, packed	½ c. golden raisins
½ c. butter or regular	2 tblsp. chopped red candied
margarine	cherries
2 tblsp. water	2 tsp. grated lemon rind
3 eggs	⅛ tsp. ground allspice
¼ c. brown sugar, packed	⅛ tsp. ground cinnamon

Sift together flour, baking powder and salt into bowl. Mix in ½ c. brown sugar. Cut in ½ c. butter until mixture is crumbly, using pastry blender or two knives. Stir in water. Press mixture into bottom of un-greased 13x9x2" baking pan.

Bake in 350° oven 15 minutes, or until golden brown.

Meanwhile, beat eggs in bowl until well blended, using electric mix-er at medium speed. Beat in ¼ c. brown sugar and ¼ c. melted butter; blend well. Stir in dark raisins, golden raisins, candied cherries, lemon rind, allspice and cinnamon. Spread mixture over baked crust.

Bake in 350° oven 15 minutes, or until golden brown. Cool in pan on rack. Cut into 3x1" bars. Makes 39.

Holiday Fruit Drops

This fruit-and-nut cookie recipe is similar to the one that follows, but this one turns out 7½ dozen gems.

3½ c. sifted flour	2 eggs
1 tsp. baking soda	½ c. water
1 tsp. salt	1½ c. chopped walnuts
½ c. shortening	2 c. mixed candied fruit
½ c. butter or regular	½ c. halved, red candied
margarine	cherries
2 c. brown sugar, packed	

Sift together flour, baking soda and salt; set aside.

Cream together shortening, butter and brown sugar in bowl until light and fluffy, using electric mixer at medium speed. Add eggs, one at a time, beating well after each addition.

Add dry ingredients alternately with water to creamed mixture, mixing well with a spoon. Stir in walnuts, candied fruit and cherries. Cover and chill dough in refrigerator 1 hour.

Drop mixture by teaspoonfuls, about 2" apart, on greased baking sheets.

Bake in 400° oven 8 to 10 minutes, or until golden brown. Remove from baking sheets; cool on racks. Makes 7½ dozen.

Holiday Fruit Cookies

Colorful fruit-filled cookies like these are perfect for the Christmas holidays. Can be dusted with confectioners' sugar.

1¾ c. sifted flour	½ c. mixed candied fruit
½ tsp. baking soda	½ c. shortening
½ tsp. salt	1 c. sugar
1 c. chopped pitted dates	1 egg
1 c. chopped candied cherries	⅓ c. buttermilk
¾ c. chopped walnuts	

Sift together flour, baking soda and salt. Mix ¼ c. of the flour mixture with dates, candied cherries, walnuts and mixed candied fruit. Set aside.

Cream together shortening and sugar in bowl until light and fluffy, using electric mixer at medium speed. Add egg; beat well.

Gradually add remaining dry ingredients alternately with buttermilk to creamed mixture, beating well after each addition, using electric mixer at low speed. Stir in fruit-nut mixture. Drop by heaping teaspoonfuls, about 2" apart, on greased baking sheets.

Bake in 400° oven 10 to 13 minutes, or until golden brown. Remove from baking sheets; cool on racks. Makes about 3 dozen.

Iced Ambrosia Drops

A creamy vanilla frosting adds a dazzling effect to these spicy, fruit-filled drop cookies.

1¼ c. sifted flour	½ c. brown sugar, packed
½ tsp. baking powder	2 eggs
½ tsp. salt	½ c. raisins
½ tsp. ground cinnamon	½ c. mixed candied fruit
½ tsp. ground cloves	½ c. chopped pitted dates
½ c. butter or regular margarine	½ c. chopped walnuts
	Vanilla Icing (recipe follows)

Sift together flour, baking powder, salt, cinnamon and cloves; set aside.

Cream together butter and brown sugar in bowl until light and fluffy, using electric mixer at medium speed. Add eggs, one at a time, beating well after each addition.

Gradually stir dry ingredients into creamed mixture, mixing well. Stir in raisins, candied fruit, dates and walnuts. Drop mixture by teaspoonfuls, about 2" apart, on greased baking sheets.

Bake in 375° oven 8 to 10 minutes, or until golden brown. Remove from baking sheets; cool on racks. Prepare Vanilla Icing. Frost cookies with Vanilla Icing. Makes about 3 dozen.

Vanilla Icing: Combine 1 c. sifted confectioners' sugar, 1 tblsp. milk and ½ tsp. vanilla in bowl. Beat until smooth, using a spoon.

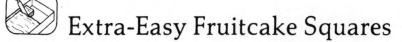

Extra-Easy Fruitcake Squares

No mixing is needed for these quickly made holiday bar cookies—all the ingredients are simply layered in the baking pan.

6 tblsp. butter or regular margarine	1 c. chopped pitted dates
1½ c. graham cracker crumbs	1 c. coarsely chopped walnuts
1 c. shredded coconut	1 (14-oz.) can sweetened condensed milk (not evaporated)
2 c. mixed candied fruit	

Melt butter in 15½x10½x1" jelly roll pan. Sprinkle graham cracker crumbs into bottom of pan, shaking pan to distribute crumbs evenly. Layer in coconut, candied fruit, dates and walnuts. Press mixture down lightly with hands to level it. Pour sweetened condensed milk evenly on top.

Bake in 350° oven 25 to 30 minutes, or until set. Cool in pan on rack. Cut into 1½" squares. Makes 60.

Refrigerator Caramel Nut Slices

A Missouri farm woman tells us that her mother made these crunchy cookies for Christmas as long as she can remember.

3½ c. sifted flour	½ c. shortening
1 tsp. baking soda	2 c. brown sugar, packed
½ tsp. salt	2 eggs
½ c. butter or regular margarine	1 c. chopped walnuts

Sift together flour, baking soda and salt; set aside.

Cream together butter, shortening and brown sugar in bowl until light and fluffy, using electric mixer at medium speed. Add eggs, one at a time, beating well after each addition.

Gradually stir dry ingredients into creamed mixture, blending well. Stir in walnuts. Divide dough in half and shape each half into 12" roll. Wrap in waxed paper and refrigerate overnight.

Cut each roll into 48 slices, about ¼" thick. Place slices, about 2" apart, on greased baking sheets.

Bake in 400° oven 5 minutes, or until golden brown. Remove from baking sheets; cool on racks. Makes 8 dozen.

 Butterscotch Oatmeal Cookies

Many farm families serve everyday favorites at Christmas along with special holiday treats. This recipe can easily be doubled.

¾ c. sifted flour	½ c. brown sugar, packed
¾ tsp. baking soda	½ c. sugar
¼ tsp. ground cinnamon	1 egg
⅛ tsp. salt	1 c. quick-cooking oats
½ c. shortening	

Sift together flour, baking soda, cinnamon and salt; set aside.

Cream together shortening, brown sugar and sugar in bowl until light and fluffy, using electric mixer at medium speed. Add egg; beat well.

Gradually stir dry ingredients into creamed mixture, blending well. Stir in oats. Drop mixture by rounded teaspoonfuls, about 3" apart, on greased baking sheets.

Bake in 325° oven 15 minutes, or until golden brown. Remove from baking sheets; cool on racks. Makes 2½ dozen.

Oatmeal-Date Cookies

Dates, coconut and walnuts add a festive touch to these yummy oatmeal cookies. Among the best oatmeals we've ever tasted.

2 c. sifted flour	3 eggs
1 tsp. baking powder	1 tsp. vanilla
¾ tsp. baking soda	2 c. quick-cooking oats
½ tsp. salt	1 c. cut-up pitted dates
1 c. shortening	1 c. flaked coconut
1 c. brown sugar, packed	½ c. chopped walnuts
1 c. sugar	Sugar

Sift together flour, baking powder, baking soda and salt; set aside.

Cream together shortening, brown sugar and 1 c. sugar in bowl until light and fluffy, using electric mixer at medium speed. Add eggs, one at a time, beating well after each addition. Blend in vanilla.

Gradually add dry ingredients to creamed mixture, mixing well with spoon. Stir in oats, dates, coconut and walnuts. Drop mixture by teaspoonfuls, about 2" apart, on greased baking sheets. Flatten each with bottom of drinking glass dipped in sugar.

Bake in 375° oven 8 minutes, or until lightly browned. Remove from baking sheets; cool on racks. Makes 5 dozen.

Date-Pecan Cookies

These pecan-topped brown sugar cookies are chock-full of pecans, dates and red candied cherries. They look and taste great!

3½ c. sifted flour	½ c. buttermilk
1 tsp. baking soda	1½ c. chopped pecans
1 tsp. salt	2 c. halved, red candied
1 c. shortening	cherries
2 c. brown sugar, packed	2 c. cut-up pitted dates
2 eggs	Pecan halves

Sift together flour, baking soda and salt; set aside.

Cream together shortening and brown sugar in bowl until light and fluffy, using electric mixer at medium speed. Add eggs, one at a time, beating well after each addition.

Add dry ingredients alternately with buttermilk, beating well after each addition, using electric mixer at low speed. Stir in 1½ c. pecans, cherries and dates. Cover and chill dough in refrigerator 1 hour.

Drop mixture by teaspoonfuls, about 2″ apart, on greased baking sheets. Place a pecan half on each cookie.

Bake in 375° oven 10 minutes, or until golden brown. Remove from baking sheets; cool on racks. Makes 6 dozen.

Refrigerated Date Cookies

Chewy old-fashioned date cookies like these are often the best. Keep in the refrigerator and bake when you need fresh cookies.

1 c. cut-up pitted dates	½ tsp. baking soda
1 c. sugar	½ tsp. salt
1 c. water	1 c. shortening
1 c. chopped walnuts	2 c. brown sugar, packed
4 c. sifted flour	3 eggs

Combine dates, sugar and water in small saucepan. Cook over medium heat, stirring constantly, until mixture thickens. Remove from heat; cool. Stir in walnuts; set aside.

Sift together flour, baking soda and salt; set aside.

Cream together shortening and brown sugar in bowl until light and fluffy, using electric mixer at medium speed. Add eggs, one at a time, beating well after each addition.

Gradually add dry ingredients to creamed mixture, mixing well with spoon. Cover and chill dough in refrigerator 1 hour.

Divide dough in half. Roll each half on lightly floured surface into 13x9" rectangle. Spread with half of date filling. Roll up like a jelly roll, starting from long side. Wrap tightly in plastic wrap or waxed paper. Refrigerate 8 hours or overnight.

Cut roll into ¼" slices. Place rounds, about 2" apart, on greased baking sheets.

Bake in 400° oven 10 minutes, or until golden brown. Remove from baking sheets; cool on racks. Makes 7 dozen.

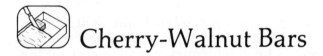 # Cherry-Walnut Bars

Delicate pink bars flavored with almond and laced with walnuts and maraschino cherries. Watch them disappear at your next party.

1½ c. sifted flour	½ c. water
⅓ c. brown sugar, packed	1 tsp. almond extract
½ tsp. salt	¼ tsp. salt
¾ c. butter or regular margarine	3 drops red food coloring
2 env. unflavored gelatin	⅓ c. chopped red maraschino cherries
⅓ c. maraschino cherry juice	⅓ c. chopped walnuts
2 c. sugar	

Combine flour, brown sugar and ½ tsp. salt in bowl. Cut in butter until mixture resembles coarse meal, using pastry blender. Press mixture into bottom of greased 13x9x2" baking pan.

Bake in 325° oven 18 to 20 minutes, or until golden brown.

Meanwhile, sprinkle gelatin over cherry juice in bowl; stir to soften.

Combine sugar and water in 2-qt. saucepan. Cover and bring to a boil over medium heat. Remove cover and boil 2 minutes.

Pour boiling sugar syrup over gelatin mixture. Beat 5 to 10 minutes, or until mixture becomes thick and begins to hold its shape, using electric mixer at high speed. Beat in almond extract, ¼ tsp. salt and red food coloring. Fold in cherries and walnuts. Pour over warm baked crust. Let stand at room temperature overnight. Cut into 3¼x1⅛" bars. Makes 32.

Northern Light Bars

A rich bar cookie featuring two layers: a walnut crumb crust and a cream cheese filling with a tart, lemony flavor.

⅓ c. butter or regular margarine	¼ c. sugar
⅓ c. brown sugar, packed	1 egg
1 c. sifted flour	2 tblsp. milk
½ c. chopped walnuts	1 tblsp. lemon juice
1 (8-oz.) pkg. cream cheese, softened	½ tsp. vanilla

Cream together butter and brown sugar in bowl until light and fluffy, using electric mixer at medium speed. Stir in flour and walnuts, mixing until crumbly. Remove 1 c. crumb mixture and reserve for topping. Press remaining crumb mixture into bottom of greased 8" square baking pan.

Bake in 350° oven 12 minutes, or until golden brown.

Meanwhile, beat cream cheese in bowl until smooth, using electric mixer at medium speed. Gradually add sugar, egg, milk, lemon juice and vanilla, beating well. Spread cream cheese mixture over baked crust. Sprinkle with 1 c. reserved crumb mixture.

Bake in 350° oven 25 minutes, or until cheese filling is set. Cool in pan on rack. Cut into 2" squares. Store in refrigerator. Makes 16.

Lemon Slices

Here's another lemon-flavored bar cookie—this one has a buttery, pastry-like crust and an egg-rich lemon filling.

2 c. sifted flour	½ tsp. salt
½ c. sifted confectioners' sugar	⅓ c. lemon juice
1 c. butter or regular margarine	1 tsp. grated lemon rind
4 eggs	¼ c. unsifted flour
2 c. sugar	2 tsp. confectioners' sugar
	Confectioners' sugar

Combine 2 c. flour and ½ c. confectioners' sugar in bowl. Cut in butter until mixture is crumbly, using pastry blender. Press crumb mixture into ungreased 13x9x2" baking pan.

Bake in 350° oven 25 minutes, or until golden brown.

Beat eggs in bowl until thick and lemon-colored, using electric mixer at high speed. Slowly beat in sugar, salt, lemon juice and lemon rind. Combine ¼ c. flour and 2 tsp. confectioners' sugar. Stir into egg mixture. Pour over baked crust.

Return to oven and bake 25 minutes, or until golden brown. Cool in pan on rack. Cut into 2¼x1" bars. Roll bars in confectioners' sugar. Makes 52.

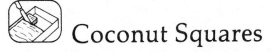 Coconut Squares

These chewy bar cookies look special, but are simple to make. The creamy lemon glaze adds a hint of citrus.

1¼ c. sifted flour	2 eggs
½ tsp. baking powder	1 tsp. vanilla
¼ tsp. salt	½ tsp. almond extract
¼ c. butter or regular	1 c. flaked coconut
margarine	½ c. chopped walnuts
1 c. brown sugar, packed	Lemon Glaze (recipe follows)

Sift together flour, baking powder and salt; set aside.

Cream together butter and brown sugar in bowl until light and fluffy, using electric mixer at medium speed. Add eggs, one at a time, beating well after each addition. Beat in vanilla and almond extract.

Gradually add dry ingredients to creamed mixture, beating well after each addition, using electric mixer at low speed. Stir in coconut and walnuts. Spread mixture in greased 9″ square baking pan.

Bake in 325° oven 30 minutes, or until golden brown. Cool slightly in pan on rack. Prepare Lemon Glaze. While bars are still warm, spread with Lemon Glaze. Cool completely. Cut into 1½″ squares. Makes 18.

Lemon Glaze: Combine 1 c. sifted confectioners' sugar, ½ tsp. grated lemon rind and 1 tblsp. hot milk in bowl. Blend until smooth and creamy, using a spoon.

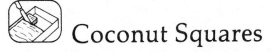 Raspberry Jam Squares

Tri-layer bars with a buttery crumb crust, a thin layer of raspberry preserves and a delicately browned topping of meringue.

1½ c. sifted flour	2 eggs, separated
½ tsp. salt	1 (10-oz.) jar red raspberry
½ c. butter or regular	preserves (1 c.)
margarine	½ c. sugar
¼ c. sugar	1 tsp. vanilla

Sift together flour and salt; set aside.

Cream together butter and ¼ c. sugar in bowl until light and fluffy, using electric mixer at medium speed. Beat in egg yolks.

Stir dry ingredients into creamed mixture, mixing until crumbly. Press crumb mixture into ungreased 9″ square baking pan.

Spread raspberry preserves over crumb layer.

Beat egg whites in another bowl until foamy, using electric mixer at high speed. Gradually beat in ½ c. sugar, beating until stiff, glossy peaks form. Blend in vanilla. Spread meringue carefully over preserves layer.

Bake in 350° oven 30 minutes, or until golden brown. Cool in pan on rack. Cut into 2¼″ squares. Makes 16.

Index